# The Art of the
# PAINTED FINISH

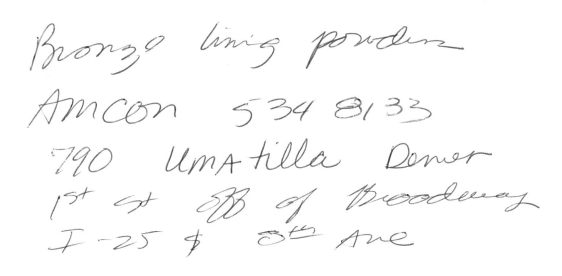

Bronze lining powder
AMCON   534 8133
790 Umatilla Denver
1st st off of Broadway
I-25 & 8th Ave

# The Art of the
# PAINTED FINISH
## for Furniture & Decoration

ANTIQUING, LACQUERING, GILDING &
THE GREAT IMPERSONATORS

## by Isabel O'Neil

*A House & Garden Book*

WILLIAM MORROW & COMPANY, INC., NEW YORK

*To Louis J. Gartner, Jr., and to my students*
*who insisted that this book be written*

# PREFACE

Little has been recorded about the art of painted finishes. Techniques employed by the master were acquired by the novice through long years of apprenticeship, or a father disclosed jealously guarded methods to a son. There remain a few treatises of the seventeenth century, written to instruct the ladies of that era who found the practice of this craft initially one of amusement and subsequently one of pride. Several manuals and a journal of the nineteenth century still exist, intended to inform the artisans of that day, which describe technique and method to be used on wall and woodwork. These works do not present much useful direction to the contemporary craftsman. The materials are obsolete, the methods are no longer feasible, and unless one is possessed of some preliminary knowledge of the craft, the instructions are for the most part incomprehensible. The few craftsmen remaining are fast disappearing, leaving no record and no trained apprentices, as this age indeed does not encourage a satisfactory economic pursuance of the craft. When labor is poorly paid, work becomes hasty and the product no longer a commercial commodity.

In our technologically impelled society, much of one's life is spent in struggle with vast intangibles; the simplest accompaniments of living are manifestations of complex scientific development. The buildings of business are warrens of steel and glass; homes are frequently beehives of poured concrete.

Thus, the beautiful painted furniture of the past has added appeal today—its patinaed surface indicative of a less sterile time, when man's use marked as his own the furnishings he treasured and bequeathed to his descendants. Man has a compelling need to make a personal imprint on the inhuman environment of steel and glass and to find individual expression in his artifacts. There is a restorative in creating through the skill of one's hands an object of beauty which exists in actuality and gives a reiterative pleasure and satisfaction to the beholder. The statement "I made this" is the affirmation of "I am."

For some years it has been my delight to discover the methods and techniques of painted finishes through research and the restoration of antique pieces. During all this search, only twice has my request for instruction from older craftsmen elicited other response than "I learned the hard way, why not you?" Perforce I did, and I wish to share these discoveries and inventions.

It is notorious that an account of technical processes written by those engaged in using them is often unreliable and that essential details are omitted owing to the writer's familiarity with them. The result is frustrating obscurity. Much of what the craftsman will learn in what follows has been the result of many trials, errors, and corrections. Mistakes have often been happy accidents and have led to charming and original techniques. The methods noted here will offer as much protection as possible from irretrievable mishap. There are innumerable modifications of each process. My goal has been both toward simplification and toward method which will provide some assurance of success.

Ancient methods in the commoner handicrafts are preserved here, and a craftsman today pursuing his task with integrity will arrive at techniques that closely resemble those of the past. For example, while doing some research at the library of Cooper Union, I chanced upon a treatise published in 1688 which detailed the exact method for varnishing that I had evolved through troublesome trial and error.

Over the years this knowledge of decorative painting has been taught in my studio to some hundreds of novices. These students are proof that a latent and modest talent can, when channeled by the disciplines of the techniques, achieve through this craft a way of personal expression. Student effort has created many of the pleasing pieces shown in these pages. Through teaching and guiding these enthusiasts to successful results, I have arrived at perfected and simplified methods.

Inspired by this experience, and prompted by letters coming from as far away as Alaska and South Africa, I present this volume, hoping that many will enjoy through this craft the satisfaction of creative experience. Whether this be small or large in measure, it is one of magical moment, the zenith of self-realization. Then, too, there is the pleasure of the concept, the pleasure of one's skill in execution, and the continuing pleasure of living with the result.

Throughout this work, it has been my desire to translate the materials of this craft into modern terms, to adjust the methods in a practicable manner; simplified as they are, they yet retain whatever is necessary for the finished product to be one of beauty and character. Paths to be pursued will be shown here, but the goal will be reached only through individual effort.

The novice, of course, will have to begin with the most fundamental techniques of this craft. They are not difficult, but he must be patient until his hand can, through practice and discipline, acquire the physical pattern and rhythm which will lead to mastery. Milton R. Stern writes, "As for classes in which skills are to be learned—they simply are not painless. Drudgery is involved—a pleasant tedium of learning, if you are willing to accept the disciplines in the interest of ultimate power, but impossible otherwise." Excellence of achievement is not attained at the first attempt and not without effort.

This craft, which is so little known, contributes to the harmony and beauty of our surroundings. It is not limited. Endless variation is obtainable in the surface patinas, the fantasy finishes, and the embellishment of the metallics. There are myriad possibilities for the use of these techniques on contemporary pieces, whose surfaces so often cry out for treatment in an original manner. Something of oneself will be manifest in each piece.

So I plead that those who share my admiration, who find beauty in painted surfaces, and who desire the pleasure of rendering them for creative satisfaction, will give themselves a "time for learning." Adults have so little patience with themselves and dogmatically demand an immediate expertise. This is the epitome of arrogance. I have taught so many whose sole equipment was desire that I know excellence can be achieved by anyone similarly embarking on this fascinating journey.

## ACKNOWLEDGMENTS

I am deeply grateful to the many friends and students who assisted in the preparation of this book. Among those who have read all of it and contributed their suggestions are my brothers John M. McDonald and Robert E. McDonald, whose assistance was invaluable, and my good friend Louis J. Gartner, Jr. I am profoundly grateful to Margaret Scolari Barr who so diligently checked the research and gave so lavishly of her time and energy. To Diane Deitchman who took hours of dictation and endlessly typed and retyped the pages of the manuscript, to Kurt Miehlmann who photographed the sample boards so beautifully, to Edward Kasper and Carol Blank who labored over the details of the drawings, to Pat Moore for her skillful copy-editing and many helpful suggestions, to Margaret Bohme who aided in the final revisions, and to Narcisse Chamberlain who brought it all together, I owe a debt of thanks.

# CONTENTS

# LIST OF
# COLOR PLATES

# HOW TO USE THIS BOOK

The text of *The Art of the Painted Finish* is organized as is the course of instruction at the Isabel O'Neil Studio-Workshop. It opens with rudimentary processes which are taught to beginning students and it progresses from one technique to the next to develop each skill the craftsman will need. As the finishes become more complex, the instructions for them assume the reader's prior knowledge of necessary techniques learned in preceding sections.

To create a beautiful painted finish is an art learned through the practice of component processes and experience in handling the tools and materials. Therefore, the newcomer to this craft is forwarned that to attempt first an elaborate finish, as described in latter parts of the book, will be altogether self-defeating. He must begin at the beginning. Every effort has been made to tell the reader what he needs to know in the sequence in which he needs to know it, so that there will not be any crucial gap in his knowledge of the craft when he advances to the more difficult finishes.

In accordance with this plan of instruction, the Subject Outline at the back of the book has been provided in lieu of an index. The progression of subject matter can there be seen in conveniently condensed form, each topic listed in the context in which it is first learned. Clearly printed headings in the text correspond precisely to the entries in the Subject Outline.

This method of presenting the content of the book has also been chosen because not everyone, certainly not beginners, would be familiar enough with the terminology of the craft to know what to look for in the alphabetical entries of a conventional index. The Subject Outline will refer the reader quickly to material studied previously on which he may need to refresh his memory, and in summarizing each section it shows what new procedures are learned to achieve the finishes in that section.

As writers on the art of cooking so often plead, that one should *read the recipe through* before beginning to cook, so this author insists even more strongly that the craftsman must not merely read but carefully study the complete instructions for a painted finish before beginning to work. In addition, there is provided at the end of each section a detailed list of materials and tools. This list is not exactly comparable to the list of ingredients in a recipe, as it includes *all* the items required for what is usually a group of several related finishes in the section. Having studied the parts of the text that he will be using and pictured each step clearly in his mind's eye, the reader should then check off on the list each item that will be needed for his purpose. Everything must be at hand from the beginning, for convenience and much greater pleasure in working and also to avoid the very real possibility of disaster should some item be missing at a strategic moment.

Finally, there are over 80 samples of painted finishes, most of them life size, among the color plates as well as pictures of completed pieces. These are an important aid to understanding the effects to be achieved and should be referred to frequently while work is in progress. (See List of Color Plates on page 11.)

The materials and tools used and their nature and function are described in the text as they first come into use. The information on labels should be read carefully when materials and tools are bought in paint, hardware and art-supply stores to confirm that the product is indeed the one required. No brand names are mentioned in the text, as the nature of each item is the pertinent information rather than the numerous brand names under which it may be sold.

## *A NOTE TO THE CRAFTSMAN:*

Flatting oil—a crucial ingredient used in many processes of the art of the painted finish—contains lead and by law may no longer be manufactured. Since the original publication of this book, the following formula has been developed for the craftsman to use as a substitute:

> 1 volume boiled linseed oil
> 6 volumes mineral spirits

*The line or curve of the edge of a leaf may be accurately given to the edge of a stone without rendering the stone in the least like a leaf, or suggestive of a leaf; and this the more fully, because the lines of nature are alike in all her works; simpler or richer in combination, but the same in character; and when they are taken out of their combinations it is impossible to say from which of her works they have been borrowed, their universal property being that of ever varying curvature in the most subtle and subdued transitions, with peculiar expressions of motion, elasticity or dependence.*

*John Ruskin,* The Stones of Venice

# HISTORICAL BACKGROUND

A background in the evolution of the craft of furniture painting will give the reader an awareness of the conventions and needs that contributed to development and change.

Embellishing with paint the artifacts and objects of daily use appears to have been almost instinctive in human beings since the earliest stages of civilization. Prehistoric man drew and painted on the rough rocks of his cave to exorcise the evil spirits, to tell a tale, and to placate the elements of nature. The Egyptians, the Myceneans, the Etruscans, and the Romans decorated their pottery, walls, and furniture with extraordinary inventiveness and a surprising variety of color and design. Unrealistic color was used by the Greeks to enhance sculpture and to emphasize architectural ornament. It was not related to nature, but was made to accord with the brilliance of the Aegean light. Before the seventeenth century, decoration of the great halls and reception rooms of Europe was usually limited to the walls, which were hung with rich fabrics, tapestries, and paintings.

In the Western world, decorative painting on church furniture developed as a by-product of the fine artist's studio. Gradually this practice spread to secular furniture such as birth and wedding trays, bed-ends, and the great storage chests called *cassoni*. Mostly this work was executed by specialized craftsmen and apprentices, but sometimes the masters themselves were not above painting a special piece for a noble family. In those days a man's requirements were few—chests, bed-ends, trestles, chairs for nobility and benches for lesser folk. Moreover, these minimal furnishings were strictly utilitarian, not pieces designed for creature comfort. The French in their successive invasions of Italy during the late fifteenth and sixteenth centuries were dazzled by the luxury of the great palaces of Florence, Milan, Mantua, and Ferrara. Francis the First imported Italian artists (including Leonardo da Vinci, no less) and commissioned them to build and decorate his palace at Fontainebleau.

By the seventeenth century, the tastes of the Italian Renaissance had become firmly established in France, and under Louis XIV the elegance of the French court with its expression of royal omnipotence dominated the Western world. Wealthy status seekers in other countries emulated the luxury of France. Grand architectural panelings, moldings, and cornices demanded fixed furnishings (*meublants*); as a result, *canapés* (sofas), imposing straight-backed chairs, armoires, consoles, and pier glasses were used to line the lofty and frigid Baroque halls. At Versailles, *enfilades* (rooms opening one into another) provided infinite vistas climaxed by the main salon where receptions and entertainments were held. In the royal apartments this furniture, richly gilded, was planned to stand against the walls of rooms and galleries. The lesser nobility were content with wood furnishings either painted white and enhanced with golden ornament or waxed and enriched with gilded fillets.

In Italy at this time, architecture dominated decoration; ceilings were elaborately painted in spectacular perspective leading far into the sky. Furniture followed the grandiose pattern, but the inferior craftsmanship of the joiners (chairmakers) was concealed with gesso (a paste of whiting) and gilt.

England's great halls in the seventeenth century were lined with fine unpainted wood paneling. The craftsmanship of their wooden furnishings was superb; gilt furniture was introduced only for originality and ostentation at the end of the seventeenth century and it continued to be used in the eighteenth century.

The Western world knew nothing of lacquer until the return of Marco Polo in 1295. Whatever minor pieces he may have brought back from China were mere curiosities. Late in the fifteenth century, however, pieces of lacquer were imported by Spain and Portugal as a result of their extensive trade with the Orient. Imitations of lacquer were produced in the fifteenth and sixteenth centuries in Venice, but only on small boxes and chests. It was not until the seventeenth century, when Europe entered into regular trade relations with China, that Oriental lacquer became fashionable. The imported lacquer ware was dismembered, then reassembled and mounted by cabinetmakers into tables, commodes, and secretaries designed in the current European taste.

*Faux Bamboo*

In their country houses the landed and wealthy peerage of England had already grasped the concept of comfort in their intimate surroundings. The chairs of the Queen Anne period were light and graceful, and small, useful tables and other furnishings had been developed. In the seventeenth century, imported Oriental lacquer pieces and English copies of them, both professional and amateur, were enthusiastically included because of their delicacy and brilliance, along with furniture of fine wood and superior craftsmanship.

The dainty Rococo style began to develop in France during the Régence (1715–23), reaching its peak during the period of Louis XV. By this time, the French had tired of the cold formality of the Sun King, and with a growing desire for personal comfort, they had come to prefer small private rooms in town and cozy country houses. With the fashion for intimate apartments, architectural grandeur was scaled down to accommodate delightful and less pretentious *boiserie* (wood paneling). This was very often painted, sometimes gilded, and sometimes embellished with decorative painting *en grisaille* (gray painting simulating sculpture), *chinoiseries* (European reflections of the exotic Orient) or *singeries* (monkeys, often costumed, imitating man's diversions). The gold and white scheme formerly used on the furniture changed to polychrome. Frames of chairs were painted to match the *boiserie*, sometimes in the pseudo-lacquer called *vernis Martin* or in a colored varnish. They were also painted to blend with the upholstery, which often established the color scheme. The decoration of the entire room was motivated by a desire for harmony through the coordination of the furnishings. The French court and the nobility of the eighteenth century, increasingly fond of luxury, encouraged furniture of unparalleled perfection. The quality and beauty of workmanship reached its apogee before the French Revolution: the cabinetmaker, the joiner, and the decorative craftsman endowing all they created with a refinement that has never again been attained.

In the eighteenth century the Venetians, no longer affluent, came to recognize the convenience of smaller dwellings in the city and the country. Consequently, these were furnished with chairs, desks, tables, and *tabourets* in a more delicate style.

The rising middle classes in western Europe found these more intimate surroundings within their means and vied with the nobility in acquiring elegant furnishings. Concurrently, furniture was scaled down, becoming light and movable—*courant* in contrast to *meublant*. Many charming grace-

*Top left, Italian casein; right, French casein.*
*Bottom, faux marbre on distressed base.*

ful pieces, less costly than the former elaborate *meublants*, were evolved to furnish private rooms both at home and at opera house or theatre. As the notion of personal comfort developed, the number and types of household furnishings broadened and the art of decoration became more creative.

In Venice, furniture in the Louis XV style was decorated with extraordinary fantasy in sensuous harmonies of color. Indeed, William Odom suggests that in Italy much of the genius of the Renaissance was diverted in the eighteenth century to the decoration of commodes, tables, and chairs. The furniture, crude and hastily constructed of inferior wood, had to be concealed by a gesso ground. This poor workmanship challenged the decorative craftsmen to that flamboyant exercise of wit and fantasy so characteristic of the Venetians. They copied and adapted, with ebullience and color, design which had been perfected by the French. But it should be remembered that originally it was the Italians who taught, and led the way for, the decorators of the French court.

The English and French used fine wood, and they had no need to disguise inferior workmanship as the skill of their craftsmen was exquisite. Consequently, the creations of their decorative painters were, so to say, redundant. For example, satinwood was further decorated with multicolored designs, and sometimes was combined with *faux marbre*.

An ingenious method of decoration—invented for the benefit of impoverished courtiers—consisted of gluing cutout and tinted designs on furniture. These were tricked out with some handwork and the whole was buried in many coats of varnish. The method was so simple that it was taken up as a fad and pastime by the gentlewomen of Europe. The Venetians coined a condescending term—*arte povera*—for this technique, which today is known as *découpage*.

In the second half of the eighteenth century a new phase of decorative painting emanated from Italy and spread throughout Europe. Neoclassic in taste, it was inspired by archaeological research and the excavations of Pompeii and Herculaneum. Rome was the center of this revival. Robert Adam, visiting there, was caught up in and stimulated by the spell of antiquity as it appeared in Piranesi's prints of Roman ruins. Piranesi and his compatriots Pergolesi, Cipriani, Zucchi, and Angelica Kauffmann were invited to England by the Adam brothers and Neoclassicism became the rage there. Neoclassic design was based on structural form. Painting and gilding contributed textural variety derived from classic ornament. Painting made possible to a very large extent the creation by simple means of graceful furniture with the pure and spare lines of classical motifs. The desire for brightness in English houses, where flamboyant gold was considered unsuitable, gave rise to the fashion of painting classic designs on satinwood. Chippendale and Sheraton hit upon the idea of lightening the heaviness of wood surfaces with real or turned bamboo, gilded, painted, and japanned. The craftsmanship of the cabinetmakers and furniture artisans of England equaled that of France. When the English "grand tour" became an established fashion, Italian furniture was influenced by English design as well as by French.

In France, decorative painting on furniture continued through the Directoire and Empire periods, then somewhat diminished. In Italy decorative painting died with Napoleon's conquest of Venice.

In Colonial America, wealthy Virginians, Bostonians, and Philadelphians imported European furniture and Oriental lacquer. In addition, the cabinetmakers of large cities—often with European training, always with European pattern books—made their own versions of painted and lacquered pieces.

Using native wood, America's itinerant decorators and local craftsmen produced country furniture with ingenious naiveté. The kind of decoration they favored was not unlike that of provincial furniture as it had flourished in Denmark, Norway, Sweden, Austria, and Germany. There, during the long winters peasants had painted their chests, chairs, and walls with vignettes and ornaments inspired by any decorative device at hand.

In the latter part of the nineteenth century decorative painting on furniture diminished as the economy of Europe became industrial. Machine-made furnishings and artifacts were produced, and craftsmanship declined in consequence. The patronage of the courts and the nobility vanished. A vast amount of tasteless wood-graining was foisted on the unsophisticated new rich. The stuffy Victorian era preferred papier-mâché tables and chairs, as well as some gold leaf on ponderous furniture. The "fancy" chair with its stenciled patterns found favor in America.

Today the term "painted" is used indiscriminately to describe a motley assortment of furniture mechanically lacquered, enameled, and plasticized, or simply sprayed with paint. The exquisite antique pieces which remain from the past are the prizes of the collector. Most modern copies available to the general public are unfortunately coarsened. Nonetheless, the sprayed surfaces of contemporary furniture and crudely wrought imported reproductions point to a resurgence of interest in ornament. Antique painted furniture lives happily in contemporary surroundings.

Contrasting with the stark lines of today's furniture and architecture, a chair pale-hued and silvered, a commode aglow with gilt, a credenza gleaming with lacquer, or a secretary softly decorated on a chalky ground provide exceptional pleasure. Smaller objects and bibelots painted in a *faux* fantasy finish, contrived with wit and exquisite craftsmanship, make delightful and amusing treasures.

The disciplined skills and time required, and the consequent prohibitive costs, preclude commercial survival in the twentieth century of the craft of furniture decoration in its finest expression. When decorated furniture is manufactured by mechanical reproduction, it is reduced to dull reiteration, and spontaneity of execution is eliminated. Only the individual craftsman can paint, gild, and decorate a piece that rivals in excellence the furniture of the past. Finally, hope lies in the person who delights in these artifacts and himself finds joy in creating them. Fortunately, in the hectic twentieth century the techniques of tradition still provide a beautiful language for the expression of the individual spirit.

# PART I

*Painting,*
*Antiquing*
*&*
*Distressing:*
*Mediums & Methods*

# COLOR

## THE VARIED ROLES OF THE PAINTED FINISH

Painted furniture supplies one of many color elements in the decoration of a room. A room—like a painting—must be composed to draw attention to the center of interest, which in this case is the occupant; the painted pieces contribute to the composition. As a decorative factor, the *pièce de vertu*—a craftsman's term for any object to be painted—is destined to serve many purposes. Its painted finish can—

> provide an area of decorative design,
> designate a point of interest,
> punctuate a color scheme,
> create a rhythm through repeated color emphasis,
> dramatize by contrast,
> lighten the tone of a room,
> subdue poor design in the piece,
> diminish the size of the piece.

A piece of furniture, even though painted to be beautiful in itself, must, in today's interiors—where scale has become so diminished—be an integrated part of the room in which it exists. The designer of today, unlike his predecessor of several centuries past, rarely has large salons or galleries at his disposal. He must remember that height, length, and breadth have been reduced in houses and apartments. He must direct his talent within this restricted framework. Such a challenge demands a subtle usage of all the three creative phases of furniture decoration—color, design, finish.

It is possible to accentuate existing beauty—or to evoke new beauty —with an original choice of color, a discriminating use of striping, and a subtle rendering of the effect of patina. Artistry and skill can refresh the shabby piece or enrich the one which is dreary. For such a rewarding experience, the novice must bring patience to the workbench: patience to follow instructions, and patience to sustain his effort while learning.

# THE VISUAL PERCEPTION OF COLOR

To successfully mix the paint to color, which is the expressive medium of painted furniture, it is essential to have some knowledge and understanding of color theory. To create finishes and decoration on furniture and objects which will enable them to live in harmony with their surroundings, one must be aware of the properties and qualities of color.

Rays of light act upon the eye and the brain and create a response of color sensation. There are manifold numbers of light-wave lengths and they vary in color. Combined, they produce white light. Pigments absorb some wave lengths from white light and reflect back only those remaining. The dominant of these is the color seen. An object that absorbs nearly all wave lengths—being devoid of color—is seen as black. The colorist, however, by mixing all pigments together will produce gray, not white.

# HUMAN RESPONSE TO COLOR

Color produces an emotional reaction in human beings. The differences in psychological response are determined by the impact of the warm hues, which range in the color arc from the yellow-greens through the red-purples, and by that of the cool colors, ranging from green through blue to purple. The warm colors are gay and exciting, apparently exuding a degree of heat, whereas the cool colors are calm, sometimes chilling, and at their nadir depressing. Actually, all colors in the dissonance or the assonance of their interrelationship can be combined to emphasize either side of this comparison. The psychological effect of color should never be underestimated.

The painter of furniture must be a colorist. He will be concerned with the juxtaposition of colors, with their reflective action and interrelation, with the illusions and deceptions created by their interaction. Josef Albers and his students have produced a remarkable book about the interrelation of color. I had been struggling for years to teach this concept of color to my students and was heartened by this confirmation. His convincing theories are applicable and most important in the pursuit of this craft.

## THE NEED FOR AWARENESS

The first concern is the seeing of color, that is to say, training the visual perception not only to differentiate between one color and another, but also to notice the difference in the appearance of one color when it is used contiguously with any number of other colors; the difference that the quantity (greater or lesser) of one color makes when juxtaposed with another; the difference made by tonality (light and dark) in two colors used together; the difference made by intensity (grayness or brilliance) of two colors used in conjunction; the difference that occurs when intensities are varied in two colors. No artist of our time was more conscious of the careful choosing and balancing of colors than Matisse. The painter of furniture must be aware of the influence of one color upon the other. He must sense that the intensity of color and the degree of value determine the influence that they exert upon each other.

## BASIC CHARACTERISTICS OF COLOR

Color as seen by the eye has three dimensions: *Hue, Chromatic Intensity,* and *Tonal Value.* Each of these can be measured separately; one can be varied without disturbing the others. *Hue* is that quality by which one color is distinguished from another—names like red, blue, and so on, are conventions for identifying hues. *Chromatic Intensity* is the measure of color strength. This factor distinguishes the brilliance or weakness of a color: whether the chroma exists in full power or has been grayed. *Tonal*

*Value* is the measure of the degree of luminosity in a hue, the quality by which light and dark colors are distinguished. When white is added, a hue becomes high in *Tonal Value* because of the increase in light rays reflected from it. As black is added to color, it decreases in *Tonal Value* since more light rays are absorbed in it. The values of the basic hues vary in themselves, i.e., yellow is more luminous, therefore higher in tonality, than is red or blue.

# EXPERIMENTS WITH COLOR

Here are some exercises that may serve to refine one's visual estimate of color. The results should be saved; they will be useful aids not only in later chapters of this book but also whenever one is engaged in the fine art of finishing furniture. For these exercises, the following gouache designer's colors should be purchased:

> Spectrum red (orange-red)
> Alizarin rose madder (purple-red)
> Cobalt blue (purple-blue)
> Cypress green (green-blue)
> Spectrum yellow
> Lampblack

White show-card paint is also necessary because a small drop must be added to each gouache color to make it entirely opaque.

## STUDY OF THE INTERACTION OF COLORS

Each of the water colors is combined with varying amounts of white show-card paint in small containers. Two 3-inch squares and two 1-inch squares of each color are painted on white index cards and cut to size. The 3-inch cards are placed haphazardly in a double row on a large sheet of white paper. By placing the two orange-red 1-inch squares in the middle of two 3-inch squares of differing colors, one finds that the orange-red square is seen differently when placed on differing grounds. As the 1-inch square is placed on the various ground colors, it will be seen that the hue of this small square is altered by the surrounding color.

## STUDY OF CHROMATIC INTENSITY

The hues directly opposite each other on the color wheel (or Color Aid; see p. 31) are known as *complementary* colors. These two hues complement each other both positively and negatively. When used in similar intensity and quantity, and placed in proximity, they each appear to heighten the *chromatic intensity* of the other. Combined in equal amounts, the complementary hues will nullify each other and produce gray. It follows that the addition of a small amount of its complement to a hue will gray or neutralize it, reducing its chromatic intensity a degree.

There is an exercise which will fix the complementary hues firmly in the memory. One-inch squares of accurate mixtures of the primary and secondary colors, true red, purple, blue, green, yellow, and orange, are painted, then are arranged on a white paper in pairs of complements. Under each of these pairs of complements are placed two other squares which have been grayed slightly by each of the complements. This proves a most effective method for comprehending the meaning of chromatic intensity.

A short cut can be taken if it is necessary to reduce the chromatic intensity of a hue selected for use on furniture: instead of mixing the complement, one substitutes the earth colors or black. The earth colors may be roughly described as clay stained with compounds of iron and manganese. Roasting the raw forms of this clay produces the burnt earth colors. The earth colors are:

| | |
|---|---|
| Raw umber | brown red-purple |
| Burnt umber | deep brown red-purple |
| Raw sienna | light yellow-brown red-purple |
| Burnt sienna | deep brown red-red-purple |
| French yellow ochre | yellow red-purple |
| Lampblack | black blue |

To neutralize, or gray, a hue, black or the earth color which contains an element of the hue's *complement* should be chosen. (For instance, yellow yellow-green, which is complemented by purple-purple red, may be neutralized with raw umber, which contains an element of red-purple.) It is possible also to turn a hue toward the secondary, tertiary, or quaternary degree by neutralizing it with an earth color which includes a *related* element. However, to keep the true chroma of a hue (actually there will be slight neutralization), it is necessary to use the exact complement.

### STUDY OF TONAL VALUE

One continues these experiments—evaluation through comparison—by painting a tonal value scale of thirteen 1-inch squares ranging in equidistant steps from white through middle gray to black. This scale is a standard for judging tonal values in color. Similar sets of squares are made for each color; their light values are achieved by the addition of white, and their dark values by the addition of lampblack.

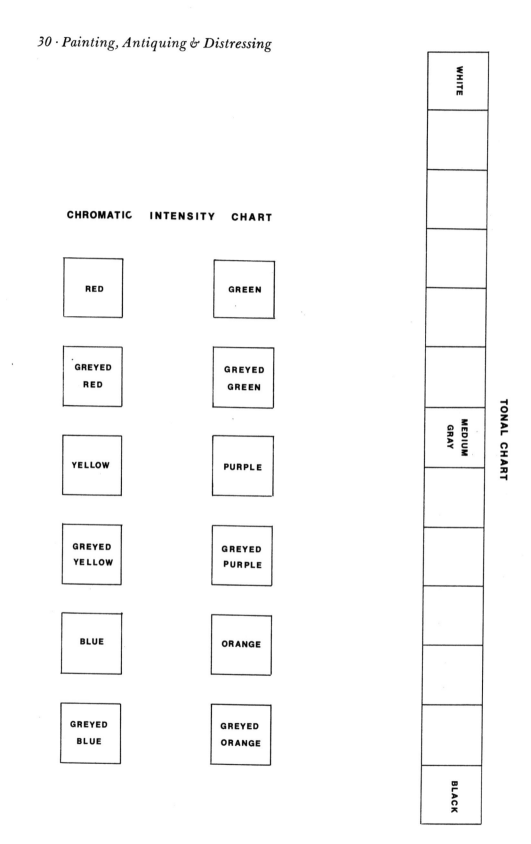

CHROMATIC INTENSITY CHART

| RED | GREEN |

| GREYED RED | GREYED GREEN |

| YELLOW | PURPLE |

| GREYED YELLOW | GREYED PURPLE |

| BLUE | ORANGE |

| GREYED BLUE | GREYED ORANGE |

TONAL CHART

WHITE

MEDIUM GRAY

BLACK

## MAKING A COLOR AID

Now a Color Aid must be made. It will consist of paint chips (made on pieces of index cards) placed contiguously around a wheel. Trained by previous exercises, the eye will readily discern any errors in progression

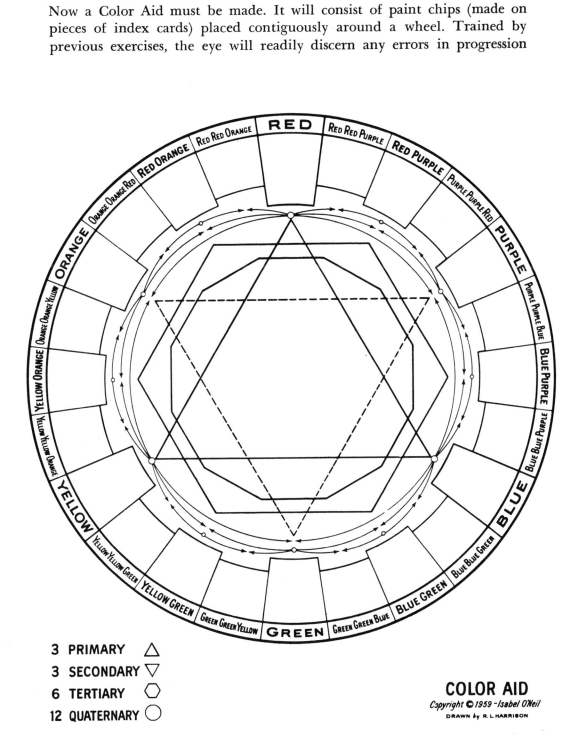

3  PRIMARY  △
3  SECONDARY  ▽
6  TERTIARY  ⬡
12  QUATERNARY  ◯

**COLOR AID**
*Copyright © 1959 – Isabel O'Neil*
DRAWN *by* R. L. HARRISON

of hue and the necessary adjustments can then be made. When completed, there will be equal steps of color change between each hue. The eye will then move easily around the circle, undeterred by the shock of an excessive gap between hues or a disparity in adjacent values.

The *primary hues* are *red, blue,* and *yellow.* They are existing basic pigments which cannot be mixed. Pure red and pure blue are unfortunately not purchasable and must be made by combining the two reds and the two blues listed above. The simplest way of preparing them for the Color Aid is as follows: alizarin rose madder (purple-red) is combined with spectrum red (orange-red) to produce a true red, leaning neither toward purple nor orange. A drop of the white poster paint is added to make the mixture opaque. In testing each mixture for pure color, one must rely exclusively on his own visual perception. This eye training is the most important aspect of the exercise.

After using the mixed pure red, one sets it aside, for the purple and orange in the red pigments used to make it will gray any other mixture of color. To continue: the hues of the Color Aid from red red-purple through blue blue-purple are now mixed with alizarin rose madder (purple-red) and cobalt blue (purple-blue). Obviously, the hue entitled red red-purple contains a preponderance of red. This pigment diminishes in proportion as the colors proceed through blue blue-purple. Because blue is the darkest value of the pigments we are using, the amount of added white is increased as the proportion of blue increases.

When one works with the blue mixture, the combination of cobalt blue (purple-blue) and cypress green (green-blue) must be neutralized with a touch of orange to produce a true blue commensurate with the preceding hues in intensity. This hue is also set aside, since the purple contained in the mixture would neutralize the ensuing hues. The arc of the Color Aid from blue blue-green through yellow yellow-green is mixed with cypress green (blue-green) and spectrum yellow. As the proportion of blue decreases, the amount of white decreases, being replaced somewhat by the yellow, which is the lightest value of the pigments used.

Yellow is mixed by adding a slight touch of cypress green to the spectrum yellow. Again, one puts aside the yellow mixture containing green, which would gray the remaining colors to be mixed. Combining spectrum yellow and spectrum red (orange-red) to mix the hues yellow yellow-orange through red red-orange completes the Color Aid. Some errors will undoubtedly be apparent because of uneven values, unequal steps between the changing hues, or incorrect juxtaposition of hues. If the squares of color are applied with stamp hinges or folded-over masking tape, corrections are easy to make.

### *STUDY OF OPTICAL MIXTURE*

To demonstrate the process of optical mixture—where two colors perceived simultaneously are visually combined and merged into a new color—the following exercise is instructive:

Strips of equal width and length are painted in primary and secondary colors which are analogous but not complementary. In looking at them, one finds that when the colors are identical in tonal value and chromatic intensity, and are placed in equal amount in adjacent areas, they fuse visually into the semblance of the color equidistant between them. This effect is corrected by reducing the dimension of one hue to half the area of the other and by lightening the tonal value of the larger area by one half and, if necessary, slightly diminishing its intensity.

It will be seen that two hues separated in the scale of tonal values exaggerate the difference of their value when they are used in conjunction —the darkness of the deeper and the luminosity of the lighter seeming more emphatic than they are in actuality. A light tonal value when used with a dark will in effect approach white, while the deeper tone approaches black. By strengthening the intensity of the pale color and bringing the values closer, the color of each will be maintained.

Two hues possessing the same dominant hue when used together will subtract the shared hue from each other and the differing elements will be prominent. (This was apparent in the first exercise involving the 1-inch and 3-inch squares.) By diminishing the quantity of the similar hue in one of the colors, the two hues will retain the intended relationship.

Color in full chromatic intensity advances toward the beholder; in low intensity, it recedes. An area of strong intensity in contrast to a background of weak intensity will seem larger than actual size. This illusion of exaggerated size can be done away with by toning down the stronger hue so that it relates less dramatically to the weaker.

# CHOICE OF HUE

In painting furniture the first concern is to distinguish shape; this is done by contrasting the color of the form with that of its background. The choice of color for painting, decorating, and antiquing a piece of furniture is made with awareness of the effect of each of the color dimensions. It is important to understand that color is subject to light and to shifting light. There is reflective action of light and color on color.

By referring to the previous color experiments, one selects the basic hue according to whether one wishes the piece to produce the effect of balance, imbalance, or neutrality.

*Balance* for the total composition is obtained by using cool color in association with warm color, light tonal value with dark, weak chromatic intensity with brilliant. *Imbalance*, which may serve to overcome monotony or to enhance and make more evident the over-all balance of the room, is achieved by overstressing the hue. Stimulating overemphasis of tonal value or a chromatic intensity lends sprightliness to an otherwise subdued room.

If the piece to be painted is overscaled or unattractive, it can be made inconspicuous by blending it into the background by the use of a closely related or a neutral hue for the base color.

Any and all hues may be combined harmoniously by the subtle adjustment of the three dimensions of color (hue, intensity, and value). Nature with her manifold contrasts and pleasing blendings superbly demonstrates this.


## COLOR GROUPS

The following definitions of color groups indicate some of the combinations available in the choice of a scheme.

On the Color Aid the hues from green onward become warm as they move toward yellow; cool toward blue.

*Warm* colors are those hues dominated by red and yellow.

*Cool* colors are those in which blue is predominant.

*Analogous* color is based on hues having a like attribute; these are either a group of three adjoining hues of the primaries, secondaries, and tertiaries, or of any three out of six if the quaternaries are included. Analogous colors are harmonious.

*Dissonant* color is achieved by a combination of hues chosen from uneven positions on opposite sides of a primary color. It creates tension.

*Consonant* color implies a balance which can be produced by using equal amounts of warm and cool color in equal dimension.

*Subtle* color is any of the tertiary or quaternary hues and is thus categorized because the mixture of pigment in each of them is variable in different lights and is influenced by adjacent color.


*Faux Natural Tortoise Shell*

*Monochromatic* color consists of variations in tonal value and chromatic intensity of a single hue.

*Neutral* color possesses neither hue nor chroma. All hues when adulterated by their complement, or by earth colors or black, are neutralized. Neutrals without hue or chromatic intensity are:

Absolute white
Gray
Absolute black

However, they do possess value—light, middle, and dark.

*Monotone* color indicates a neutral hue used in conjunction with another of the same tonal value and chromatic intensity.


## USE OF WHITE

As the enormous breadth and lavish potential of color is sensed through continual experiment and increasing awareness, students are led to exciting concepts and to the creation of myriad combinations. Yet there is always the person who feels so ignorant—so insecure—when he surveys the vast field of color that he chooses to paint "white from fright." It offers little as a factor in a color scheme.


## COLOR

*Materials*
  Gouache colors
    Spectrum red
    Alizarin rose madder
    Cobalt blue
    Cypress green
    Spectrum yellow
    Lampblack

  Jar of white poster paint
  Unlined index cards
  White paper

*Tools*
  #6 sable brush

*Miscellaneous*
  Masking tape or stamp hinges


*Basic Antiquing and Striping*

# PREPARATION OF SURFACE:
## Basic Tools and Methods

### ORGANIZATION FOR WORK

When the craftsman starts his project, he should wear a smock or coverall and comfortable shoes. He coats his hands liberally with a protective cream and allows it to dry. When the day's task is over, he rubs a cleanser containing lanolin well into his hands and wipes it off with a paper towel. He then washes his hands in warm water and applies hand lotion.

Work should be executed in a light, roomy area where the project and equipment may be left undisturbed until completion. There should be enough space around the object so that the worker can stand directly in front of the particular area on which he is working. To avoid tiring backaches, the piece should be placed on a table or sawhorses. However, if a surface to be worked on is above shoulder height, the piece is removed to the floor, for sanding, painting, and antiquing need the downward swing of the arm for control.

All hardware, such as handles and escutcheons (keyhole plates), must be removed before painting; hinges are best left on. Hardware is mounted on long nails inserted in a block of styrofoam for easy painting.

# SANDPAPERS—THEIR USE IN PREPARING SURFACES

60   garnet opencote cabinet paper—for hard finished surfaces, enamels or lacquer.

100   garnet finishing paper—for varnished or flat painted surfaces.

220   garnet finishing paper—for filled areas, for feathering, and for sanding between paint coats.

The numbers 60, 100, and 220 refer to the number and size of garnet grits per linear inch that have been sifted through screen mesh and glued to the paper—the finer the mesh, the more grits there are per inch. Therefore, the higher numbers indicate the more numerous and smaller grits found on the finer finishing papers.

The classifications *cabinet* and *finishing* refer to the weight of the paper on which the grits are mounted. Cabinet is a heavy paper for rough use. Finishing paper is light and pliable.

*Opencote* indicates the area between grits which prevents the paper from becoming rapidly loaded or clogged. It should be specified on a purchase order. Finishing paper is always opencote.

Sandpaper is sold by the sheet or in sleeves which consist of 100 sheets.

*Sanding blocks* of various sizes (1½" × 2"; 3" × 4½") are helpful for flat surfaces. Felt is glued to them; this cushions the stroke when sandpaper is wrapped around the blocks. Rubber sanding blocks are also available at paint stores. Except when used for wrapping a sanding block, the paper is divided into small squares, a sheet being torn four times each way against a steel edge. For sanding narrow moldings or similar areas, strips are preferable. A sharpened typewriter eraser makes an extra fine abrasive for carvings.

## *SANDING—PROCEDURE*

A light sanding to abrade the surface, thus creating a bond for the paint, is all that is required to prepare most pieces for painting. Sanding should be rhythmic, with an easy movement which uses the muscle at the back of the shoulder, the same muscle which is used in playing the piano, or in golf or tennis. Actually the sanding and painting arm is propelled by energy originating in the center of the body. The arm acts as a peripheral extension possessing no independent energy. The rhythmic shifting of body weight directs the operation and controls the lightness or firmness of the pressure. This method eliminates much body fatigue. A light steady stroke will accomplish more than short aggressive jabs that are elbow-, arm-, or wrist-directed. A little more pressure is needed to eliminate a deep scratch. The beginner should learn to discriminate between those dents and agreeable irregularities which contribute to a look of antiquity and the blemishes that have resulted from abuse, such as scratches, ring marks, and gouges. The sandpaper should be changed when it is full of residue. Sandpaper is less valuable than human energy.

Strokes must be kept even; any deviation will show through the paint coats at the final moment of antiquing. Sanding must follow the direction of the grain of the wood. There is one exception to this rule: when the line of a piece indicates that the design should go in a direction contrary to the grain, sanding arbitrarily follows the direction in which the section will later be painted. *Example*—The grain of the wood in the drawer of an apron (support to a table top) flows vertically—that of the apron, horizontally. If it is decided to keep the apron area unbroken in painting, the direction of the sanding of the drawer must correspond with the direction of the grain of the apron. Sanding and painting are always done in the same direction.

On painted surfaces there may be chips which require *feather edging*. This means sanding the edges of the chips, first with 100 garnet sandpaper, then with 220, so that the bare wood and the remaining paint surface blend smoothly together. In the restoration of an old piece, this is, of course, essential.

A keen sense of touch is indispensable. The tips of the fingers are used to feel the surface *lightly*. If pressure is heavy, only that pressure is felt and not the texture of the surface. It is possible to *feel* a roughness which cannot be seen. Repair or filling should be sanded absolutely level with the surface. A repair that is obvious is as unacceptable as the original damage.

## FILLERS—THEIR USE IN REPAIRING SURFACES

A *coarse wood filler* is used for large holes, cracks, and broken moldings. Any such cavity is lined with resin glue before it is filled. If an outside edge needs repair, a small nail is driven into the cavity. This provides the necessary extra support to hold the coarse filler in place. After the filler has dried, it is sanded with 100 garnet sandpaper and then surfaced with *fine filler*. When this top filler is dry it is sanded with 220 garnet sandpaper and shellacked. If the coarse filler dries out in the can, lacquer thinner should be added as a moistener, and the can is stood upside down overnight; the filler will then be ready for future use.

A *fine grain filler* or a *vinyl filler* is used for filling joining seams, fine cracks, small holes, and porous surfaces. The surface of the grain filler is first scraped with a palette knife moistened in water until a thick paste forms on the knife. Water is never put directly into the container.

Vinyl filler can be used directly from the can; it is applied with a palette knife, orangewood stick, or finger; after a brief wait, the residue is wiped off. When dry, the filled-in surfaces are sanded with 220 garnet sandpaper and shellacked. The vinyl filler may also be used for shallow filling, as in, chipped veneer, or to fill an open-grained wood such as oak. It is applied with a palette knife and then is evened off with a wet finger or a cloth run diagonally over the surface. If the vinyl proves too stiff for this purpose, it can be thinned with water. Sanding with 220 garnet sandpaper and shellacking follow after the vinyl filler has dried.

Later on, after the first coat of paint, an overlooked crevice can be filled with the vinyl filler combined with the paint being used.

*Water putty*—a soft-bodied filler—is used when a missing piece of carving is to be duplicated. The putty is made as directed on the can. Grease (oil or petroleum jelly) is applied to an existing piece of carving that is identical with that to be duplicated. It is then coated heavily with coarse filler. This coating forms a negative mold, which is removed when dry. The cavity of the mold is greased and filled with putty. As soon as it has set, the *positive* is removed, allowed to harden, and pointed up with a sharpened carving tool. After shellacking it is ready to be glued in place.

*Glue with resin base* (polyethylene glue)—any good brand—is used for regluing broken carvings, etc. Each of the broken sides must be coated; then they are pressed together, and any residue is wiped off with a damp cloth. The carving is secured with masking tape and let dry overnight.

## SHELLAC—ITS USE IN SURFACING

Shellac is a substance derived from the hardened secretion of insects which swarm on the trees of India and Thailand. This substance is melted, purified, and chipped into small flakes.

*Orange Flake Shellac* is unbleached gum that is cut (dissolved) in alcohol to make orange shellac.

*White Shellac* is *bleached* orange shellac gum dissolved in alcohol.

White or orange shellac should be purchased in a *5-pound cut*; this term indicates that five pounds of shellac gum have been cut into a gallon of alcohol. Orange shellac is somewhat less expensive than white but, though adequate for preparatory work, is more difficult to apply. Because shellac deteriorates and discolors, it should be purchased in small quantities.

There is yet another shellac, one incorrectly called *French varnish.* I imagine that this name resulted from use of this shellac for the French polish so popular on French furniture in the nineteenth century. French varnish is the most refined of the shellacs; it is less yellow, thus does not affect the hue on which it is laid. This medium will be specified by its popular name—not as shellac—whenever its use is required.

Before shellac is used, it should be further cut with an equal amount of *denatured alcohol.* And unless otherwise stated, it should be understood that whenever shellac is mentioned in this book, this fifty-fifty solution is intended. It should be stored in a reasonably warm room away from light, and in a glass container, as a metal container would cause the shellac to darken. The shellac container is never shaken because agitation creates bubbles that dry as imperfections in the surface. Shellac must only be stirred.

Shellac is never applied in damp weather; dryness is essential for successful shellacking. If the surface is damp or the atmosphere is laden with moisture, a milky, cloudy film called "bloom" will appear on the surface. Therefore, windows should be closed and shellac applied in a dry room with an approximate temperature of 70° F.

A paint coat may be applied after a single coat of shellac has dried for an hour.

One brush is reserved for shellac only. A 1½-inch or 2-inch "cutter," a white French bristle brush, is the most suitable. The end bristles of this brush are chiseled to facilitate flow of the medium. Immediately after use this brush should be cleaned in denatured alcohol. Should the bristle harden, it can be cleaned in a solution of ammonia and water. Soap should *never* be used.

To apply a good coat of shellac is no easy matter. After the brush is loaded, the excess is pressed out on the *inside* of the container, because, when the brush is drawn across the top of the container, air bubbles are created. Quick, even strokes with no overlap are essential. The first stroke begins with the tip of the full brush placed in the center of the area to be covered; it is moved lightly to one end. Then the brush is lifted, returned to the center, and stroked to the opposite end, thereby dispersing the initial puddle. The brush generally retains enough liquid to repeat this process on the following stroke. When the brush is less full, pressure on the heel of the brush is required to complete the succeeding strokes, which now go clear across the surface from edge to edge. If the brush needs reloading, this should be done quickly, repeating the steps just described. For carved pieces, the work proceeds rapidly and with a minimum brush load, the brush pouncing from both sides of a center point to avoid any edge-drying. Pouncing in this instance means jabbing with the shellac brush, the long bristles of which will seek out the depths of the interstices. A fine shellac coat requires precision, quickness, deftness, and skill.

## RAW WOOD—PREPARATION

A piece fresh from the cabinetmaker still requires sanding. There may be whiskers of wood or tool dents—these must be sanded with 100 garnet paper. Exposed nail heads are sunk with a nail set, and the holes repaired with fine filler (wood or vinyl). Joining cracks are similarly filled, and when dry are sanded with 220 garnet paper. Any residual glue is chipped off with a razor. Rough areas of the wood are sanded until smooth. The entire piece is then ready to be dusted, tack-clothed, and shellacked. Shellac seals the surface of raw wood, preventing the paint from sinking in. If the wood has a wide open grain, as in the case of oak, a fine wood or vinyl filler serves to seal the whole surface. Before the filler sets, the surface is scraped diagonally—with a palette knife held at about a 45-degree angle —so that the filler remains only in the grain. When dry and sanded, this type of filled surface requires two coats of shellac. *Only raw wood pieces should be shellacked in their entirety before painting.*

## VARNISHED WOOD—PREPARATION

Varnished wood is first washed with denatured alcohol, which cleanses it of foreign matter. Wood appearing to be varnished is often, instead, shellacked. The denatured alcohol will also remove that surface. Then it is sanded with 100 garnet paper to provide a surface "tooth" to hold the first coat of paint. It is unnecessary to expose the bare wood. It is enough to roughen the hard varnish. Carving and grooves need only cursory sanding. If the veneer has buckled or raised, the warped areas are cut out or split with a razor. Glue is inserted in these spots. Any pieces of veneer that have been removed are replaced and held firm with masking tape to dry over-night. Chips in the veneer are repaired with vinyl filler. All filled areas are sanded and shellacked as explained earlier in this chapter. The piece is then ready for painting.

## PAINTED WOOD—PREPARATION

If a piece to be reworked has been painted with skill in the past, it need only be sanded with 100 garnet paper. If the painting was somewhat inept or if the mediums used were enamel or lacquer, the heavier cabinet paper (60) will produce—when used lightly—a good abraded surface. Drips and roll-overs (a painter's term for the ridge of paint that occurs when the brush tips off by mistake on the surface adjacent to the one being covered) are scraped off with a single-edge razor. Chips in the paint are feathered out with 100 and 220 garnet paper. A moderate sanding is needed in this preparation. After the sanding, the piece is completely washed with alcohol to remove any foreign matter. If there is filling to be done, those areas only, after drying, need be sanded and shellacked. At this stage the piece has been properly prepared for painting.

## A HORROR—PREPARATION

A "horror" is an article painted many times by inexpert workers. Paint remover is necessary only in this instance. A heavy-bodied paint remover which remains where laid on should be used. The worker, wearing rubber gloves, applies the remover with a fully loaded stiff-bristle 2-inch brush—not brushing on but *patting on* with the flat side of the brush a cover at least ¼″ thick. He waits—as directed on the container—until the painted surface bubbles and shows signs of wrinkling. The old paint is then re-moved with scraper, putty knife, razor, brass-bristle suede brush, old tooth-brush, and "tired" (previously used) steel wool. A test patch is tried first to gauge the timing. Only a small area is covered at a time so that the process is not arduous. For a complete job the operation must be repeated. When finished, the piece is washed with denatured alcohol. It is then sanded with 100 garnet paper wherever the surface is rough. The usual filling, sanding, and shellacking follow. The piece is now properly prepared for painting.

# PLASTER, MARBLE, STONE, LEATHER— PREPARATION

Chips or blemishes on any of these materials are preferably repaired with a vinyl filler after a thorough preliminary cleaning with either soap and water or alcohol. Two coats of shellac are applied to fill the porous surface sufficiently for painting. The final coat is lightly sanded with 220 garnet paper; the piece is then properly prepared for painting.

# METAL—PREPARATION

A metal oil primer, a type of varnish specifically designed for protecting metal surfaces, prevents rusting and provides a surface for painting. This coat must dry overnight. Hardware (knobs, door pulls, handles, escutcheons) to be painted should also be coated with this primer. Old metal previously painted is prepared by removing all old paint with 60 garnet opencote cabinet paper, wire brush, and scraper, or with paint remover. Emery cloth is excellent for removing rust. If an antique object is dented, it is possible to have the damages filled in with metal at an automobile body shop. Finally, old metal is washed with denatured alcohol and the primer applied. Such a piece is now properly prepared for painting.

The importance of dusting a piece before the application of each and every coating cannot be overemphasized. All surfaces must be free of dust and other alien matter. A whisk broom or a small hand vacuum may be used for the initial dusting. This is then followed by careful rubbing of every minute area with a tack cloth. This cloth (sometimes called a tack rag) is sold at paint stores. It is a piece of cheesecloth impregnated with resinous varnish which remains sticky as long as the cloth is kept warm (at ordinary room temperature). It should be stored in a closed jar and may be used as long as the tackiness remains.

Whatever its former state, a piece after this dusting is now in condition for the craftsman to embark on the creative phases of this decorative craft.

# PREPARATION OF SURFACE

*Materials*
60 garnet opencote cabinet paper
100 garnet finishing paper
220 garnet finishing paper
Emery cloth
Coarse wood filler
Fine wood filler or vinyl filler
Water putty
Glue (any resin-base glue)
Denatured alcohol
Lacquer thinner
Paint remover
White or orange shellac (5-pound cut)
Metal oil primer

*Tools*
Shellac brush, 2″ or 1½″
Palette knife
Scraper or putty knife
Single-edge razors

Wire suede brush
X-acto knife (carving tool)
Orangewood sticks
Nail set

*Miscellaneous*
Sanding blocks
000 steel wool pads
Masking tape
Block of styrofoam
Typewriter eraser
Petroleum jelly
Whisk broom
Tack cloth
Rags
Newspaper
Cans and jars
Assorted nails
Glass containers
Rubber gloves
Toothbrush

# PAINT

## COLORS OF THE PAST

Before a paint color is chosen—whether for chair, commode, or some other object—it is interesting as well as enlightening to have some knowledge of the colors prevalently used on such a piece in the past. Painted furnishings did not exist before Louis XIV and even during his reign they were rare. At that time furnishings keyed to the architecture (*meublants*) were gilded. During the Régence, they were apt to be painted in white and then parcel-gilt (adorned with gold moldings, carvings, and the like). Obviously, such furnishings were found only in the great halls of the nobility. Under Louis XV, white went out of fashion; favored instead were reticent pastel shades —lilac, yellow, green—with contrasting pastel stripings, and carving rendered in a polychrome of natural color. Combinations of yellow and silver, yellow and red, red and gold, green and gold, as well as green and rose were frequent. The colors matched the painted *boiseries* which lined the walls or they were keyed to the upholsteries. The entire ensemble of the room and furniture was an example of harmony executed with exquisite refinement of taste. In Venice during the 1700s, furniture at mid-century was more effulgent in color. Blue, green, ivory, and yellow were decorated with lively abandon in a galaxy of colors which were brought into a harmonious golden tone with a varnish glaze. Under Louis XVI, pastel shades were abandoned in favor of more vivid effects, and white came back into fashion. The Directoire period produced a palette of green, mauve, blue, and yellow, embellished with a variety of stripings. The Empire, with its lavish ornament, was restrained in color, using cream or gray with gold decoration. In England during the eighteenth century, the designs of Hepplewhite combined green, blue, black, and buff with multicolor decoration. Sheraton and Adam favored pastel green, fawn, pink, and mauve, with white and gold enrichment. Multicolor decoration and *faux marbre* were often combined with satinwood.

Originally the colors of the eighteenth century were fresh and bright; time has grayed and softened them. The paint of the period of Louis XV was glossy while that of the Louis XVI period was mat. If a chair was caned, the caning was painted the same as the wood frame and often was decorated with two or more striping tones. The magazine *Connaissance* mentions a chair with a landscape painted on the caning. It is amusing to note that during the French Revolution the great furniture dating back to Louis XV and Louis XVI was often painted over as a matter of prudence, its appearance rendered less rich through the use of black or a shade now referred to as Trianon gray. Knowledge of traditional pieces is one guide to color selection —another is the craftsman's own inventiveness.

In a group of painted furniture having antique lines, only one piece should be painted and antiqued in any single method. It should seem that each piece has been garnered from some distant place and joined with the others to create a harmonious effect.

## MATERIALS—THEIR USES AND MAINTENANCE

### FLAT WHITE OIL PAINT
A flat white oil paint containing a titanium and silicate base is most suitable as a substance (tinted with color) for painting the surface of a piece intended to receive an antique patina. As the body of this paint is softer than that of an enamel or alkyd, it lends itself to fine sanding. This paint must dry overnight between coats. It requires six months to achieve a completely hard set but the piece may be used in the interim.

## CARE OF FLAT PAINT

Flat paint is best stored upside down since this makes it easier to mix. It must be stirred thoroughly before use, turpentine being added when thinning is necessary. Palette knives made in various lengths are convenient for stirring. These should be cleaned immediately after use with tired—previously used—steel wool. A few drops of turpentine added to each paint can before closing will prevent the formation of a skin, or crust, on top. If such does form, it should be removed carefully with a palette knife and discarded.

## JAPAN COLORS

The term "japan" is now used to describe colors ground in quick-drying synthetic varnish. Formerly, the term designated colors ground in japan, a spirit varnish made of natural gum dissolved in a solvent containing no oil. Today's japan colors are opaque, quick-drying, and mat, and are used to tint white paint. They may be purchased in sixteenth (half-pint) size cans. Thus the term "japan color" in this book always refers to japan taken directly from the can in which it is bought.

A basic assortment might include:

> Liberty red medium—red red-purple
> Signcraft red—red-orange
> Chrome yellow light—light yellow
> Cobalt blue—blue blue-purple
> C.P.* green medium—blue blue-green
> C.P.* green light—green green-yellow
> Raw umber
> Burnt umber
> Raw sienna
> Burnt sienna
> French yellow ochre
> Lampblack

For striping and decorating, the japans are preferable to oil colors, which consist of pigment ground in oil and are therefore transparent. In this book, the term "oil color" refers to artists' tubes.

Smooth coverage is achieved with one thin, flat coat. Japan colors are also used as a wash by diluting them with turpentine. These colors, if the tonal value is above middle value, appear darker when wet than when dry; if below middle value, they appear lighter when wet than when dry.

* In old manuals, C.P. is a holdover of the term "coach paint" which described this green.

### DILUENTS AND SOLVENTS

A diluent should have the power to dissolve the vehicle, disperse it uniformly, and maintain solution without harming the paint materials. It must evaporate from the freshly laid-down film in such a fashion that a uniform coating of maximum over-all adhesion is deposited upon the surface.

*Denatured alcohol* is a solvent to dilute shellac and to clean brushes used to apply shellac.

*Sealed turpentine* is a solvent made from the gum of the terebinth tree. It is a diluent for paint and certain varnishes.

*Thinner and mineral spirits* are solvents and diluents derived from petroleum, minerals, and other substances.

*Flatting oil (soybean oil)* is sometimes used to dilute paint. It delays the drying time and therefore enables one to brush out the paint to a smoother surface. This oil is non-yellowing and does not alter the color of the paint.

*Japan drier* is a quick-drying agent used to accelerate drying and add cohesiveness to pigment. Japan drier, in a proportion of 10% of the mixture, is added to any paint mixture consisting largely of japan color. In addition, turpentine is used to thin the mixture to proper consistency for painting.

*Liquid detergent Triton X100* combined with mineral spirits (4 ounces detergent to 1 quart spirits) makes a solution for further cleaning brushes after paint has been removed from bristles.

*Brown naphtha soap* is a strong cleanser used for the final cleaning of brushes.

### BRUSHES

Brushes are made of various bristles held together by a metal ferrule which in turn is fastened to a handle. The *tip* of the brush is the free end of the bristle and the *heel* of the brush is the end near the ferrule. A long-handled brush is selected as its length allows it to be held loosely midway up the handle. This forces the use of the trapezium muscle in the back of the shoulder, the same one mentioned in the discussion of sanding. Practice eventually leads to maximum control of the brush. Long-bristled brushes are designated because they are flexible; moreover, because of their length they carry a load of paint sufficient to eliminate frequent dipping into the paint can. Brushes fresh from the manufacturer contain size, which preserves their shape prior to use. It is necessary to flick them with one's fingers in order to remove this size as well as any loose hairs.

Since brushes are the most important tools of this craft, they should be kept in perfect condition. The rule to remember when *cleaning brushes* is that the agent indicated to reduce or cut a given medium is the solvent in which the brush used for that medium is cleaned. After a brush is used, it is wiped out well on newspaper and is then cleaned with mineral spirits and detergent to remove the paint, varnish, or wax—or with alcohol to remove shellac. In the studio, two cans of the detergent solution are used, termed Bath 1 and Bath 2. Sieves are hung by wires in the upper third of each can. When the brush is rubbed out against the sieve, paint dislodges and drops to the bottom of the can. This leaves the upper part of the bath clear and the solvent continues to dissolve the paint from the bristles. The brush is dipped repeatedly in Bath 1 and is wiped each time on rough cloth, such as an old turkish towel. Now the brush is dipped in Bath 2, which obviously will remain clearer. When a residue of color no longer shows on the towel, the bristles are worked well in the hand and rinsed out in warm water. In order to remove any paint that stubbornly clings to the heel of the brush, a steel brush comb (or dog comb) is used repeatedly. Finally the bristle is scoured briskly on a cake of brown naphtha soap and again rinsed in lukewarm water. A little soap is left in a paint brush to point and shape it. This acts as a substitute for the manufacturer's size and must be flicked out before reusing. After the bristles have been shaped, the brush is set to dry; it may be stood on handle-end in a can or suspended on wire strung through a hole in the handle. If the brush is to be stored or transported, foil or paper is wrapped around the bristle except at the very end. This allows the brush to dry yet maintain its original shape.

*Shellac brushes* are exclusively reserved for shellac and are cleaned immediately after use. This must be done with alcohol; the brushes are dipped and wiped several times. They must never be washed with soap. If a shellac brush should become stiff, it may be cleaned in a mild solution of ammonia and water.

*Varnish brushes* are reserved for varnish. If the varnish brush is in daily use, it may be suspended in a container of turpentine or mineral spirits, care being taken that the brush tip does not touch the bottom or sides. The solvent fills the container to the point where the entire bristle is immersed. If, on the other hand, the brush is to be stored, it is cleaned thoroughly in the solvent of the specific varnish employed. Absolutely no other cleaning material can be used.

*Fine sable brushes* used for striping and decorating have a delicate bristle which bends easily. They should be cleaned in turpentine and soap and water immediately after use and shaped to a point.

Brushes should never be used to stir paint. Brushes should not be left standing on their tips. All bristles are delicate; they will easily bend out of shape and lose the resilience without which fine brushwork is impossible.

# PAINTING—PREPARATION

### COLOR TEST
A sample of the color to be mixed should be glued to half fill a 1" × 2" aperture cut in a sheet of white paper. By moving this sheet around the Color Aid, any divergence from the hue of the sample color will be apparent. The sample should be further compared with the Tonal Value chart and Chromatic Intensity chips which have been previously made. The comparison with the Color Aid will be a guide to the selection of the pigments to be mixed. The comparison with the Tonal Value scale will determine the quantity of flat white paint needed. Obviously, if the tonal value is light, the mixture starts with flat white paint and then the japan color is added. Conversely, if the hue is deep, the mixture starts with the japan color. The comparison with the Chromatic Intensity squares indicates how much of the appropriate complement or earth color must be added to neutralize the color sufficiently for it to match the sample.

A study of dry color samples of the japan color should be made before beginning any color mixing. Since certain japan colors have greater strength than others, a small amount of them suffices to tint a mixture. Experience will teach the individual potency of each color. Mixing color in this way and understanding the resources of a single pigment will lead to a knowledge of the possibilities of each color. There is a point in color mixing when one additional drop of color will produce the hue sought; too much added at this stage will overbalance the proportion and ruin the mixture. Remembering that the wet value of japan color differs from the dry, one should proceed with caution and make a dry test after every addition of color. These tests are made on newspaper or white blotter, which absorbs paint, enabling it to dry quickly. Each test is placed in the opening of the sample sheet, and the comparison is then made in north light, under a daylight bulb, or in any clear light which does not distort the color.

### JUDGMENT OF PAINT QUANTITY
The quantity of paint needed for a piece is difficult to assess. Experience counsels that it is better to err with too much than too little. For three coats on a 48-inch three-drawer chest, a quart will be more than adequate; for a chair frame, a pint will suffice.

### DILUTION OF PAINT
When the color has been matched, the paint is thinned with turpentine to the consistency of thin cream. To insure that the pigment has been completely disseminated in the mixture and any foreign particles have been

removed, it is strained into a wide-mouthed jar through a piece of nylon hose held by a rubber band over the opening.

### ADDITION OF JAPAN DRIER
If the paint consists primarily of japan color and has little flat white paint content, japan drier is added to the mixture (10% of the quantity of paint) in order to give additional cohesiveness to the color.

### STORAGE OF PAINT
Wide-mouthed jars with screw tops are excellent for storing paint. A small amount of petroleum jelly rubbed around the rim before the jar is capped makes reopening easy. If the paint is to be stored for more than a short interval, the surface of the paint is thinly coated with turpentine. If a scum or crust forms on the paint despite this precaution, it is removed carefully before using to avoid the necessity of re-straining the entire mixture.

## PAINTING—PROCEDURE

It is essential that each technique be executed with skill and artistry. Until long practice and experience have permitted the acquisition of expertise, care and exactitude are substituted to achieve a professionally excellent piece. Perfection is always the aim but, with the knowledge that it is not humanly possible, less must needs be satisfactory. A critical faculty must be developed. When the desired effect has been all but achieved, restraint must prevent that last finicky touch which inevitably results in ruin. This is a nicety which is not easy to learn. If a mishap does occur, a knowledge of materials combined with ingenuity will find a way to recover the beauty that has been temporarily lost.

As the painter sets up his materials, he should provide himself with several boards of masonite, cut 8″ × 11″. These panels are executed in the same manner as the furniture. They serve as a guide and a testing ground for each process. A tack cloth is used to remove all dust particles from any surface before paint or any other type of medium is applied.

### APPLICATION OF PAINT
As painting begins, the brush is dipped into the container to just half-way up the bristles and pressed against the inside of the container to

remove the excess load. Roll-overs (laps on edges adjacent to the brushed surface), sags, and drips often result from too much paint on the brush— these are the signature of the amateur. The 2-inch bristle brush is best used for broad surfaces, the 1-inch for small areas. A fine oxhair brush, though expensive, produces a smoother surface, making brush ridges less discernible. The brush is held well up on the handle so that it becomes an extension of the arm, and the body movement described in the discussion of sanding is brought into play. This method may seem clumsy at first but leads eventually to mastery of the brush. The energy for the brush stroke starts from the center of the body and proceeds through the trapezium muscle of the shoulder. By shifting his weight from one foot to the other and using the brush only as an extension of the arm which is moved by the body, the painter is able to flow the paint on the surface with light strokes.

The surface is rapidly covered with a fully loaded brush. Regard for the direction of the grain at this initial depositing of the paint on the surface is not necessary, for this coverage is followed immediately by long, even strokes which reach from one edge to the other and which *are* brushed *with* the grain. (The only exception to this stroking with the grain is in those instances where the direction of the grain is discordant with the design of the piece—as on the apron of a table, where the grain is often vertical whereas a horizontal direction would be more pleasing.) This stroking is executed repeatedly, with a light touch, without bending the bristles, with the brush held at a 45-degree angle to the surface. The result is a smooth coat with few brush marks. The purpose of this stroking is to level the paint and smooth out any irregularities. If the brush wavers or is lifted in the stroking, the surface will be marred with flaws and unevenness which will be apparent when the final process of antiquing is reached. Should the paint run over on an adjacent side, it must be wiped off before it sets and produces a blemishing thickness.

### CORRECTION OF ERRORS

On the completion of each area, the painter checks for drips, sags, and roll-overs. Drips descend from carvings, indentations, corners, and at the joinings of arms and legs; sags droop on flat surfaces; roll-overs lap over corners and edges. A dry 1-inch bristle brush is used to catch these errors while they are still wet. When the paint begins to set, the stroking stops, as the brush bristles will roughen the drying paint. Roll-overs occur on edges where the brush tips over on a surface adjoining another at an angle. If the grain of adjacent surfaces follows in the same direction, the simplest method of correction is to draw a dry 1-inch bristle brush down the corner edge. If the paint has begun to set, the edge can be smoothed with the finger. Should the overlapping paint indeed have set, it must be gently scraped with a razor held perpendicular to the surface. In case the graining on the two surfaces is not parallel, the brush—with a very light paint load—is held evenly against the edge of their juncture and is drawn its full length, with care not to tip over on the adjacent edge. Most of the beginner's difficulties are caused by a surplus of paint on the brush; if the ferrule is kept dry, the chances are that the paint load will be correct.

## ORDER OF PAINT APPLICATION

The order to follow when painting a piece is first to apply the paint to the legs of a chair or the sides of a chest; if beginning errors occur, they will be least seen in these areas. The front of chair backs and the tops and fronts of chests should be reserved for last, when technique will have been perfected. Care exercised during these first steps prevents future problems and contributes to the excellence of the finished piece. The excitement of the first application of color is stimulating to the creative faculty. The transformation effected is the beginning of a personal expression and is one of the satisfying and pleasure-giving phases of this craft.

The first paint coat must dry overnight or possibly longer if the weather is exceptionally damp or humid. At this point, the hardware is painted unless its quality and design permit it to remain uncovered.

## SANDPAPER PROCEDURE

Before any succeeding coats of paint are applied, the preliminary coating is sanded. This is done both to remove any dust or foreign particles that may have settled on the wet paint and to reduce the differing levels of the brush strokes. Before the surface has been sanded, it feels slightly gritty; after sanding, it feels satin smooth. The work is done with 220 garnet paper used with a light, even pressure. For eliminating waves in the paint on a large, flat surface, the sandpaper is wrapped around a wood block.

Sandpaper loses its "cut" with use. This is detected when the surface of the piece begins to show polish as it is rubbed. To test the texture of the surface, the fingers are run lightly against the grain. With heavy pressure the sensitivity of the fingertips is reduced. With light pressure the faintest deviation in the surface is perceptible. The sound of sanding is soft and sustained when pressure is even. A harsh, grating, erratic sound indicates energetic—but ineffectual—sanding. To avoid sanding through the paint coat on edges and corners, the sandpaper is rolled back over the forefinger

and held between the thumb and the third finger with the remaining fingers braced against the edge of the surface for support. As a further precaution against losing the paint coating at the edges, sanding proceeds from within an area to the periphery, leaving the edges almost untouched. Drips and roll-overs which have been overlooked are removed by gentle, patient scraping with a razor held at right angles to the surface. Areas that were not sufficiently sanded before the first coat of paint are now apparent. They should be sanded further. If the grain of the wood itself is still apparent, a paste mixture of the base paint and vinyl filler is applied to the surface against the grain and scraped diagonally as smoothly as possible. The filling must of course dry overnight and be sanded smoothly with 220 garnet paper before the next application of paint.

### CORRECTION OF "BLEEDING"

In painting an old varnished piece, a problem often arises if the original varnish contained red aniline dye. This is usually a constituent of the mahogany or cherry coloring used before the invention of wood stains. The strength of the dye may come through the first paint coat as a pinkish blush called "bleeding." A mixture of 2 volumes titanium powder and 4 volumes white shellac applied over the area seals the discoloration. If the dye is discerned before the first coat of paint, it is of course preferable to apply the mixture then.

### CREATION OF PAINT "BODY"

Before the application of each coat of paint and after sanding, the piece is dusted and rubbed with a tack cloth. Paint for the second and each succeeding coat is thinned with a half-and-half combination of flatting oil and turpentine. Flatting oil retards drying sufficiently to allow the paint to flow together, resulting in a smoother coat. As the painter has in effect "gone to school" while sanding the first coat, the errors discovered and corrected will therefore be avoided in the application of the second coat. This second coat must also dry overnight, be sanded as described before, and then be dusted and rubbed with a tack cloth before the application of a succeeding paint coat. Many coats of paint—each well sanded—confer a handsome body to the piece. "Body" implies paint of such thickness and depth that it integrates with the piece and at the same time gives to it a substance over and beyond the wood of which it is made. Four to five coats are required to achieve this. The developing sense of touch will soon lead to an understanding of this quality, which in itself provides delight. People instinctively feel a beautiful piece of furniture, unconsciously seeking the pleasure of the tactile sensation induced by the depth of the paint body and the smoothness of its surface.

## STRIPING

The second creative process in the enhancement of a piece is the application of decorative stripes in a color that differs from the ground hue. The line and form of the piece and its purpose in the realization of the concept of the room are factors determining the placement of striping. Line can be improved, size diminished, weak form strengthened, poor form disguised, and drama created through striping. A layout in chalk serves as a dress rehearsal. If there is some uncertainty about the areas where striping would be most effective, at first only those lines should be sketched in experimentally which seem convincingly expressive. Then, study of the piece from a distance allows it to "speak," in effect, and the places where further striping is needed are obvious. Arbitrarily imposed lines out of harmony with the design of the piece, as well as the delineation of obvious elements which are not necessarily pleasing, should be avoided. For example, too numerous moldings encircling a chair leg, or jutting knobs, or obtrusive blocks are poor choices for striping. On the other hand, in instances where a piece has an uncompromisingly square or uninteresting form, an over-all pattern of striping—parallels of varying widths, plaiding, diapering (diamond-shaped diagonals), or a Mondrian-inspired series of geometrical forms—will elevate the piece from mediocrity to stylized sophistication. Uninteresting legs are given style by applying the striping color to the two inner sides; often broad elements, such as a chamfered corner, painted in entirety bring distinction. Embellishment through striping and design is never an end in itself but a means to enhance the underlying form by emphasizing its graceful qualities and by camouflaging or understating its poor ones.

Color for striping is chosen with reference to the principles discussed in the chapter on color. Here in particular the purpose of color is to distinguish the piece of furniture from other elements in the room. Striping color should be tested on a sample board painted with the base hue so that the compensation necessary to discount the influence of that color can be made. When the mixture is satisfactory, it is thinned with turpentine and strained. A very small amount is required for striping. Varying effects are achieved in the following manner:

1. A thin striping fluid of watery consistency produces a faded stripe varying in value. Where desirable, the variation may be emphasized by patting or wiping the wet paint with tissue or—on completion of the striping when it is semi-dry—by rubbing it lightly, at random, with a pencil eraser.

2. A fluid of thicker density is used to obtain a worn effect. The stripe is rubbed through here and there against the grain with 220 garnet paper as soon as the paint is "surface set."

3. A fluid of the usual painting consistency is used to achieve a chipped effect. The striping is allowed to dry hard—overnight—and is then sharply hit at points of normal abuse with the wooden handle of a screwdriver or similar instrument to cause the paint to chip.

Should the striping be executed in white, the paint must be thick enough to cover the base color. All of the methods described are effective; the choice is determined by a consideration of which will be most suitable and becoming to the piece.

## STRIPING—PROCEDURE

A long-haired #6 sable brush is used for striping. If a line less than 1/16″ is desired, a #3 brush is needed. The brush is filled and the excess paint tipped off on the inside of the container. Keeping elbow, wrist, and fingers relaxed, and with arm extended, the artist stands far enough from the piece to allow the shoulder muscle free play when striping. As the muscle pulls the brush along, a straight clean line is produced provided the eye is kept on a point ahead of the brush. The brush is held well up the handle at as great a distance from the point of the bristle as possible. The greater the length of handle between the fingers and the point of the brush, the longer the sweep that can be taken. The resulting stroke is free and continuous. Nervousness may cause an initial wobble but the brush must not be lifted in an attempt to correct any inaccuracies so occurring, as this action produces a tentative, amateurish line. It is essential both to *maintain an even pressure* and to *continue.* Hesitation shows. Practice will produce control over the evenness and the width of the striping. Slight discrepancies, however, attest to the hand of the craftsman and add a certain charm.

The long bristle of the brushes holds a load of paint which is sufficient to insure a stripe of considerable length. Very light pressure of the brush will effect a hairline stripe; for a ⅛", ¼", or ½" stripe, heavier pressure must be exerted. It is wise for the striper—no matter how expert—to have tissues at hand for wiping off the inadvertent slip immediately; then it can easily be eradicated with 220 garnet paper later on.

Location of the striping will to some degree affect its execution. Examples follow.

1. *Incised or raised molding striping*—In this instance the indentation is used as a guide and the brush tip rests against it. Through the exertion of enough pressure to spread the bristle to the width of the molding, an even stripe may be executed without difficulty.

2. *Edge striping*—The brush is placed at a 45-degree angle against the edge. With the little finger used as a rest, a clean line automatically follows. To fill in the stripe evenly, the brush is again run along the same line.

3. *Free striping*—Where there is no molding and a single edge is to be used as a guide, or when striping is placed within a margin, a cardboard gauge is used. This is made by notching the straight edge of a cardboard strip as follows: One quarter inch, or the width of the desired stripe, is marked on the straight edge of the cardboard and cut in 1 inch. A diagonal cut to this point removes a triangle, which leaves a convenient measuring gauge. With this the width of the stripe is marked from the edge of the surface with the tip of the paint brush every 6 inches. The brush is pressed

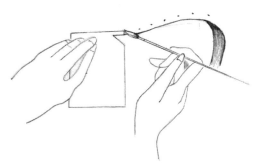

to the measured width at the first mark and, aimed at the mark ahead, the brush is pulled quickly along the edge. Extra support is provided by resting the right elbow on the worktable and supporting the hand with the little finger on the surface, or by steadying the wrist with the left hand. The commercial sword striping brush and the striping rest are not relevant here because a free striping stroke is the aim. It is imperative that the brush pressure be kept constant to achieve a free stripe of sufficient evenness. Eventually after practice, the marking gauge is used only as a check for the width of the stripe on each succeeding area.

Errors are corrected immediately on completion of the striping. Irregularities are rubbed away whether wet or dry with 220 garnet paper and pencil eraser. If any part of the striping is too narrow, it may be corrected with additional paint. Retouching of the base color is kept to a minimum because even in a few days paint fades. However, when this is necessary, the edges of the touch-up are feathered out with 220 garnet paper or blended in with the finger.

If the directions above are followed carefully, discipline in time will lead to mastery. Clean, even striping results from manual skill, which develops only through practice. However, it must be remembered that individual expression and freedom of execution are the goal, not mechanical perfection. The remaining treasures of this craft are valued today because they are the result of the artistry—with all its deviations—of the skilled hand of man.

## PAINT

*Materials*

Flat white oil base paint with a high proportion of silicate japan colors (pigments ground in japan, which is a flatting agent)

*The combination of these two substances makes a mat color.*

Turpentine (sealed)

Japan drier

Flatting oil (a soybean derivative)

Titanium powder

Shellac

Denatured alcohol

Mineral spirits (for cleaning brushes and thinning certain varnishes)

Ammonia

Detergent (for cleaning brushes)

*Tools*
  Palette knives
  Spoons
  Screwdriver
  Ice pick
  Brush comb
  Painting brushes—
    2″ sash with long handle, or
      oxhair brush of same size
    1″ hog bristle with long handle
    1½″ or 2″ oxhair
  Decorating brushes—
    #3 and #6 long-haired
      pointed sable
    1″ shellac brush

*Miscellaneous*
  Tin cans fitted with sieves
  Screw-top jars
  Nylon hose
  Rubber bands
  Tack cloth
  Newspaper
  Pink pearl eraser
  Tissues
  Liquid detergent
  Brown naphtha soap
  Rough fabric cloths
  Cardboard
  White blotters
  Masonite boards (8″ × 11″)
  Petroleum jelly
  Razor
  Tired steel wool
  Test brushes

# ANTIQUING

## THE EFFECTS OF ANTIQUING

The time for the artificial ·re-creation of the patina of centuries past (antiquing) has been reached. The preceding steps are the preparation for the emergence of a simulated eighteenth-century treasure.

The antiquing medium to be used will create the charming effect of long use and wear. As this is truly a creative process, it requires sensitivity and patience. The thrill of metamorphosis lies ahead. The effect to be sought should give the illusion that the maid and the housewife in the daily "once over lightly" have given the surface a soft polish, leaving dust in the corners and the crevices of carving. Arms have been rubbed and worn, legs and edges nicked and dented gently because inadvertently. Doors, drawers, and backs of chairs have become stained and darkened by much handling. Surfaces are soft and satiny to the touch. Colors somewhat faded by the sun are gentle and mellow to the eye. All is pleasing and harmonious. The application of antiquing softens any sharp rigid line with subtle shading and draws the beholder's eye to the rhythmic curve of the piece. Nothing should be obvious, nothing hard. This subtle artifice produces the patina of gracious age. The finished piece casts a spell as it brings the past into the present.

# ANTIQUING—PREPARATION

### *PREPARATION OF SURFACE*
After the piece has been striped and let dry overnight it is cleaned carefully. Kneaded erasers, pink pencil erasers, or 220 garnet paper are used to remove smudges. The piece is then dusted and wiped with a tack cloth.

### *APPLICATION OF VARNISH SEALER*
Now a colorless flat varnish with a high wax content is applied. This is used as a protective coat before antiquing. The varnish is stirred well but not thinned. If stroked on evenly, it does not change the paint hue perceptibly. On deep values it may dry with a whitish film, but this is easily removed when the wax medium or antiquing fluid is added.

The varnish brush is well loaded, the excess tipped off *inside* the container. The surface is coated lightly with long, even strokes in the direction previously established in the painting. A thin application is essential. Pools, sags, and roll-overs dry with a discoloring yellow tint. Although the varnish dries rapidly, it is safe to go back over the surface and pick up any excess with a brush—this is continually wiped dry on a cloth. Varnish requires overnight drying.

The sealing will protect all the work done heretofore, will allow the removal with steel wool of any errors made during the application of the antiquing medium, and will permit easy blending of that medium. "Antique" may then be applied without the fear of possible ruin of the work previously done. It is possible for an expert to "antique" directly on the painted surface, but this requires knowledge and technical proficiency because it leaves no margin for error.

## CHOICE OF COLOR

To determine the color for the antiquing of a piece, these principles should be followed:

1. The chromatic intensity of the color must be less than that of the base hue.

2. The tonal value of the color must be deeper than that of the base hue.

A color tone is chosen which will lessen the intensity of the base hue and yet not alter it to a different hue. The tone is then neutralized with dust color, or the earth colors, or black.

A treasured antique piece never looks dirty. Dust blended with faded and deepened color creates the tone. This is achieved by the addition of a deeper, related value of the base hue to the mixture of neutral color. This addition is delicately modulated to avoid any obvious contrast to the base hue of the piece. When the medium is applied, it creates the illusion that the hue of the piece has faded and become somewhat discolored.

There follows a detailed description of materials, mediums, and techniques that are used in antique finishes. The entire section should be read carefully before one begins this phase of the work.

## FORMULATING THE MEDIUMS

The following mediums are used because they can be easily controlled in application and blending and because they dry quickly. Through them a wide range of varying and muted effects are produced which possess the added advantage of preventing a piece from looking like a dirty or smeared antique with its finish obviously applied rather than the result of time and use.

### DRY COLOR (POWDERS) AND WAX

This combination is used as a mixing agent. Inexpensive powder pigments come in a full range of color and in earth colors, and they include rottenstone. Though rottenstone is a polishing agent, it is also a color, that of dust—a beige gray frequently used for antiquing white or pale-hued furniture. Rottenstone was known as Tripoli in the eighteenth century. It is a siliceous residue from a type of limestone. The wax used with the dry colors is bleached and has a high turpentine content.

On wax paper with a palette knife (see drawing opposite page), rottenstone, gray, or earth color, plus a dry powder related in hue to the base color, are mixed with wax. The amount of dry color determines the strength of the resulting hue. Too great a proportion of powder makes a grainy mixture; too much wax, a greasy, colorless mixture—neither of which is desirable. Only a test with a brush on newspaper discloses these errors. Too much powder is indicated by loose grains which fail to adhere. Too much wax forms a greasy ring beyond the application. One part dry color mixed with 2 parts wax usually combines to the proper mixture; however, it must be tested for color with a light stroke on a sample board. If it is necessary to keep the medium for a period of time, it is stored in an airtight tin. This

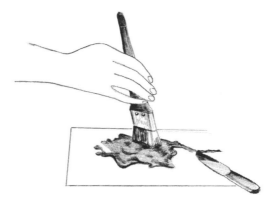

tin is placed in a pan of water and heated before re-use. However, the contents should not be used in a liquid state, but only after it has cooled to a paste. This medium adapts admirably to stroking and pouncing.

### JAPAN ANTIQUING FLUID

To make this medium, 3 volumes of paint are combined with 1 volume of colorless flat varnish. It is strained before use. If it is to be stored over a long period, the surface is coated with turpentine. An excellent basic antiquing color is a warm gray, which is made as follows:

3 volumes flat white paint
2 volumes raw umber japan color
½ volume lampblack japan color

The quantities may be varied in relation to any base hue through the differing proportion of white, black or raw umber. To this mixture the relating deeper value of the base hue is added. Any of the earth colors, or black, is suitable if becoming to the color of the piece. One volume of flat varnish is always added to the mixture. This medium is also tested lightly on the sample board for color; it too adapts for stroking or pouncing.

### JAPAN ANTIQUING FLUID COMBINED WITH WAX

The antiquing fluid described above is combined with wax (bleached and with a high turpentine content) into a smooth paste. This is mixed on wax paper with a palette knife. Too great an amount of wax weakens the color. This mixture is also stored in an airtight tin and later softened—if necessary—by warming. It should be tested as directed on the sample board for color, and it may be applied by stroking or pouncing.

### JAPAN SPATTERING FLUID

The following mixture is prepared:

> 1 volume paint (japan color with flat white
> paint if necessary)
> 3 volumes flat varnish
> 3 volumes turpentine

This fluid can now be used for spattering. When it is further diluted, with one more part of turpentine and one of varnish, it is suitable for pouncing. This, too, is tested on the sample board.

### TECHNIQUES OF APPLICATION

There follows a description of the techniques of application to be used:

*Stroking*, a striated grain, is especially becoming to the rustic and simple line of Provincial and Early American furniture.

*Pouncing*, a scumbled film, is the choice for eighteenth-century French and Italian furniture, any piece with decorative carving, or delicate Adam, Sheraton, or Hepplewhite pieces.

*Spattering*, a spray which shades and produces a sleek effect for Regency, French Directoire, and Chippendale furniture.

As we shall see, all of these methods and all mediums may be combined to create varied, interesting effects for traditional and antique pieces. Further, it is possible to originate contemporary finishes by applying the mediums evenly with any of the above methods, thus creating tone and texture.

For all the antiquing methods, wax paper is used as a palette. The medium is poured out and the brush is loaded directly from the paper. When the medium has been applied throughout, it is blended with either 000 steel wool or 220 garnet paper. No attempt should be made to correct errors until they are completely dry.

## ANTIQUING—PROCEDURE

### STROKING

The 2-inch paint brush is lightly loaded. Held high on the handle, it is stroked out on newspaper without pressure until a fine striation (grain) flows from the bristles. It is then applied to the surface and brushed in the direction of the grain of the wood (or the direction established by previous painting) with long, light strokes. Stroking of a recessed area starts from

the center. The brush is slightly lifted off the surface as the edge of the frame is reached. This avoids heavy deposits of the medium in the edges of the recess. Each time the brush is loaded it is first stroked out on fresh newspaper before approaching the surface. Application continues until there is an even depth of tone over the entire piece. The result is a broken striation of the surface with few if any obvious brush strokes. Then, with a 1-inch brush, corners, recesses, and areas of use are re-stroked to deepen the tone. With the stroking method, the heavier the application of the medium the cruder and more provincial the result will be. Stroking may be used with any medium. Each of them produces a slightly different effect.

## POUNCING

For this method, a 1½-inch oval sash brush is used. The quantity of antiquing applied is controlled by the brush load as well as by the degree of pressure used in pouncing. The brush is held high on the handle and perpendicular to the surface. It must be tapped lightly, yet with enough force to spread the bristles. The brush is constantly turned and also moved in an advancing and retreating fashion—overlapping so that all areas are equally pounced.

To begin, the brush is loaded and tapped out on newspaper. When the antiquing medium left by the brush produces a soft, even tone, it is the moment to proceed to the surface of the piece. The brush is not whisked or dragged as it makes contact with the surface or the medium will smear. Instead, it is patted up and down on the surface with enough resiliency so that it almost bounces. After each reloading, the brush is pounced out on a fresh piece of newspaper. When all areas of the piece are covered with

an even tone, the edges, corners, and crevices are re-pounced to deepen the tone. It is advisable to circle inward from the outer edges of a given area with the freshly loaded brush, working toward the center as the load decreases. To achieve a highlighted effect on carvings and hardware, their raised parts must be wiped with a soft cloth immediately after the application of the medium. The pouncing method may be used for any medium, and also in combination with stroking.

When the medium used for pouncing contains wax, it is first stroked on to form a thin covering coat—this is immediately followed by pouncing with a dry brush. Deep carvings are best handled with a wax medium pounced on.

When the thin spattering medium is used for pouncing, it is thinly but evenly brushed over the entire surface. This application is immediately pounced with a dry brush.

## SPATTERING

For this method a stiff brush with bristles cut off to a length of 1″ is used. Since this brush carries a thin medium, it must be well tamped out on a wax paper palette before application. The brush is cradled in the palm of

BASIC ANTIQUING: *Top left, pounced, wax and japan antiquing medium;
right, japan spattering fluid.
Bottom left, flyspecks, wax and powder; right, striation, wax and powder.*

the left hand, with the handle resting along the inside of the left arm and the brush directed toward the object. The narrow end of the ferrule rests on the left index finger with the left thumb holding the top edge of the ferrule near the bristle. To steady the brush, the right thumb is placed on top of the left. The index finger of the right hand (protected with a rubber finger guard) is drawn slowly down the bristles, directing them

downward toward the surface. By separating the bristles in this manner, a spray is projected. With little fluid on the brush, a slow movement which releases only a few bristles at a time with the pressure of the finger creates a fine spray. A quick movement, ending with a jerk at either end of the bristles, produces larger spatter. To achieve a large, loose spatter, the brush is struck against a wooden block. A more irregular spatter results when the handle of the spattering brush is knocked on the handle of the pounce brush.

For the fine spray, the arm holding the brush continually moves across the surface so that the spray falls evenly; otherwise, the effect will be spotty. The index finger is lifted gently off the bristles, as a jerking motion will project a large uncontrolled spatter. The index finger accumulates fluid; therefore, it is kept dry by frequent wiping to avoid unexpected blobs dropping on the surface. Practice leads to an even spatter accurately placed. To achieve the patina most becoming to the elegance of Regency furniture, a fine spattering is rendered on each surface, and this is immediately followed by a light pouncing. The process must be repeated a number of times

DISTRESSING: *Top left, distressing in three colors; right, peeled finish.*
*Bottom, left and right, peeled finishes.*

to achieve the desired patina. So long as the spattering is as fine as peppering, no drying time is necessary.

A form of spattering frequently used in conjunction with other media is fly-specking. To produce these sparsely spaced specks, only one or two bristles are moved quickly as the arm holding the brush moves rapidly across the surface. India ink, or preferably black japan spattering fluid, is used for this process. If the specking is too heavy, it should be allowed to set before the excess is removed with steel wool.

Spattering is an excellent means of rendering subtle shading and emphasizing elements of form in the piece. A thinned solution of the japan antiquing fluid which has previously been applied by stroking or pouncing is used for this.

Spattering may be treated in a variety of ways:

1. The spattered surface is brushed lightly and diagonally across the grain in both directions with a whisk broom or a stiff brush just before the paint has set.

2. When a spatter is half dry, it is followed by a turpentine spatter; this dissolves the fluid slightly, producing a softer effect. Dissolution is controlled by patting the surface with ooo steel wool or a soft pad of cheesecloth.


## LIGHT AND HEAVY APPLICATIONS

The first distribution of antiquing medium on the surface should result in an even patina. Emphasis where deeper shadings are required follows. When a medium combined with wax has been used, repeated applications in the same area must be postponed until the first distribution has dried. This requires at least a 30-minute wait. Only then can additional wax combined with medium be added without removing the initial application.

Accumulations of antiquing medium should appear in the crevices of moldings and carvings. For these places, wax combined with medium may be used and applied by pouncing. As an alternative, the japan antiquing medium may be converted (by adding 3 volumes flat varnish, 3 volumes turpentine) into a thin wash and brushed over the carving. To achieve a light antique effect, the surfaces of carvings are wiped with a soft cloth almost immediately after the application of the medium. Hardware antiqued in this fashion and then buffed with steel wool shows the glint of the metal in a pleasing way. The lightness or heaviness of the application of any antiquing medium, as well as the length of the drying time, determines the end effects. A light application with brief drying time gives the piece soft and delicate patina. A heavy application with an overnight drying time creates a cruder aspect with greater contrast. The latter is desirable for reproducing a piece of great age.

The antiquing medium must be surface dry before it is rubbed off. This requires half an hour on a dry day, longer in a damp atmosphere. If longer drying time is permitted, the antique patina is darker and heavier.

### SELECTION OF ANTIQUING METHOD

Experience provides the best directive in choice of antiquing medium and method. It enables the painter to consider well the purpose and the future installation of the piece, and to take into account his own empathy for it. Until this state of grace has been achieved, the following suggestions will be of assistance.

*The Louis XV and Louis XVI period and the designs of Adam, Sheraton, and Hepplewhite* produced furniture of delicate and refined line. Pieces fashioned after this furniture emerge with great beauty if the mediums combining powder and wax, antiquing fluid and wax, or spattering fluid thinned further as previously described are applied by pouncing. All of these are blended with steel wool after a brief drying time.

*Provincial* is furniture of rustic and simple line, indigenous to various European countries and the Americas, and demands a cruder finish. Antiquing fluid is applied with the dry brush method and allowed to dry overnight, and then is blended with 220 garnet paper. An alternate method calls for spattering fluid to be applied in an over-all coating; this is rubbed off lightly with steel wool before drying and is further blended the next day. For smaller pieces, antiquing fluid—with or without wax—is applied by stroking and is slightly blended with steel wool.

*Directoire and Regency* furniture is sleek and elegant. It is enhanced by a spray of spattering fluid, pounced when semi-dry, and both operations repeated until a dual tone is built up. This application is briskly polished with a flannel cloth, and finally gloss varnish coats are applied to produce a high gloss.

# BLENDING

The process of blending the antique patina makes it possible to bring out the subtlety of the line and at the same time to soften the form. Thought, study, and patience are essential in the blending process. The desired final effect is one which simulates the aging of color with areas of base color to suggest fading, with darker areas where many hands have rested, and with dulled carvings where the dust of centuries has accumulated. The acme is a duality of tone wherein the base hue of the piece is seen in differing intensities through the antique medium. Distant viewing helps one to judge how much patina is sufficient to make the gradations of tonal value discernible and any offensive blemishes imperceptible. Emphasis of line and form by means of antiquing serves to make the piece convincing. The lesser or greater depth of patina required to be subtly evident in the light of the final environment must be considered.

There are two methods for blending—one for a slender, elegant piece, and one for a more crude provincial piece.

To achieve a soft patina, ooo steel wool is used. This blending method may be used for any antiquing medium after it has dried for half an hour on a dry day or longer if the day is humid. No matter what the method of application—stroking, pouncing, or spattering—the optimal moment for blending is when the antiquing medium on the entire piece has just surface-dried and is completely free of any tackiness.


## BLENDING—PROCEDURE

A pad of steel wool is first unrolled, and one end wrapped around the forefinger. Then the centers of areas are lightened with the steel wool and blended gradually to depth in the corners and at the edges. A light stroke in any direction, against or with the grain, will eradicate brush marks, uneven blotches, or other obvious errors. Any so-called "happy accident" is treasured, for it provides interesting variation in the over-all texture of the surface. The protruding surfaces of carvings and moldings are lightened so that only a slight film of the antiquing patina remains. As soon as the steel wool becomes impregnated with the medium, it turns into a polishing rather than a blending implement. This is the reason for using steel wool unrolled to its full length rather than tearing off small segments which rapidly become sticky little wads. In every area, the base color must show through the antique coat, more on places of use, and less in corners, bottoms of legs, and joinings. If wax is contained in the medium, the blending pressure is kept light or the result will be a polish instead of a shading and will produce an unsightly, dark, shiny streakiness. To correct such a mistake, this area is stroked lightly with 220 garnet paper and then brushed over equally lightly with steel wool. Hardware on all pieces is buffed with steel wool to show a pleasing glint of metal on the raised edges.

The dry powdery appearance of the cruder provincial finish is produced over a coat of japan antiquing fluid or spattering fluid, either of which has been allowed to dry overnight. Blending is done with 220 garnet paper used with a light over-all stroking touch. This method, too, employs a motion either with or against the grain. It permits the correction of over-long striations of the medium or any other irregularities. This is not a sanding though sandpaper is used; it is a gentle feathering and pulling of the antique medium.

When either method of blending has been completed, should a further gloss be desired, it can be obtained by polishing the piece with a soft flannel cloth.


## ANTIQUING

*Materials*
Inexpensive dry powder pigments
Bleached wax with high turpentine content
Flat varnish
Clear gloss varnish
Turpentine
Japan colors
Flat white paint

*Tools*
000 steel wool
220 garnet paper
Spatter brush
Pounce brush (oval sash brush)

Whisk broom
Bristle brush (1″ or 2″)
Varnish brush
Palette knife


*Miscellaneous*
Wax paper
Newspaper
Cheesecloth
Flannel cloth
Rags
Finger guard
Tack cloth
Erasers

# VARNISHES

## GLOSS AND MAT

Both gloss and mat varnish are required for this craft.

Gloss varnish must be crystal clear, strong and elastic, heat- and spot-proof, and as near alcohol-proof as possible. It is used as a protection on all flat, horizontal surfaces on which objects are constantly placed. To lock up color on furniture, the Venetians used a glossy and durable oil varnish, then dried it in the sun.

Mat varnish is less durable but offers sufficient protection for chair frames and other furniture subject only to contact from the body. Mat varnish contains wax, pulverized mica, and talc to reduce its luster.

Gloss varnish is cut 40 per cent with the diluent indicated on the can, generally turpentine or mineral spirits. The surest way to test the tone of any varnish is to apply it to a light value of red red-purple (pink). When dry, any yellowing tendency will be clearly discernible. If a water-clear varnish is unobtainable, compensation for the yellowing film must be made in the mixture of the base color or by tinting the varnish itself with a tinge of cobalt blue oil paint. Varnish is warmed so that it will flow on a surface with ease. This is done by placing it in a pan of water and heating it for a few minutes to about 70° F. For the best results it is applied on a clear day in a dust-free room where the temperature is about 70° F.

# VARNISHING—PREPARATION

Antique patina requires a two-week drying time before varnish of any type is applied to it. This insures *thorough* drying.

The varnish brush is a chiseled oxhair and ranges in size from ½" to 3". For most purposes a 2-inch brush is satisfactory. A surface must be carefully rubbed with a tack cloth before varnish is applied to it. One method of reducing floating dust motes is to place the object on damp newspaper. To lacquer in a dust-free setting, Oriental craftsmen went to sea in a sampan.

# VARNISHING—PROCEDURE

A description of the proper method for applying varnish appears in *A Treatise of Japanning, Varnishing, and Gilding*, written in 1688 by Stalker and Parker:

> Be mindful to begin your varnishing stroak in the
> middle of the table or box that you have provided
> for that work, and not in full length from one end
> to the other; so that your brush being planted in
> the middle of your board, strike it to one end;
> then taking it off, fix it to the place you began
> at, and draw or extend it to the other end; so must
> you do till the whole plane or content be varnished
> over. We have reasons too for this caution, which
> if neglected, has several faults and prejudices
> attending it; for if you should undertake at one
> stroak to move your pencil from end to end, it
> would so happen that you would overlap the edges
> and mouldings of your box; this overlapping is, when
> you see the varnish lie in drops and splashes, not
> laid by your brush, but caused by your brushes being
> at the beginning of the stroak overcharg'd and too
> full of varnish, and therefore we advise you to
> stroke your pencil once or twice against the sides
> of the Gallipot, to obstruct and hinder this super-
> fluity; small experience will discover these mistakes.

These delightful directions are proof that integrity in the pursuit of exper-tise in a craft leads to the appropriate method.

### LOADING THE BRUSH

Here is a more modern explanation of the varnishing technique. The brush is dipped into the jar up to one third the length of its bristle. The excess is pressed out on the inner side of the jar, since dragging the bristle across the top edge forms unwanted tiny air bubbles. They also occur if the pressure of the brush on the surface is too heavy.

### STROKING TECHNIQUE

When the brush is newly loaded, the stroke starts in the *middle* of the surface and moves to one edge. The following stroke overlaps the central heavy deposit and brushes it out to the other edge of the surface. This initial stroking keeps the edges of the surface free from pools of varnish, which are apt to sag or roll over. It is continued until the brush load diminishes. Then the strokes go all the way across the surface from edge to edge until it is necessary to re-load the brush. This entire procedure is repeated until the surface is covered.

The first application of varnish is stroked as described but only *with the grain* in order not to disturb the antiquing medium. Each of the successive coats is brushed *three ways*: first with the grain, then across the grain, and finally with the grain. The almost-dry brush on the final stroking

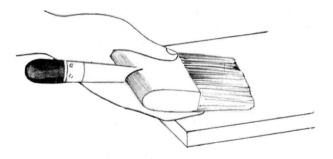

is held close to the ferrule to make possible the lightest touch of the brush— the bristles staying unbent. If this procedure is followed, "holidays" (skips) and brush strokes are virtually eliminated.

Each varnish coat must be as scant as possible. The entire purpose of varnishing is to build up a series of extra-thin coats, thus providing the object with the greatest possible protection. After the first varnish coat, a pad made of nylon hose may be substituted for the brush. Such an applicator insures the thinness of the successive coats. Twenty-four to 48 hours must be allowed for drying time between each varnish coat—longer if the weather is damp. Varnish must not be dried in intensive heat, artificial or natural, as blisters—not only of the varnish but of the painted surface beneath—will result.

The varnished surface must have an impervious smoothness, affording no minute receptacle for dust. An even gloss is the sign of properly applied varnish. However, a satiny luster is the most elegant cloak for antique pieces, preferable, indeed, to the hard enamel-like gloss resulting from the mechanical spray processes used commercially.

### *"TUFBACKING"*

Varnish is rubbed down only after the application of the first two coats, in order to avoid any possible damage to the antique patina. Careful rubbing with 600 wet-or-dry paper and a sudsy solution of non-detergent soap and water (patted on with a synthetic sponge) is followed by the use of the tack cloth which precedes each succeeding coat of varnish. Caution is the watchword in rubbing, since each varnish coat is only a thin film.

Wet or Dry Waterproof Silicon Carbide with Soft Back 600 is a fine abrasive of silicon carbide grit fastened to tough and pliable paper by means of waterproof plastic. Formerly this type of paper was marketed as "Tufbak," a word appropriated as a verb in my school. As it is no longer a trademark name, its use as a verb will be continued throughout this book. (The word has an interesting origin, which became clear to me after reading a nineteenth-century volume written and used in Holland. In describing the preparation of a brush for a certain technique, the author required that the bristles be ground "on the wet tuff." At first my students and I were totally mystified by this terminology. Further thought led to the realization that brushes in those days were ground on wet carborundum, and that this was "wet tuff." The member of the contemporary firm who suggested this term for wet-or-dry paper must have been scholarly. Its derivation understood, the word has become a delight.)

An emulsion of non-detergent soap flakes and water is patted on the surface with a sponge. As an abrasive to smooth the surface and rid it of any dust particles, either 0000 steel wool or two pieces of 600 wet-or-dry paper (one on top of the other; both face-down) may be used. The two pieces give greater purchase when rubbing. The emulsion acts as a lubricant, helping to prevent scratches from the steel wool or the wet-or-dry paper and lightens their abrasive quality. The surface is frequently washed off and dried to ascertain the progress of the work. The grain of the paint application is followed during the rubbing (departure from this rule comes only after much experience). When the surface is smooth it should be washed and dried, and rubbed with a tack cloth before the next coat of varnish. The rubbing with steel wool or the tufbacking not only levels the surface but also provides "tooth" for the succeeding coat of varnish. When varnish does not adhere successfully, it peels in ribbon-like sections. It is then necessary to tufback after each coat of varnish is applied. For surfaces on which alcohol might mar the finish, at least seven coats are indicated.

### POLISHED FINISH

For the finest possible finish and to obliterate any faint scratches produced by the wet-or-dry paper or the steel wool, a further rubbing is necessary. A light paste of rottenstone and lemon oil is mixed and rubbed with a circular motion over the surface with the palm of the hand or a pad made of nylon stocking or felt. A paste of rottenstone and lemon oil, used on the final varnish coat without tufbacking, produces a superb finish. Craftsmen of old, including the Orientals, used the palm of the hand or the fingertips; the resulting heat of the light friction gave the surface a beautiful soft finish.

### MAT FINISH

A mat varnish is used on the arms and backs of chairs to protect them from the hazards of daily use. It is also recommended as the final coat on the surfaces of tables and chests if a flat, non-glossy finish is desired. The mat varnish selected for this purpose should contain less wax than that used on the piece prior to the antiquing medium. This will provide a harder surface. A mat varnish requires only two coats with the usual 24-hour drying period intervening. As it is a very thin film, it needs no rubbing.

It is generally thought that varnish should not be applied over a waxed surface. However, if six weeks of drying time is allowed after the application of an antiquing medium combined with wax, varnish can successfully be applied.

### WAXING

A final finish for varnish-protected surfaces is a coat of thin-bodied wax—one with a high turpentine quotient. After this wax has been well rubbed into a damp cloth, the surface is rubbed over and allowed to dry for 20 minutes; the application is then repeated. When dry, the second coat is polished with a water-dampened cloth to the desired degree of gloss. If polishing with the damp cloth is repeated on successive days, an even luster is more readily attained. For antique furniture a soft sheen is the best. However, if a mat finish is desired, the wax coat is not polished at all. For a high gloss, the surface is buffed first with 0000 steel wool and then with the damp cloth.

## SEASONING

The piece is now finished. A fine painted surface requires aging before it approaches perfection. Six months' seasoning is necessary for paint to reach maximum hardness. This process is not affected by everyday use. During the hardening period, dusting with a dry, soft flannel cloth will contribute to the patina. Later, if the surface becomes defaced in any way, it is possible to gently clean it with mild soap and water or to polish it softly with a lightly waxed cloth. Disfigurations should be removed carefully with 0000 steel wool. With such care the furniture mellows and takes on additional character as it is enjoyed.

# VARNISHES

*Materials*

Crystal-clear gloss varnish

Mat varnish for final protective coating

600 wet-or-dry paper (waterproof silicon carbide with soft back)

0000 steel wool

Turpentine

Mineral spirits

Non-detergent soap flakes

Clear wax (with high turpentine content)

Rottenstone

Lemon oil

Cobalt blue oil paint

*Tools*

Chiseled oxhair varnish brush (½″ to 3″—size commensurate with piece)

Tack cloth

Synthetic sponge

*Miscellaneous*

Lint-free cloth

Flannel cloth

Nylon hose

Felt

# DISTRESSING

## SIGNS OF AGE

Noble furniture of great age shows signs of physical damage even though
it has been cared for tenderly. Normal use and the passage of time add a
gentle rounding to the sharp edges and clean-cut carvings that once pro-
claimed its youth. Families of worms have left holes that mark their some-
time abode in the framework. Household mishaps have contributed dents
and scars. The simulation of all these signs of age is termed *distressing*.

As one looks back, it seems probable that the system of overpainting one
color upon another to create variations in depth and hue was not restricted
to the painter of pictures, but also was used by the painter of furniture. An
oil painting was an elaborate structure, its layers usually consisting of an
underpainting and then a succession of glazes and scumbles (semi-opaque
paint films). The undertone was most often painted in monochrome. The
scumbles and glazes added color and gave richness of texture to the paint,
but what lay beneath the last layer of paint might be of equal or even
greater importance in influencing the total effect. When the ground was
covered entirely with opaque paint, the ground hue was still apt to have
its influence—appearing in the interstices between the brush strokes or
being seen through patches of paint which through accident or lapse of

time were not entirely opaque. These notes were culled from the *Painter's Workshop* by W. G. Constable. They offer the only grounds for explaining how eighteenth-century furniture was painted, for where it has chipped, several different color tones are revealed beneath the exterior surface. Their paint covering is ancient, and seemingly the several coatings were executed at the time of the original finish.

Let us imagine that furniture so painted endured the rigors of changing temperatures and frequent handling through several centuries. Such wear and tear caused the painted surface to chip so that the various hues of the coats of underpainting were revealed. Our generation finds these indications of age in furniture pleasing. The methods described here to simulate the effects of wear were evolved through the experience of restoring old pieces while respecting and retaining their aged, mellow appearance. With knowledge of the properties of modern materials, it is possible to emulate antiquity and, incidentally, to evolve original finishes for contemporary furniture.

# PHYSICAL DISTRESSING—PROCEDURE

With a new, or relatively new, piece of furniture, the framework is initially aged with tools and various other devices. This is termed physical distressing.

## *BLUNTING*
The first step is to round all the edges and corners with files and rasps. A round-headed hammer is used lightly to further break down and soften the edges and corners. Sections of frame or molding that jut out from the general structure of a chair or other object would be the areas most blunted by daily use. These hammer blows can be so mingled and superimposed as to conceal any indication of the tool employed. The hammer is also used to flatten protruding carvings. When these operations have been completed, the edges are sanded with 60 garnet paper followed by 220 garnet paper to blunt the mutilation.

## *SCARRING*
Irregular yet convincing scars are produced on a flat surface by striking it with an uneven bunch of 1-inch link chain or with many keys threaded on a wire hanger. A heavy glove or toweling is recommended to protect the right hand. The scarring action, though brutal, should be tempered with

reason, for the indentations should not be too close together or too obvious. Another excellent way to create this kind of blemish is to drop from a height of 2′ or 3′ a rough brick onto the piece, one corner directed toward the surface to be marred. Scarring with a brick gives variety to the distressing, which is desirable since flaws look artificial when too much alike. Bricks are also used as a hammering tool to blunt carving and the volutes which terminate a molding. Another scarring tool is made by pounding fragments of chain, bent nails, and other metal objects with irregular surfaces into one face of a 3-inch wooden mallet. The objects are embedded at irregular intervals. The rough face of the mallet is used for chipping corners and scarring surfaces. Other uses will be described later.

### WORMHOLES

The woodworm beetle invades buildings and the female lays her eggs in furniture. The grub feeds on the wood, making a small tunnel from $\frac{1}{32}''$ to $\frac{1}{16}''$ in diameter during the two years which it takes to arrive at the pupal stage. Signs of these active worms are small holes; some artisans manufacture them with BB shot. Under normal circumstances, if a householder were alerted to these holes by the telltale sawdust, he would be horrified and go to great effort to eliminate the perpetrators before their appetites resulted in a total collapse of the furniture. However, in our endeavor to create the look of antiquity, we assume that the worms have been exterminated and contrive a facsimile of their past residence. Failing a BB gun, satisfactory holes are produced with an ice pick, red-hot from a candle flame, hammered deep into the wood. It is withdrawn in a rotary movement to eliminate any betraying wood whiskers. The characteristics of wormholes should be studied, but it can be noted here that they are often clustered, sometimes single, sometimes adjacent.

As the physical distressing is concluded, the damaged areas are carefully examined, softened where they are too obvious, and eliminated by sanding when unconvincing. If the deliberate flaws are too obscured by the successive coats of paint, they may, with finesse, be brought back by using the same tools at any stage before the final paint coat.

### DARKENING

The piece is now colored with deep brown in order that the modern wood may acquire the appearance of age. For raw wood, a solution of 1 teaspoon of walnut aniline powder dissolved in 1 pint of alcohol is combined with an equal quantity of undiluted orange shellac (5-pound cut) to make an apparently authentic coating; after an hour's drying, it is bound with one coat of undiluted gloss varnish. If the piece was previously painted, a mixture of burnt umber japan color (1 volume to $\frac{1}{10}$ volume japan drier and $\frac{1}{2}$ volume turpentine) is applied to give the impression of old wood. This coating dries overnight, then is sealed with two coats of diluted orange shellac, the second one applied after the mandatory hour of drying time.

The object, whatever its previous condition, now appears to be a darkened, well-worn heirloom.

## DISTRESSING—PROCEDURE

The following processes are based on a system of paint coats alternating with binding coats. The latter differ in function: some reserve the underlying paint, while others act as a deterrent to the consistent bonding of a succeeding paint coat. When the principles involved are well understood, they may be used to evolve other interesting finishes.

### *SIMPLE DISTRESSING—ONE COLOR*

Distressing in one color is the least complex process. Two heavy coats of paint are first applied to the piece. Each is allowed the usual overnight drying period; each is well sanded with 220 garnet paper to level the brush strokes. Now begins the initial distressing of the painted surface, not to be confused with the physical distressing of the piece which has been described above. The processes of distressing continue at each operation to restate and emphasize the areas of wear and abuse.

On a distressed painted surface, chipping occurs in small or large areas depending on how accessible a particular one might have been to the ravages of use. Characteristically the edges of such chips are irregular and angular. On rounded and protruding areas, particularly at the base of an object, the brown wood is most frequently exposed. Indeed, the piece may appear to be of sufficient age for the exposed wood to be seen extensively at any point where the paint is unprotected by a jutting molding or a joining member. A touch of realism is added by paint chips that linger here and there on the exposed brown wood. They should be large enough to be discernible at a distance. The paint adjacent to chipped areas contains fractional nicks which prophesy the future cracking off of the contiguous paint. These nicks act artistically as a transitional element from the exposed ground to the remaining painted sections.

To obtain these effects, an orangewood stick and a #8 bright hog-bristle brush are used. A portion of semi-paste paint remover is poured into a flat container. The end of the bristle is loaded sparingly, and it carefully deposits the remover on areas which might be legitimately worn. The application should be limited to small areas at a time. The aim is to produce irregular and uneven edges. At the first deposition of the paint remover, the orangewood stick is used to push the blob of liquid into jagged edges.

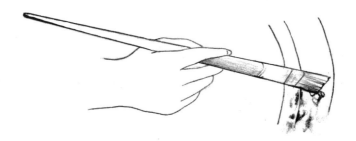

The remover remains on the surface until the paint wrinkles—instantly then the lifting paint is sharply rapped with a heavy wad of turkish toweling. This arrests the action of the paint remover before it has cut through the initial brown coating. Wiping the surface would smear the disintegrating paint and remove too large an area, hence the necessity of a forceful, precise blow. Only through experiment can one determine how much is needed between the application of the remover and the stopping of its action. If the stopping occurs too soon, the result will be a crazing rather than a lifting of the paint. This is sometimes a desirable effect on large surface areas. The complete lifting of the paint coat requires a longer time span and is preferable on the protruding elements where greater abuse would have occurred. The paint coat is mutilated on every area that has been physically marred, for the obvious reason that any damage to the body of a piece must first break through the paint coating. Paint remover burns the skin intensely but immediate application of cold water will relieve the sensation.

After the paint distressing, the piece dries overnight and any decoration may be applied. The decoration should be partially worn off with 220 garnet paper at all points of distressing. After the 24-hour drying period, the piece is coated with a protective mat varnish of high wax content. It is now ready for the final antiquing.

*Distressing*

### SIMPLE DISTRESSING—COARSE VARIANT

Should a more coarse and extended version of distressing be desired for a one-color piece, paint remover is pounced with a 1-inch stiff-bristle brush over the entire object with the exception of any slim (1″ to 1½″) areas protected by molding or form. This application is allowed to dry overnight without stopping the action of the remover. The next day the entire piece is lightly scraped with a razor in a somewhat haphazard way. The dry chipped paint is allowed to remain wherever it falls on the piece, thus adding a rough texture to the final finish. To hold the chips, a heavy coating of paint is immediately applied. Indentations from previous physical damage need not be filled with the paint as they would obviously be visible. When this coat has dried overnight, the resultant surface is rough and uneven. Design or striping rendered on such a surface is inevitably uneven, too, and augments the appearance of age. After the 24-hour drying time a sealer of mat varnish is applied in preparation for over-all antiquing.

### COMPLEX DISTRESSING

Complex distressing begins with the following steps:

1. Physical distressing
2. Brown coat
3. Binder
4. Application of the first two coats of paint, then two protective coats of shellac
5. Application of the third coat of paint
6. Distressing with paint remover
7. Overnight drying

A coat of mat varnish with a high wax content is then brushed on. The piece is now ready for a final coat of paint, which will also be distressed.

(Commercial finishers use soap, wax, crayon, or petroleum jelly as a quick substitute for the varnish. These, too, act as a preventative to the bonding of the succeeding coat of paint. They are placed haphazardly on points of wear and permit the superimposed coating of paint to be easily knocked off. I prefer the waxy varnish because the chipping which follows the final coat of paint is more readily controlled.)

After the mat varnish coat has dried overnight, the fourth coat of paint

GLAZING: *Top left, striated; right, blended with cheesecloth.*
*Bottom left, patted with sponge and spattered; right, sponged.*

is thickly brushed on and, when dry, sanded with 220 garnet paper. It is now chipped with an orangewood stick, distressing mallet, or razor.

One kind of damage simulated by complex distressing is attributable to extreme changes in the atmosphere. The interior core of wood expands in the heat and contracts in the cold, but old paint cannot stretch or shrink accordingly and therefore flakes off in large areas. Age and misuse are indicated by the chipping on corners, edges, and other points of wear, which discloses the brown base coat or an underlying coat of paint. The total result of these effects is an uneven surface broken through to several levels.

A razor, held perpendicular to the surface and run lightly down the edges of the piece and across the grain of any molding, easily produces the

ragged chipping desired. On the flat surfaces, a razor lightly used across the grain reveals only the places already roughened by the paint remover. Care must be exerted to avoid scratching the surface. Scratches proclaim too clearly the tool and the manipulation of man; so do chips on the edges when reiterative in width or shape. Over the years, the arms of an antique chair or settee would be polished to smoothness by the rubbing of many hands. This is easily fabricated with 280 garnet paper followed by 0000 steel wool.

An orangewood stick is the preferred tool for chipping large areas where one wishes residual flakes of paint to remain. It is also effective for small scars in the center of the surface and for the tiny breaks adjacent to larger exposed areas which foretell future chipping. When the distressing is complete on the painted surface, a coat of mat varnish is applied preparatory to the antiquing which makes obvious the different levels of the surface.


### THREE-COLOR DISTRESSING

To create depth and variations of hue, a complex distressed finish has been developed that employs three different color hues. The colors are chosen in accordance with their probable origin. They are tantamount to the underpainting of a canvas or panel. Artists have found that successive warm tones enhance one another; warm over cold tones weaken one another. Complementary colors in combination result in dull tones; similar values over each other become lifeless. Cennini and Vasari advocated the "three dish" system for rendering any part of a painting in a series of three values. Three mixtures were compounded: one of 2 parts dark and 1 part light; the second of 2 parts light, 1 part dark; the third a fifty-fifty combination of each of these. The values were laid on in this order: dark, middle, light. Then the painting was highlighted with white, accented with dark. Today's translation of this system into a method for three colors requires that the values should be exaggerated, three different hues substituted for light, middle, and dark values of one hue, and highlight and accent values used for striping and decoration. Since the palette of three hues is based on the "three dish" value system, one must be constantly aware of the interrelation of color. The first hue chosen is two values lighter than the brown primary coat; the second and third colors are each increasingly lighter in value— and by at least two intervening steps. In a combination of opaque color tones, the first underpainting is the most intense in order that its presence affects the final outcome. The second coating is either remotely analogous to the first or complementary—depending on whether one's aim is to enhance or to neutralize the first color. Similarly, the third and final coat is either analogous to the second coat or is its complementary hue. However, in those cases where the second color is a complement of the base color, the final color must be analogous to one of the two preceding colors.

These complex types of distressing begin with the procedure described in detail earlier: physical distressing; staining of the wood; and two coats of flat paint (*color one*) both sanded. This done, it may be desirable to emphasize some part of the physical distressing once again. The two coats of color one, having been sanded with 220 garnet paper, are sealed with two applications of the thinned shellac most related to that color. Of course, the drying time of one hour is allowed for each coat of shellac. These act as a binder for the first color and will also delay the action of paint remover when it is applied.

*Color two* is now brushed on with an oxhair brush. This coat is heavy enough to conceal completely the initial color except where indentations from physical distressing occur. These scars, which have been brushed over without an attempt to fill them, retain the initial brown coat of the first body covering. After color two has dried overnight and been sanded with 220 garnet paper, the surface is distressed with paint remover in the manner previously described. In this case the object is to cut through color two to color one, and—at the points of greatest wear—to the brown undercoat.

A chip of color two should remain on exposed areas of color one as well as chips of color one on the brown undercoat. (It will help to have studied antique painted furniture that has become naturally distressed, for the careful observer will detect on them areas of brown wood ringed by a jagged and uneven border of the first color, which in turn is surrounded by the second.)

Experiment determines how long it will take the paint remover to craze the surface or to remove color two or color one. The areas so exposed must be large enough so that when they are again exposed after the application of color three they will show in an effective contrast. Should the distressing be manipulated in a timorous or picky fashion, the end result tends to resemble a woven tweed rather than naturally chipped paint, the reason being that when small areas of color are evenly distributed, they merge, blend, or neutralize visually. On the completion of the step executed with paint remover, the piece is allowed to dry overnight. It is then coated with flat varnish high in wax content (or with a substitute material) and left to dry overnight.

A heavy covering coat of *color three* is added. This time, too, filling of the physical dents is avoided. After overnight drying the coat is sanded with 220 garnet paper or 400 wet-or-dry paper, and any striping, gilding, or decoration is rendered. When the piece has dried, an orangewood stick, razor, or distressing mallet is used to expose once more the areas of distress and wear. Chipping now reveals color two in addition to color one and the base brown undercoat. The roughness caused by the paint remover indicates the areas to be re-disclosed. Should an unsightly or ill-placed chip or scratch be inadvertently produced, such errors are touched up with heavy paint, which, when almost dry, is smoothed by the fingers to blend with the surface. Finally, the piece is coated with mat varnish and permitted to dry overnight before the application of antiquing.

It should now be clear that these methods are based on paint applications alternated with binding coats of various types. For instance, a protective binder resists the solvent action of the paint remover. A surfacing film (mat varnish) does not provide a foothold for the succeeding paint coat. Either of these acts as an intermediary application to enable manipulation of subsequent paint coats into dried and brittle paint that has flaked and chipped. With this type of procedure, many other varied effects are possible.

## PROVINCIAL DISTRESSING

Among the simulations achieved through this technique is the peeling paint observed on objects which have been subjected to the inclemencies of weather. A peeled and flaked finish is particularly successful on simple early

American country furniture and Canadian and European provincial pieces. The method employs two colors, and it begins with the steps previously described: from physical distressing through the applying of the two paint coats of color one. After the first-color coats are sanded with 220 garnet paper, the piece is coated with mat varnish of high wax content. When it has dried, a heavy covering coat of the second color is applied. This finish is most successful when the value of the first color is deeper than that of the second. The underbody can be revealed as soon as color two has surface dried. This is accomplished by using 220 garnet paper and a razor to pull the top layer off in broad, broken striation following the grain of the wood. The areas of the exposed underbody should range in width from ⅛″ to ½″ and should consist of varying lengths commensurate with the scale of the piece. The remaining top surface of paint, which comprises about 60 per cent of the surface, is intermittently joined and separated, always parallel with the grain. When complete, the piece receives an isolating coat of thinned shellac to prepare it for a heavy antiquing.

## *PROVINCIAL DISTRESSING—CONTEMPORARY VARIANT*

A variant of the method described above may be rendered in an elegant fashion on contemporary furniture or on period furniture possessing straight sleek form. In this case the physical damage is of course omitted. One begins instead with an application of body color in a light value. Three to four coats are required, each finely sanded with 220 garnet paper or 400 wet-or-dry paper. A reserve coat of thinned shellac or gloss varnish follows. When dry, a final coat of deep value is applied. As this coat dries to a mat surface, a very fine striation is effected by careful and even pulling with 000 steel wool in the direction of the grain. Any decoration or striping follows after this final surface finish has dried. A piece of furniture so finished may be then coated either with a mat varnish or with two coats of gloss varnish. The latter must be tufbacked and waxed.

# ANTIQUING

The most effective means of creating a patina on a distressed piece is with japan antiquing fluid mixed with paste wax. This waxy compound seeks out uneven levels and textures and reveals all surface deviations. The mixture is brushed on a section of the piece with a stiff-bristle brush of a width commensurate with the piece. The application is then pounced with a 2-inch stencil brush to eliminate and blend any previous brush strokes. On damp days, the force and speed of pouncing is tempered, as the resultant antiquing must be blended rather than lightened. The antique coating is applied *evenly and heavily* (without any lumps), since the blending methods to follow will remove a great part of it. When the antiquing has dried, a small, bristle kitchen brush is used in a rotary motion over the piece. This operation both embeds the antique film into the surface and partially removes it. Should the brush scratch the surface, the medium has not yet dried sufficiently. It is quite safe to blend on the day following the application of the antiquing medium. When this operation is completed, the piece is buffed to a final finish with felt.

After a lapse of several days, if a heavier patina is desired, a second antiquing in another related color is added. Either a heavy japan antiquing medium is stroked on with a dry brush, or a very thin one is applied by the spattering method and then is lightly pounced.

The antiquing described is enhanced by daily use and generally requires no protection. However, to preserve the patina of a chair frame from the friction of the human body it is necessary to coat the surfaces with mat varnish. To protect the tops of tables or chests from normal household mishaps, the usual varnishing procedure is necessary. These top surfaces are finally coated with mat varnish to maintain their worn, lean appearance.

For a crude finish on the provinical distressed surface which has been shellacked, a japan spattering fluid thinned out with mat varnish and turpentine is applied in an over-all coating. When the surface has dried overnight, it is blended and striated with 220 garnet paper. Or, if a heavier patina is desired, the piece is again shellacked, and japan antiquing medium mixed with wax (using the method described before) is applied. In this case the patina coat is blended with steel wool and the entire surface finally polished with flannel.

The foregoing systems of various paint layers with intervening coats for bonding and isolating can also be constructed with a series of glazes and scumbles. The possibilities, in fact, are manifold.

# DISTRESSING

*Materials*
Walnut aniline powder
Shellac (orange and white,
  5-pound cut)
Flat paint
Japan colors
Paint remover
Mat varnish with high wax
  content
Mat varnish for final
  protective coating
Gloss varnish
Turpentine
Alcohol
Japan drier
Paste wax

*Tools*
1½″ or 2″ oxhair brush as required for the size of the
  piece
1″ stiff-bristle brush, or as required for the size of the piece
2″ shellac brush
2″ varnish brush
1½″ sash brush
2″ stencil brush
Spatter brush

Small stiff-bristle kitchen
  brushes
#8 bright hog-bristle brush
Orangewood sticks
Straight-edge razor blades
60 garnet paper
220 garnet paper
280 garnet paper
400 wet-or-dry paper
000 steel wool
0000 steel wool
3″ wooden mallet
Bent nails
Round-headed hammer
Chains
Bricks
Fine wood files
Ice pick
Rasps
Keys
Wire hanger

*Miscellaneous*
Turkish towel
Flat lids
Felt
Flannel polishing cloth
Candle
Heavy glove

# PART II

# Glazes, Lacquer & Casein: Old Techniques Updated

# GLAZES

## DESCRIPTION

A glaze is a carefully controlled transparent film of color superimposed on opaque color. It effects a transformation that may vary from the subtle to the dramatic. A glaze interposes a thin transparent layer between the eye and the object, independently of the object's surface color. Artists of the past often applied glazes on their paintings to enrich the deep color and make translucent the light one. A glaze on graceful pieces of furniture enhances them in the same way. Blooming faintly over the raised and rounded elements, lightly tinting the center field of the flat areas, and emphasizing the line and limits of form, glaze is distributed to accentuate the depths of shadows and the brilliance of highlights. As the artist's desire to reproduce in a picture the luster of satin, the richness of velvet, the brilliance of a jewel, led him to the technique of glazing, a similar desire to exalt the beauty of a piece of furniture may be the explanation for the craftsman's use of glaze in the eighteenth century. Furniture of the late eighteenth century, Neoclassic in style, designed with restraint and purity of form and line, and for the most part free of carved ornament, is admirably enriched by a glaze. Pursuing the theory that several techniques of the fine artist were incorporated in the craft of decorative furniture painting, we can regard glazing as yet another heritage from the painters of the Renaissance. In their works, the use of an oil glaze created an atmospheric quality softening the form, modulating the transitions, enriching the shadows; the eye could penetrate the depths of a picture rather than be arrested at its surface.

Glazing is the application of color, transparent in nature, over a ground hue calculated to assist the final color in value and intensity. Such color seen through color enchants the beholder with the beauty of combined yet unmixed hues. An internal light is represented by the light ground over which transparent colors are passed. Light is here seen from within rather than as a reflection from the surface.

## PRINCIPLES OF GLAZING

The principles followed by artists who paint in oils may be of assistance to the furniture craftsman.

> Glazes that are deeper in value than the ground increase the warmth of a surface as long as any inner light is visible.
>
> A cool deep glaze over a warm ground creates a rich depth.
>
> A warm glaze over a darker warm tone produces a cool silvery effect.
>
> A light neutral glaze over a dark surface creates a warm intensity.
>
> A light glaze thinly applied over a dark tone effects a cold tone.

Degrees of warmth and coolness are obtained through the interaction of one tint with another. The colors respond to each other in terms of value and intensity as well as altering the final hue. Creating the depth peculiar to oil painting—which is so delightful when transferred to furniture—depends essentially on a constant awareness of transparency.

## GLAZED EFFECTS ON FURNITURE

A glaze may be applied evenly on a piece of furniture to produce a special color illusion or a nuance of tone in keeping with the general effect of the room. This method was prevalent in the period of Louis XV. The beautifully fashioned painted furniture of that time was most often finished with a tinted varnish, in essence a glaze. This may have been an inept attempt to simulate the then fashionable Oriental lacquer, or again it may have simply been a protective coating tinted to harmonize with upholstery or *boiserie.*

On a piece with good lines, glaze emphasizes the grace of structure and proportion. Points of reflective light varying in extent should be visible as the glaze deepens in conformity with the shape of the piece.

## GLAZE AND COLOR

Traditionally, a glaze presupposes a light opaque undertone, which it tints, deepens, or modifies. In some cases the color of the undercoat unites with the color of the glaze. If the glaze is a hue analogous to the body color, the result will be a delicately modified and deepened tone. If the glaze is a complement of the body color (e.g., orange over blue), the result will be a neutralized tone, although this could be mitigated somewhat by an imbalance of values. When a glaze of a primary or secondary color is placed adjacent to the hue of the base color, it modifies the original tone of the surface and creates an optical illusion—a mixture of the two hues.

Glazing lends itself to myriad effects. When it is employed on contemporary furniture, liberties may be taken with the traditional concept of a light undertone deepened by a glaze, particularly when striation is employed. Strong hues when differing in value from the surface hue have tremendous impact (e.g., a brilliant green glaze over a blue ground, or an intense orange over an intense purple-pink). To soften and diffuse the harshness of a large and rigid piece, a neutral ground coat of gray glazed with a lighter neutral of beige is effective.

Study of the foregoing methods has led to other interesting color effects. A tinge of color over a gray ground achieves a reticent and harmonious result. A thin film of red-orange over a pale ground heightens luminosity.

## GLAZING—PREPARATION

The piece to be glazed is prepared with utmost care, special attention being given to filling and sanding. Four to five coats of the ground color are applied with a fine-bristle oxhair brush in order to minimize brush marks. Each coat is allowed to dry for the usual 24 hours. Every second coat is sanded where necessary with 280 garnet paper. The last coat is tuf-backed with 600 wet-or-dry paper and a soapy solution to a satin smoothness. The end result is a body of paint which totally envelops the object. This exacting care in preparation is essential as the thin glaze will catch in any irregularities or brush ridges on the surface and thus prevent the desired film-like effect. The surface is now isolated with a protective coating in order that any unfortunate errors arising in the application of the glaze may be removed with mineral spirits without damage to the underbody. The binder is a fresh solution made of equal parts of French varnish (the most refined bleached form of shellac) and denatured alcohol. This is more easily applied if a fine linen or cotton bob is substituted for the brush. (See chapter on gilding.) After drying overnight, the binder is gently rubbed with 0000 steel wool.

In decorative furniture painting, japan color is the preferred tinting ingredient. The slight thickness which it gives to the glaze film makes its contrast with the underpainting more effective. It is *essential* that a glaze medium be evolved which accords with each individual's method of working, his rate of speed, and his dexterity. The consistency must be such that the medium can be applied evenly and its placement controlled. The thin transparent medium must also allow further manipulation so as to achieve dual tonality.

### FORMULA FOR A GLAZING FLUID

The proportions of the formula suggested below should be adjusted to personal requirements.

> 2 ounces flatting oil (soybean oil)
> —to slow drying and to provide elasticity and richness.
>
> 2 ounces undiluted gloss varnish
> —to control tackiness.
>
> 3 ounces thinner (a refined type of mineral solvent)
> —to augment transparency.
>
> 2 to 6 drops of japan drier
> —the amount will vary; increasing with ideal weather conditions and/or the craftsman's progress in dexterity.

### COLOR MIXTURE

To color the glazing vehicle, ½ ounce of a mixture of japan color and flat white paint, if required, is added.

To reiterate, the balance of the ingredients of the glaze must be varied to accord with each individual's facility. The aim is to cover the surface with as small an amount of color glaze as possible. Deep hues require a richer consistency (more flatting oil) of the glazing vehicle.

The color mixture and the glazing vehicle are kept in separate containers and are combined only when required for immediate use. A small amount of color when combined with a large volume of liquid separates and clumps into particles. If the requirement of the day is a very small quantity of glaze, a teaspoon may be used as a measure.

## GLAZING—PROCEDURE

### APPLICATION OF "LEAN" GLAZE

An age-old adage counsels the artist to proceed from "lean" to "fat" when coating a surface. These terms indicate the lesser or greater quantity of oil in a formula. Before application of the fat glaze made to the formula given above, a colorless lean glaze consisting of 2 volumes turpentine combined with 1 volume flatting oil may be laid on the surface with a cotton bob and allowed to dry for 24 hours. When sufficiently skillful, one can eliminate the isolating coat of varnish or shellac and use only the colorless lean glaze as a preliminary to the tinted fat glaze. Or instead of the lean glaze, an equal combination of flatting oil and turpentine may be spread over the surface; this is wiped off immediately with a cloth before the glazing.

### APPLICATION OF "FAT" COLORED GLAZE

A small amount of the tinted glaze mixture is spooned into a low container. One method of application is with an oxhair brush moved over the surface with–against–with the grain to spread the coating as thinly as possible. Finally, the surface is stroked lightly with the tip of the bristle to even out and dry the glaze.

Another method uses a fine natural sponge (e.g., a cosmetic sponge) as an applicator. As the glaze film is patted on, the sponge is manipulated in the advancing and retreating movement used in pouncing. With a dry sponge used similarly, the film is blended evenly. At first, the glaze will look spotty, but should even out to a very sensitive mottling. The edges of each portion must be patted heavily with a dry sponge so that they will be transparent and the adjoining sections will not form a ridge. A pad of cheesecloth or a blunt round brush are also used to apply glaze in this manner.

Only experiment will determine the procedure most appropriate to each individual. A totally different method may be invented which will prove more efficient. To repeat, glazing, in both formula and method of application, is a personal technique.

### TECHNIQUE OF BLENDING

Blending is a most delicate operation, and must be done at the moment before the glaze has reached the mat stage of drying. The blending may be handled in several ways to achieve different effects. Should one desire the delicate striation which is seen on pieces of *vernis Martin* (French lacquer), a dry oxhair brush is drawn firmly and evenly over the surface with pressure on the ferrule of the brush. The resulting accumulation of medium is wiped off the brush. The action is continued until the surface has an even tonality consisting of fine lines of glaze alternating with fine lines of the exposed background. This is the method recommended for contemporary pieces.

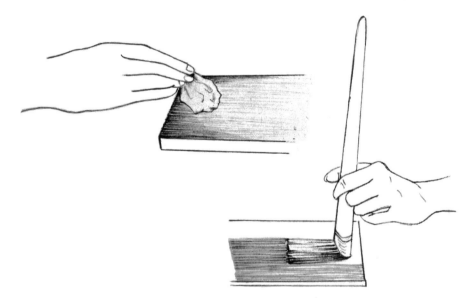

Another type of blending is the more subtle shading from dark to light of the artist's panels. Four-inch squares of cheesecloth are necessary for this. The square is held by its corners to blend the glaze. The cheesecloth is changed frequently to avoid re-depositing accumulated color. At first a very

*Lacquer*

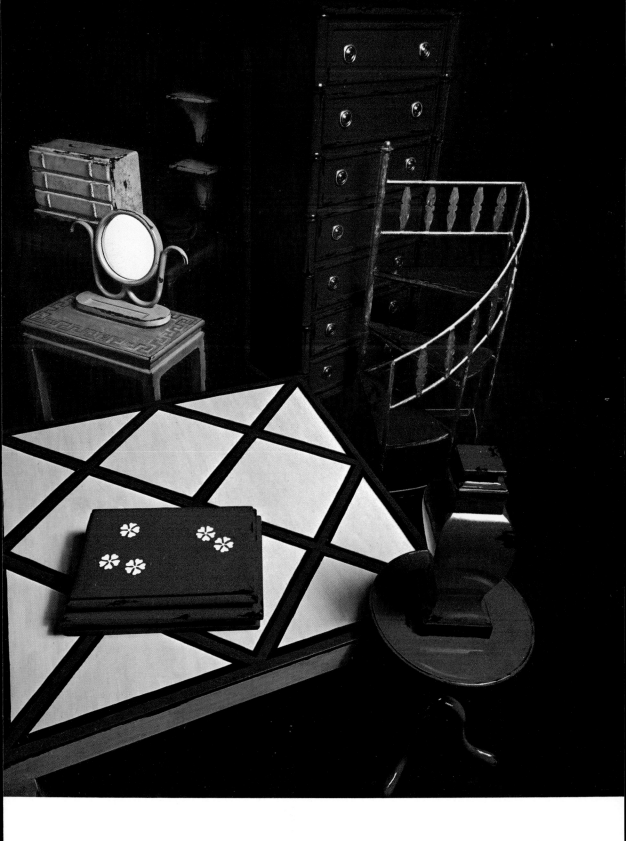

light pressure is sufficient to manipulate the glaze, but as it dries the pressure is increased. A transparent film of glaze remains on the center of the surface. This type of blending proceeds from the center outward, going to each end following the grain. The length of the strokes on each successive whisk is shortened, thus creating a light oval center surrounded by a deeper bordering tone. Then the juncture between the oval and the darker border is lightly pounced with a fresh cloth. Again the glaze is whisked from the center in both directions, this time through the bordering deep tone. With added pressure at this stage, the dark border is next pulled into the center, blending the outer deeper tone into the light. The result is a delicate, transitional, shading. If any dark streaks mar the harmony of the toning, a little more pressure is used to eliminate them when the glaze is almost dry. The final effect is a veil of color deepening as it nears the edge of an area or the juncture of form.

In a third method of blending, a badger blender pounces the glaze. The blender must be held perpendicular to the surface. Reiterative marks are avoided by continually revolving the tool between the thumb and finger.

After the blending, any glaze must be allowed to dry for a week because of its high oil content. Should an additional glaze seem desirable, the initial glaze must be bound with an isolating varnish. Succeeding glazes might follow any of the premises mentioned at the beginning of this chapter. Indeed, they might simulate the priming coats used by the Italian artists to hold an underpainting or to counteract the eventual yellowing of varnish; these are discussed in the chapter on distressing.

## DECORATION ON GLAZED SURFACE

When the glaze coats have dried, decoration, gilding, or striping may be added. It is preferable to use casein (water-soluble) paint for the decoration; then without damage to the glaze finish an error may be easily removed with a cotton tip moistened with water. If any other medium is used for decoration, the glazed surface must be protected with thinned French varnish. When the painted decoration is thoroughly dry or any gilding has been antiqued, the entire piece is surfaced with flat varnish, and finally is antiqued overall.

LACQUER: *Top left, variant; right, coromandel.*
*Bottom left, dragon's blood; right, antiqued Chinese linen.*

## A SCUMBLE

Scumbling is a method of toning that somewhat resembles glazing. A scumble is a layer of paint used to modify the color of the surface to which it is applied; it differs from a glaze in that it is opaque rather than transparent. The thin overlay of color is lightly applied so that some light penetrates here and there and reflects back. Over a dry paint coat or one brushed with isolating shellac (French varnish), a scumble is stippled, striated, or daubed with a brush or rag, and then is partially rubbed off.

To effect a semi-transparency with delicacy, scumbling is done on a surface previously moistened with varnish or flatting oil. The medium for this is usually a lighter tone over a dark tone, resulting in a cool tint. It may be applied—either by brushing with a large brush or by pouncing—over a ground hue which has been isolated with shellac (French varnish). In the next step, a large badger blender is used to flatten and tone the color, or a cloth or 0000 steel wool is used to wipe the surface to a uniform coating. A piece so rendered is coated when dry with mat varnish in preparation for antiquing.

## ANTIQUING

The antique patina on a glazed piece must be subtle to enrich and to soften, but not to extinguish, the variation of color. A thin solution of japan spattering fluid made to this formula is appropriate:

1 volume japan color
4 volumes mat varnish
3 to 4 volumes turpentine

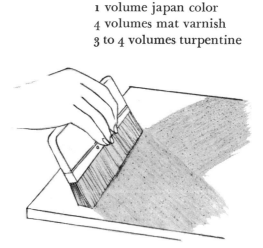

This solution is spooned out on a heavy wax paper palette. The pounce brush (1½-inch oval sash brush) is lightly loaded and tamped out on white paper. A small portion of the surface is then lightly dappled with a pounce brush. A dry wallpaper brush is immediately whisked over the area in criss-cross fashion (see drawing opposite). The result is a light film of antique patina which appears to be totally embodied in the paint surface. When the antiquing has dried for two weeks, the surface may be further protected with several coats of protective mat varnish or gloss varnish.

Another kind of antiquing medium, particularly recommended for a striated piece, is a sparse spattering of an antique aniline solution (see chapter on antique patina for leaf) which is lightly pounced. This method resembles that seen on pieces finished in *vernis Martin*. Over a piece finished in this manner, a gloss varnish is effective.

## GLAZES

*Materials*
French varnish
Flat white paint
Japan color
Mat varnish with high wax content
Mat varnish for final protective coating
Flatting oil (soybean oil)
Clear gloss varnish
Turpentine
Denatured alcohol
Thinner (a refined type of mineral solvent)
Japan drier
Casein color (water-soluble)

*Tools*
2 1½" or 2" oxhair brushes as required for the size of the piece

2" shellac brush
2" varnish brush
1½" oval sash brush
3" badger blender
Blunt round brush
Wallpaper whisk brush
600 wet-or-dry paper
0000 steel wool
Cosmetic sponge
280 garnet finishing opencote paper

*Miscellaneous*
Cheesecloth
Flat containers
White paper
Heavy wax paper
Spoon
Cotton or linen bobs

# HISTORY
# OF LACQUER

A lacquer finish is shining, reflective, and of impeccable smoothness. It provides a gleaming cloak for any object, mundane or sophisticated. Furniture of merit wears this garb with exquisite grace, its mirror gloss both reflecting its surroundings and adding richly to the ambiance of a room. A lacquer surface moreover is impervious to acid, alcohol, and average heat and cold. As long ago as 2000 B.C. the value of lacquer was appreciated to such an extent that it served as a temple offering and was even acceptable as payment of taxes.

The religious philosophy of the artist-craftsman of the Orient directed him to avoid imposing a form on his material and encouraged him instead to stress its own intrinsic quality. Lacquer is by nature destined to serve as decoration to form, whether used to cover a surface or to embellish it through design. It follows therefore that a lacquer finish of the highest quality is never allowed to become an end in itself.

The art of lacquering was first developed in China. By the fifteenth century the Japanese, who had been instructed by the Chinese, excelled in the technique to the point where the Emperor of China esteemed their gifts above the handiwork of his own craftsmen. In China the art had deteriorated and attempts to copy the excellence of the Japanese pieces failed. China, once the master in the art of lacquering, now became the pupil of

Japan. That the Japanese retained leadership in the art is evidenced by the fact that the East Indian trading companies imported nothing but Japanese lacquer for the European market.

In the Western world there was a great confusion about this beautiful finish called lacquer. Some part of the confusion arose from the fact that in India there was a material used for coating metal and wooden objects called "lac." The term had evolved from the Sanskrit numeral *laksha*, meaning 100,000, for this was the number of insects (*Coccus lacca*) needed to produce the resin lac. These insects fed on the juices of various trees and with their secretion formed an incrustation around the young branches. After being duly processed, this substance became what we today call shellac and what the people of the seventeenth century knew as seedlac. But the lacquer so admired by the European collector and misnamed by him was the product of a totally different substance.

The lac tree *Rhus vernicifera*, from which lacquer is obtained, is a sumac tree related to the vinegar plant and also to the terebinth tree, from whose resin turpentine is made. Trees between fourteen and fifteen years old supply the best quality of lacquer. Tapping occurs from June to September, the sap being obtained by a horizontal incision in the bark. Small branches are cut off and then barked by soaking in water. When the bark is pierced or removed, a resinous substance exudes slowly from the stem, turning from transparent white to gray and then to black when exposed to the air.

An *inferior lacquer*, which dries more slowly but is harder, is made by boiling down the small branches. All raw lacquer is sold by the producers to merchants, and they in turn sell it to the manufacturers who process it into various secret formulas. The sap, which is thick, is stored in wooden pails and protected against dust and light. Impurities are removed by constant boiling, stirring, and skimming. It is then strained through hemp cloth to remove more impurities and stirred for many hours in shallow vessels over a slow fire or in hot sunshine so as to make the excess moisture evaporate. After this thickening process, the lacquer could be colored with dye, combined with a little egoma oil, and then used for coloring or surfacing. Inferior lacquer is used for preparatory coats, and is sometimes combined with ground powder of brick, stone, or clay into a filler. Finally, the product is retailed to the lacquer workers.

A description of the procedure used in the Far East may serve to clarify the methods devised in this book to emulate lacquer. Wood is the most common support for lacquer—a wood free from knots and preferably containing little resin. In Oriental practice, the object to be lacquered was first carefully smoothed and all cracks and joints were filled. It was then covered with cloth or paper, not only to strengthen the joints but also to isolate the base, thereby preventing the sap of the wood from mingling with the lacquer. The piece was next surfaced with many layers of the lacquer composition, and each layer was smoothed after it had dried. When preparation was complete, the piece was so totally encased by these basic layers that no detail of its structure was apparent.

Lacquer has the extraordinary characteristic of attaining its maximum hardness only in a damp atmosphere, such as that of a cave or cellar. After the basic preparation, it was never exposed to the air. Twenty-two coatings made up the foundation layers, and each one was polished and smoothed after intervening drying periods of varying extent—twelve hours to three days. This was followed by three or more coatings of black lacquer with similar drying and polishing periods. After this, seven to fourteen coats of clear lacquer were applied; these were smoothed and polished finally with oil and deerhorn ashes applied with the fingers. Since each layer was polished to smoothness, the total thickness of the layers was minimal even in the case of the thirty-three to forty layers essential to fine lacquer. After this time-consuming process to produce a flawless surface, decoration was added. It might have consisted of further lacquering in various colors, these incised or carved out to reveal underlying color at different levels. It might have consisted of raised relief decoration, painted or gilded, or of inlay—decoration embedded in further coats of lacquer. Innumerable variations depending on the quality and purpose of the object were effected by the color, the decoration, or the carving or inlay.

Lacquer with its flawless surface, polished to a mirror gloss, impervious to scar and scratch, dazzled the Europeans. The undeniable perfection of craftsmanship, the tasteful and exotic decoration, the novelty and the scarcity of imported lacquer pieces reserved them for royalty. They were gifts as acceptable as jewels.

The vogue for lacquer reached a high point throughout Europe as the Dutch and the British developed their East Indian trade. Confusion existed in the Western mind about the term lacquer. This can be accounted for by the fact that lacquer was rarely shipped direct to Europe from the country of its origin but found its way to some intermediate trading station—such as Dutch Batavia, the Coromandel coast of India, or the port of Canton—where cargo was collected for transport. Therefore, the English designation for a type of lacquer did not necessarily describe the place of an object's conception or even the country of its origin. Europeans universally regarded the East as a region of elegance and fantasy. Regardless of whether its provenance was China, India, Korea, or Japan, lacquer was termed Japanware, Bantamware, Japan Black, Coromandel.

The designation in the case of Bantamware derived from Bantam in Java, where lacquer was collected for transport to Europe, even though produced in Japan or China.

Coromandel lacquer was so called after the island of Coromandel off the coast of India. It is a combination of lacquer, carving, and painting. The technique consisted of overlaying a base of wood with a composition of fine white clay, a coating of fibrous grasses, and then three coats of finer clay which were rubbed down to smoothness. Following this, lacquer was painted on in sufficient coats to insure a body for rubbing down and polishing. The design was carved in intaglio, revealing the chalky layer and reserving the black lacquer as defining lines of the pattern. The portions hollowed out were brightly colored with gamboge, red ochre, cinnabar, carthamin, and gilt, which contrasted with the dark lacquer around them.

Japanning was used to describe the imitation of Oriental lacquer by the English craftsmen, amateur and professional, during the sixteenth, seventeenth, and eighteenth centuries. The term was also used in America. It covered a variety of techniques, including the coating of papier-mâché or decorated tin with imitation lacquer.

As a result of haste on the part of the Oriental craftsman and his desire to accommodate European taste, the fineness and beauty of the imported lacquer varied in quality. Although a whole summer is hardly sufficient to bring lacquer to perfection, the workmen of the Far East did not even begin production of export ware until the ships that would carry it back to Europe had arrived. Then they worked hurriedly, fully aware that the European purchasers were not connoisseurs. The volume of this export was so great that the European trade finally petitioned against it, maintaining the danger of being utterly ruined. In the early part of the eighteenth century a duty was levied.

The demand for Oriental lacquer mounted. The Dutch East Indies Company brought back chairs and boxes, also panels to be incorporated in the structure of Western furniture. Still the supply was inadequate, so Holland and England began to produce imitations. Traders brought Oriental workers to Holland to teach the decoration of lacquer. Patterns were created in Europe and reproduced in the Orient. Designers were sent to the East to produce models for the European market. However, Western shapes were not understood in the East, and when produced there, they were ornate and clumsy. Europeans attempted to obtain the actual lacquer substance but it appears that the Eastern merchants sold them an inferior product—doubtless out of a sound instinct for self-preservation. Efforts to solve the mystery of the material continued through succeeding centuries without success. The tree from which lacquer is obtained was not brought to the Western world, possibly because of sumac's poisonous vapors, which can cause rashes and inflammation similar to poison ivy. It must be noted, too, that the cost of production and the painstaking technique involved made genuine lacquer commercially prohibitive despite the low wages of European artisans.

Lacquer, with its brilliant color and entrancing decoration, appealed especially to the English, who were weary of the dark tones of oak and mahogany prevalent through the period of Queen Anne. Indeed, the fad was so great that books were published with instructions for the layman, and many amateurs practiced the art. In the seventeenth century, Stalker and Parker published a treatise for the instruction of young ladies in the art of lacquering, which the authors described as "Japanning." Children were taught the subject in school. Fashionable ladies concerned themselves with the art as a polite occupation. Lady Walpole regarded her pieces of Japanning so highly as to designate the recipient of each one in her will.

English Japanware was one of the facsimiles of lacquer on papier-mâché or on tin coated with a varnish consisting chiefly of asphaltum dried in an oven. This was common ware, molded mechanically and decorated primarily with transfers. In copying the decoration, the English were more repetitious than the Orientals, often designing pairs in exact reversal without the endless Oriental variations. They restricted their decoration for the most part to gold and silver design on a ground of lacquer of various colors—black, red, bistre, and green. The English framework consisted of borders of repetitive surface motifs rather than the inlaid or incised design of the Orient. The surface of Oriental lacquer was smoother and more brilliant, the gold gleaming, the details sharp, and the lines fine. The myriad types of Eastern lacquer were beyond the skill of the Western copyist. Indeed, according to a noted Orientalist, "for the most part, European lacquer, which professed to imitate the Chinese, is simply glorified coach-painting at its best, and at its worst, a mere daubing of paint surfaced with shellac polish either applied with a brush or a rubber."

After 1725, the craft was firmly established in England. Chippendale, fascinated by the Orient, filled the great houses of England with his fantasies. Adam joined him in designing and manufacturing such pieces. By 1760 lacquer was primarily used for coaches and commercial objects and by the end of the century was almost abandoned except for accessories and small articles.

The lacquer of France reached its zenith in the eighteenth century. However, it was only one of the painted finishes used on the furniture of that period. The French mounted Oriental lacquer panels in ormolu on their cabinet pieces. Near mid-century the four Martin brothers invented an imitation lacquer which was as highly valued as the authentic; indeed, after 1740 a royal decree granted them a monopoly on its production, owing perhaps to the appreciative interest of their clients Madame du Pompadour and Madame du Barry. The Martins created many boxes and bibelots for the court, lacquered their coaches, and decorated the *petit appartement* for Marie Antoinette in Versailles. Their lacquer, called *vernis Martin*, consisted of copal varnish over many layers of color, often the blue of lapis or the green of emerald decorated with transparent gold in striations or waves. This was then subjected to heat. No record remains of the formula.

Italian lacquer was inferior in quality to that of France, England, and Holland. However, compensating for its lack of smoothness and brilliance were ebullience and variety of color and beauty and originality of pattern. The high point of Venetian lacquer occurred somewhat later in the first half of the eighteenth century. All painted and decorated furniture at this time was finished in "lacquer." Although the Venetians' lacquer was not comparable to that of the English, French, or Dutch, its decoration was more expertly rendered in *chinoiserie* with rocaille scrolls. Decorations of fanciful garlands and scenes were delightfully painted on the lacquer ground. They were as finely rendered as those embellishing porcelain, and in full color rather than the black and gold to which the English rigidly clung.

In America, Japanning was not executed until the 1730s, and whether professional or amateur it was little more than clear varnish over painted wood. Imitation tortoise shell which combined streaks of black on vermilion with gilded decoration sometimes in slight relief was its most charming achievement.

The first flush of ecstatic admiration for all things Oriental subsided after the seventeenth century, only to revive again in the mid-eighteenth in a more whimsical fantasy of chinoiserie. A graceful flight of fancy characterized this somewhat naive expression of the Occidental's dream of the mysterious East. *Chinoiserie* is often more appealing to Western eyes than is the perfection of Oriental decoration. Similarly, the European imitations of Oriental lacquer, though lacking its unblemished and impervious surface, are appealing—their very flaws enchant the eye.

Although fine lacquer work deteriorated in Europe toward the end of the eighteenth century, technical proficiency improved. Toward 1800 a lacquer industry was built up in Germany producing Japanned tin ware and papier-mâché similar to the English kind. This continued well into the nineteenth century, when the vogue for lacquer revived, this time in the form of a relatively inexpensive mass product which by now had little in common with its beautiful Oriental ancestor.

Obviously it is impossible to duplicate Oriental lacquer without the lacquer resin. Fortunately, through experiment in the studio, it has been possible to create an acceptable facsimile.

# LACQUER
# TECHNIQUES

## NEGORO NURI

One of the earliest and simplest types of Oriental lacquerware is *Negoro nuri*. It was developed by the priests of the Japanese monastery *Negoro-dera* as early as the fourteenth century, and included the vessels used for their simple meals. The bowls were first lacquered in black and then in red. Sometimes part of the red was polished away to reveal the black as a form of decoration; sometimes the red just became worn with use and the black underneath came to light with a lovely effect. This type of lacquer finish is becoming to straight-sided chests, commodes, Queen Anne or simple Chippendale chairs, and small objects of clean design.

## PROCEDURE

### BLACK LACQUER–UNDERCOAT
The surface of a piece to be rendered in a manner resembling that of *Negoro nuri* is coated with four layers of the following paint medium, which simulates the black lacquer base:

> 5 volumes flat black paint
> ½ volume burnt umber japan color
> ⅓ volume japan drier
> ¼ volume spar varnish

The mixture is strained, and then applied to the surface with an oxhair brush. After each two coats the surface is tufbacked with 600 wet-or-dry paper with non-detergent soapsuds as a lubricant. The black is then protected with two coats of thinned orange shellac, each of which after an hour's drying is lightly smoothed with 0000 steel wool.


## RED LACQUER—OVER-COAT

The enveloping red lacquer is imitated with the following mixture:

> 1 volume true red japan color
> ½ volume orange-red japan color
> ¼ volume flat white paint
> ½ volume turpentine


## EXPOSURE OF BLACK UNDERCOAT

When the red mixture is completed, it is strained. It should be fairly heavy and yet spreadable, so that, if possible, a single smooth covering can be evenly applied with an oxhair brush. But, if necessary, a second thin coat may be spread on when the first is surface dry. As the paint sets to mat dryness the surface may be tufbacked with 600 wet-or-dry paper and a soapy emulsion to remove any ridges left by the brush. This tufbacking, though done with delicacy, will undoubtedly reveal shadows of the black base. If pleasingly located, they indicate areas to be further revealed as decoration or as evidence of wear. Rubbing with a soap emulsion and 000 steel wool against the grain completes this operation.

On the other hand, the procedure of revealing the black may begin by rubbing with 000 steel wool and the soapy emulsion. A word of caution: this is apt to produce too gross an area of black and must be used carefully. This rubbing must be delayed until the paint is set, otherwise steel wool particles will be caught in the surface. The rubbing attempts to produce irregular edges of the red coating in imitation of actual wear, which is never uniform. Tufbacking the entire surface with 600 wet-or-dry paper and a soapy emulsion completes this process. After the red coating has dried overnight, and to effect a semblance of age, it is spattered with a thin solution of Antique Aniline Warm (see chapter on antique patina for leaf) diluted with an additional volume of alcohol. The spattering should be large and irregular. The spatter is blended by patting it with a slightly alcohol-dampened cloth. For further antiquing, the following are combined:

> 1 volume orange-red japan color
> 1/4 volume burnt umber japan color
> 4 volumes mat varnish
> 3 volumes turpentine

This mixture makes a very thin spattering fluid, which is pounced on the surface. When the antiquing has dried for several days, a series of varnish coats—lightly tinted with cadmium red oil paint—is applied. As they build up, these tinted layers simulate the glowing depth of lacquer. If the red tint begins to discolor the black, clear varnish should be substituted. Varnishing continues with the usual intervening tufbacking until a translucent surface is obtained. The final varnish coat is polished with a paste of rottenstone and lemon oil. The Orientals polished with their fingers and palms, but the effete Westerner will probably wish to use a felt pad.

### VARIATION—YELLOW OVER-COAT
An agreeable variation of this technique substitutes a golden yellow lacquer for the red one:

> 1 volume chrome yellow medium japan color
> 1/4 volume raw sienna japan color
> 1/2 volume turpentine
> 1/10 volume japan drier

The procedure described for red lacquer is followed, including the application of the warm antique aniline. For the japan spattering fluid, a mixture of 1 volume yellow ochre japan color and 1/4 volume raw umber japan color is substituted. The varnish for this variant is tinted with raw sienna oil paint until it begins to discolor the black.

### VARIATION—GESSO AND LINEN GROUND
Another type of *Negoro nuri* calls for the object to be coated with gesso (see chapter on burnishing), then covered with coarse linen. The cloth is affixed with rabbit-skin glue solution. (To make this, a scant 1/3 cup rabbit-skin glue granules is soaked overnight in 14 ounces water; the jelly is dissolved the next day over a pan of hot water; then 2 ounces of the stock are added to 1 pint boiling water.) When the glue-soaked linen applied to the gesso has dried overnight, the piece is smoothed down with the fingers from the center out. Then the lacquering procedure continues as previously described. When the final coating of color is rubbed with wet-or-dry paper or steel wool, the black-coated mesh of the linen is revealed here and there. Obviously, this type of lacquer must be varnished until the mesh of the linen is levelled.

## VARIATION—BLACK UNDERCOAT WITH RICE GRAINS

Another variation involves a pattern of rice grains. Over a base of black, an additional coat of black is painted on. While it is tacky, rice grains are pressed into the surface and left to dry overnight. The rice grains are then flicked off the surface, and two coats of thinned orange shellac are brushed on. After these coats have dried, a color coat is applied. When dry, the surface is sanded through with 220A silicon carbide paper until the colored depressions left by the rice kernels are revealed in the black surface. The whole is then given a series of gloss varnish coats until the surface lies smooth and even.

## VARIATION—OVER-COAT IN NON TRADITIONAL COLOR

To relate the technique of *Negoro nuri* to the contemporary scene, a variety of color substitutions may be made. The undercoat continues to be black or a deep value of color. These are tufbacked and held with the two coats of thinned shellac before the application of a hue of lighter value. In this variation, the undercoat may be revealed in a precise decorative pattern. This rendering also receives many coats of tinted varnish.

# NEGORO NURI

*Materials*
- Flat black paint
- Burnt umber japan color
- Japan drier
- Spar varnish
- True red japan color
- Orange-red japan color
- Flat white paint
- Mineral spirits
- Orange shellac
- Denatured alcohol
- Non-detergent soap flakes
- Cadmium red oil paint
- Rottenstone
- Lemon oil
- Chrome yellow medium japan
  color
- Raw sienna japan color
- Antique aniline
- Yellow ochre japan color
- Raw sienna oil paint
- Turpentine
- Mat varnish with wax content
- Raw umber japan color
- Gloss varnish

*Tools*
- 0000 steel wool
- 600 wet-or-dry paper
- Oxhair brush
- 000 steel wool
- 220A silicon carbide paper

*Miscellaneous*
- Coarse linen
- Rice grains
- Rabbit-skin glue granules
- Felt pad

## EGGSHELL INLAY

A lacquer ground inlaid with eggshell, somewhat resembling a mosaic, is one of the decorative treatments created by Oriental craftsmen. It is not known when this finish first evolved, but since the 1930s it has had a certain vogue among lacquer connoisseurs. The popular name for this type of lacquer is *Tamago-ji*, but the literal name is *Keiran nuri*, from *kei* meaning chicken, *ran* meaning egg, and *nuri* meaning lacquer(ware). According to Taro Maruyama, who today practices the technique of eggshell inlay on lacquer in Matsumoto, Japan, this art originated in China and came to Japan via Korea.

Cennino Cennini, a chronicler of the Renaissance, describes eggshells crushed down on a roughened ground, then colored with a paint brush. No example of this is extant. Vasari, another chronicler and painter, attributes eggshell mosaic to Gaddo Gaddi. Examination by experts of the only existing example by him has proved it to be rather a mosaic inlaid with minute-sized tesserae of marbles, lapis, and other stones.

## MARUYAMA TECHNIQUE

Taro Maruyama's experiments and the technique that he developed are described in the March–April 1962 *Craft Horizons*. Here is the Maruyama process: A thin coat of adhesive is first brushed on a surface on which a piece of eggshell is placed. The eggshell is broken with the pressure of the finger and is set by tamping with the rounded end of a bamboo stick. After the fragments have dried in place for six hours, their edges are filed and smoothed. A paste of lacquer thickened with ground whetstone is next applied to the surface with a stiff brush. When dry, the surface is sanded through to the shell. The process is repeated perhaps three times, each application followed by sanding. Then applications of clear lacquer build up the surface to an even smoothness. Each layer is sanded and polished.

Photographs of Maruyama's beautiful lacquer inlay plus the few specimens from antiquity that I have actually seen show inlays of an exquisite fineness—a delicate web of cracks appearing within each segment of shell.

## O'NEIL STUDIO TECHNIQUE

### *EGGSHELL—PREPARATION*

Relying on an empirical method, my students and I have developed a technique which, despite the absence of lacquer, produces a pleasing effect.

Shells taken from cooked or raw eggs—and preferably broken in large pieces—are rinsed in cold water and then put to soak in Clorox (sodium hypochlorite) for at least two days. The Clorox dissolves a number of layers of the membranes which form the shell, reducing it to a thinner consistency. After this soaking, the shells are rinsed in hot water and spread out to dry for several hours. Additional soaking in vinegar further reduces the thickness of the shell. The pieces are sorted by size into separate containers, including the tiniest pieces, which are kept for fill-ins. Larger pieces are broken by hand into sections about 1½″ long. Preferably these sections are from the long shallow curve of the shell. The deeply rounded end is less manageable for flat areas, but is recommended for curved surfaces.

The piece to be inlaid with the shell is prepared with three coats of flat paint, the last of which is tufbacked to smoothness. The surface should be in a color of deep value to contrast with the shell, thus making the pattern easily discernible. (The final coloring of the base will derive from the grout.) The ground colors most often used by the Orientals were black, brown, green, and red.

## OVER-ALL INLAY–PROCEDURE

*Gluing the Shell.* A white polyethylene glue is the best adhesive for affixing the shell to the surface. With a ⅜-inch red sable blunt-edged brush dipped first in water, the adhesive is applied sparingly to the inside of the shell, which is then placed upon the prepared surface. A square of wax paper

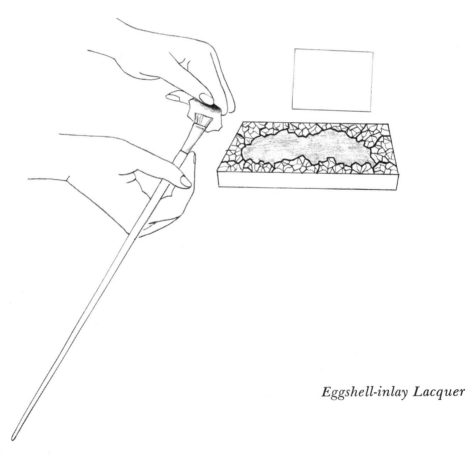

*Eggshell-inlay Lacquer*

or clear plastic is laid over the shell, and pressure from the center to the outer edge is applied with the fingers or a tool (the bowl of a spoon or a tweezer with a diagonal edge) to produce the myriad cracks. After the paper has been removed, the shell is further crushed with a metal tool and the fragments are slightly separated or pushed into better position with the point of a dressmaker's pin. The scale of the cracking within each segment

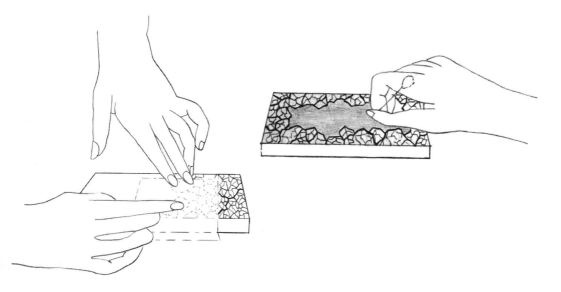

is determined by the size of the object. A small object that will be picked up and examined in the hand should be covered with pieces of shell no larger than $\frac{1}{2}''$ in size; each of these is crushed to a fine web-like cracking. On a larger piece, such as a table, the pieces of shell should be approximately $1\frac{1}{2}''$ in length; these are cracked to fragments about $\frac{1}{4}''$ in size. As the various sections of shell are added to the surface, the dividing lines between them should be at least $\frac{1}{32}''$ wide. The division *between* the sections, no matter what the size of the subject, is slightly wider than the fragmentation *within* a section, thus emphasizing the larger units over the smaller interior particles. In sum, the dividing lines are scaled to the piece—being barely discernible on a small article; and their width is maintained consistently.

*Shaping the Shell.* To facilitate the matching of the sections, the following procedures are used. After all the fragments within particular sections have been affixed to the surface and allowed to dry for six hours, small

LACQUER: *Top left, vernis Martin; right, rice kernel.*
*Bottom left, antiqued Chinese; right, with eggshell inlay.*

irregularities are cut away from each section's periphery with a #16 or #26 X-acto knife. The blade must be very sharp and frequently changed. In addition, before placement of an adjoining section, its peripheral edge is shaped to fit with a #6 triangular file or an emery board. An application

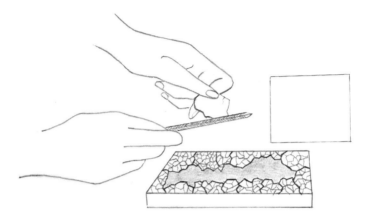

of glue which has been allowed to dry on the shell makes it possible to cut the edge with a nail clipper or small scissors without fragmenting the piece. This cutting and shaping is kept to a minimum. The pleasing irregularities of shell shapes are retained wherever possible unless the shell is being laid in a predetermined geometric pattern.

*Patching the Inlay.* When a number of sections have been placed, it is necessary, despite the evened edges and careful selection, to fill in the gaps with particles of shell. For this procedure the glue is applied to the surface rather than to the shell. From the tiny particles which have been kept separate, one of the proper shape is chosen and picked up either with a dressmaker's pin which has been dipped in the glue or with a water-moistened wooden matchstick. A square of clear plastic is used to press the piece into the space. As pressure is exerted to force the particle into position, any overlap will chip but it can be easily lifted off with the X-acto knife. The flat side of an emery board has also been found to be excellent for pressing the shell in such cases.

The procedure just described continues until the entire surface is covered. It is wise to lay the shell from the edges of the area into the center and to ignore any patching until the surface is completed. When the piece has dried overnight, protruding edges and corners are trimmed and filed. There is a possibility that some glue may have remained on the surface of the shell. Therefore, when the piece is completed, it is wiped with a turkish towel dampened with warm vinegar. Then it is cleaned again with a towel slightly moistened with water.

The procedure described is exacting and time-consuming. However, it is as absorbing and fascinating as a jigsaw puzzle without benefit of picture. The eye sharpens to discern the relation between form and space. Time evaporates when one is thus engrossed.

*Varnishing the Inlay.* Because of its porosity, the shell surface is protected with two coats of gloss varnish, lightly tinted with ultramarine oil paint to counteract the inevitable yellowing tone of varnish. Only enough paint is added for the varnish to show the faintest tinge when tested on white paper. After each of the varnish coats has dried overnight, the surface is completely covered with a grout to fill the cracks.

## PREPARATION OF GROUT

The grout is prepared by combining casein (water-soluble) paint, mixed to any desired color, with $\frac{1}{16}$ volume of polyethylene glue. This mixture is thinned with water until it reaches the consistency of sour cream. It is now compounded into a thick paste by adding dry color powders (purchasable by the pound) which have been mixed to the same color. The grout is pounced, with a 1-inch stiff-bristle brush, into the crevices until they are filled. A piece of straight-edged cardboard held perpendicularly scrapes away most of the excess grout. It is best to scrape diagonally across the surface. At this point there is no need for alarm if the entire eggshell inlay is lost to view.

## COMPLETION OF EGGSHELL INLAY

After the grout has dried for an hour, the surface is sanded with silicon carbide paper 220A until the eggshell is again evident. A small sanding block is used when the surface is large and flat. When partially sanded, the surface looks like a jumble of pebbles; when the sanding is carried a few steps farther, it resembles snakeskin. If either of these effects seems desirable,

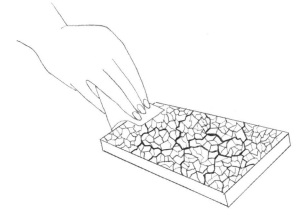

the sanding should be stopped. However, if the piece is to simulate the Oriental eggshell lacquer, the sanding is continued until the very fine cracking in each segment becomes apparent. Of course, so much sanding produces a great deal of dry powder and the object will seem somewhat discolored and soiled. This can easily be wiped off with a cloth slightly dampened in water or vinegar; if the cloth is too wet, the grout will dissolve. The surface is then sprayed with a clear waterproof mat fixative to prevent the least bit of powder from discoloring the subsequent varnish coat. The spray can must be held perpendicularly to the surface, at a height of 12 inches. The spray is applied with a smooth side-to-side motion that ranges beyond the object, thus avoiding puddles and over-spraying. Successive coats of the same ultramarine-tinted gloss varnish previously applied are now added. After each varnish coat the surface is smoothed with 600 wet-or-dry paper lubricated with non-detergent soapsuds. When the surface is totally level, any additional design is transferred to it with chalk transfer paper and a stylus. It may be raised and burnished, mat gilded, inked, or japan painted.

## INLAY DESIGN—PROCEDURE

*Patterning and Gluing.* Eggshell inlay may be used as a decorative element on any lacquered piece. A template of the design to be inlaid is cut out of clear plastic and painted with a bright color that will show effectively on the surface to be decorated. The design is then outlined on the surface. Next eggshell is laid on a section of architect's linen larger than the pattern.

A piece of acetate is laid over the shell and smoothed out carefully with a small roller or spoon. The acetate is cautiously slipped off the eggshell to avoid lifting any pieces. The template design is traced on the eggshell. With an implement (sharp scissors or X-acto knife) held at an angle away from the design, the pattern is cut out. This procedure leaves the shell with a slightly beveled edge which will glue more readily to the object. Again the acetate is placed over the design and the surface is smoothed before it is glued to the prepared surface. After the shell has been cleaned with vinegar, protected with varnish, and grouted, it is treated as previously described.

*Tinting the Design.* If the aim is to emulate what we suppose to have been the polychrome effect of the eggshell mosaics of the Renaissance, each shell particle is tinted with gouache in acceptable marble colors before application of the fixative spray. The design might include portraits or scenic compositions. The design application, after the fixative spray, is followed by continued varnishing until the soft, lustrous surface of a lacquer finish has been attained.

## EGGSHELL INLAY

*Materials*
Architect's linen
White polyethylene glue
Eggshells
Japan colors
Clear gloss varnish
Ultramarine oil paint
Casein
Clear waterproof mat
   fixative (spray can)
Dry color powders
Gouache colors
Clorox
Vinegar

*Tools*
Stylus
400 and 600 wet-or-dry
   paper
3/8" blunt-edge brush
   (red sable)

Spoon
Tweezers with diagonal edge
Dressmaker's pins
#16 or #26 X-acto knife
#6 triangular file
Emery board
Nail clipper
Small scissors
Wooden matchstick
1" stiff-bristle brush
220A silicon carbide paper
Sanding block
Small roller

*Miscellaneous*
Non-detergent soap flakes
Plastic containers
Clear plastic squares (acetate)
Wax paper
Cardboard
Turkish toweling

# COROMANDEL LACQUER

Coromandel lacquer involves many layers of material, the last of which is coated with lacquer. Gesso or casein may be used (see chapters on burnishing and casein). Into this thickness, figures or designs are cut in intaglio. In some instances three or four levels are colored in varying hue and the cutback controlled to reveal the particular stratum required by the design. In other instances the design is cut back at different levels to the whitish material (the gesso or casein) which is then tinted in various hues. Fine retaining lines of the surface lacquer define each element of the design. Either of these techniques requires great skill and extraordinary patience.

There is, however, one characteristic of Coromandel lacquer which may be readily achieved, and that is its color, which appears to be a combination of black and mahogany. This makes a very handsome background for decoration with various tones of gold leaf.

## *PROCEDURE*

A base hue is prepared according to the following formula:

> 1 volume red red-purple japan color
> $\frac{1}{2}$ volume burnt sienna japan color
> $\frac{1}{4}$ volume orange-red japan color
> $\frac{1}{10}$ volume (of above mixture) japan drier
> $\frac{1}{4}$ volume turpentine

Four to five coats are applied to the surface, and the last coat is tufbacked to satin smoothness with 600 wet-or-dry paper and a soapy solution. The piece then receives two binding coats of diluted orange shellac, each of which dries for an hour before being lightly rubbed with 0000 steel wool. Over this is applied a coat made to the following formula:

> 1 volume raw umber japan color
> $\frac{1}{4}$ volume lampblack japan color
> 7 volumes glazing medium (see chapter on
> glazes)

With an oxhair brush, a heavy coating is applied in a broad streaked manner that allows the base hue to show through. When it has dried, 000 steel wool with a solution of soapy water is used to rub the surface smooth with long strokes. This creates the ambivalence of tone characteristic of Coromandel. The surface is varnished with two coats of clear diluted varnish, and is tufbacked before the application of design in tones of gold that are most appropriate to the base. Over this go the many finishing coats of gloss varnish. They must be tufbacked with 600 wet-or-dry paper and, finally, polished with a paste of rottenstone and lemon oil.

## COROMANDEL

*Materials*
    Red red-purple japan color
    Burnt sienna japan color
    Orange-red japan color
    Japan drier
    Turpentine
    Raw umber japan color
    Lampblack japan color
    Thinner
    Orange shellac
    Clear gloss varnish
    Denatured alcohol

*Tools*
    600 wet-or-dry paper
    ooo steel wool
    oooo steel wool
    Oxhair brush

*Miscellaneous*
    Non-detergent soap flakes

## EUROPEAN LACQUER

The Western world never produced a convincing facsimile of Oriental lacquer. Europe's craftsmen used materials which dried more rapidly than true lacquer, and their workmanship was neither as skilled nor as painstaking as that of the Orientals. However, their efforts achieved an individuality and charm which are often more appealing than the utter perfection of the Far East. Interestingly enough, the processes for European lacquer are undocumented; thus innovative methods have had to be worked out in the studio to approximate the extant examples.

Pieces to be lacquered should be chosen with attention to their basic form, which should be simple and elegant in line and without ornamental carving. The foregoing would include Oriental forms, pieces from the period of Queen Anne, and from that of Louis XVI in its simplest style, some Georgian pieces, and certainly those of our own period.

The colors most often used in the Orient were black, brown, dark green, vermilion, red, ochre, purple, yellow, and light brown. In France: white, green, blue, yellow, and orange-red. In England: black, blue, red, chestnut, bistre, and olive. In Italy: green, black, red, and yellow.

### *ITALIAN LACQUER—PROCEDURE*

The Italian version of lacquer was executed over a gesso support (see chapter on burnishing). In the studio, we have used casein as a facsimile of gesso. For this preparation, reference should be made to the chapter on casein.

The piece having been prepared with its casein base is finely sanded. It is now ready for the application of color.

Water-soluble aniline powder is dissolved in hot water. If a light value of color is required, cold water is added. With a fine-grained natural sponge, the solution is rubbed over the white underbody and immediately wiped off with an absorbent cloth. In the manner of glaze blending, rounded portions may be highlighted, leaving the connections at joinings and edges deeper in value. The application dries for two hours and is then coated with thinned white shellac once daily for five days—the weather, of course, must be clear. Each coating of shellac is rubbed down gently with oooo steel wool. An antique patina can be added with a thinned-out japan spattering fluid. When this is dry, two coats of clear gloss varnish are applied. The latter one is rubbed down with a paste of rottenstone and lemon oil. This lacquering approximates the Italian method of the eighteenth century.

## FRENCH LACQUER—PROCEDURE

In the seventeenth century the French version of lacquer consisted only of tinted varnish coats over a base hue. The final coat was not rubbed down, so the finish had a high luster. In the mid-eighteenth century the Martin brothers invented a type of varnish—said to contain garlic juice—which hardened with heat and resulted in a beautiful glossy finish. Often their pieces were first coated with a striation of glaze deeper than the base hue. Then minute particles of gold were distributed over one of the varnish coats while the surface was still tacky. The end result was an effect of translucent lacquer, lovely in itself though utterly dissimilar to its Oriental forebear. By the end of the eighteenth century, French lacquer deteriorated and became simply a highly varnished finish. The following method is used to facsimile the famous *vernis Martin*.

The piece is given five coats of paint of a hue of middle value; then the surface is tufbacked with 600 wet-or-dry paper to satin smoothness. Over this, a reserving coat of thinned French varnish (shellac) is applied and allowed to dry. A glaze deeper in value than the base hue (see formula in chapter on glazes) is now rendered in striation. After a week's drying time, a coat of thinned clear gloss varnish is lightly applied with an oxhair brush and allowed to dry overnight. When a second coat of this clear varnish has partially dried, the piece is ready to be sprinkled with flitters of gold.

A sheet of gold leaf is crushed with a gilder's tamper to form the particles. A tube of heavy paper is cut diagonally across one end and the other end is covered with fine-meshed cheesecloth to act as a sieve. The particles are poured into the tube. They are then dispersed sparsely over the tacky coat of varnish by tapping the tube with the finger. When this coat has dried, two more coats of varnish tinted with a related oil color are applied. The surface is then tufbacked with 600 wet-or-dry paper and a soapy solution. Additional coats of varnish, each one tufbacked, are added until the desired translucency is achieved.

## *ENGLISH LACQUER—PROCEDURE*

In England, small objects of Japanware or Bantamware (the popular designations of Oriental lacquer) were most frequently rendered in a black-brown tone. Chinese black lacquer was first colored with lampblack and then with iron or a compound of iron, thereby acquiring a slightly brown cast. Japanware was the type of lacquer ware which amateurs were most apt to decorate. Its finish contained asphaltum (a tar derivative) and was subjected to heat to attain the appearance of a lacquered surface.

The surface for English lacquer is coated with four to five coats of a mixture made to this formula:

> 5 volumes flat black paint
> 1½ volumes burnt umber japan color
> ½ volume japan drier
> ½ volume clear gloss varnish
> mineral spirits if needed for thinning

It is then tufbacked with 600 wet-or-dry paper and non-detergent soap solution. Should an edge of the base wood be inadvertently revealed, it may be retouched with India ink. Finally, a coat which combines asphaltum in this mixture is added.

> ¼ volume raw umber japan color
> ¼ volume lampblack japan color
> 2 volumes asphaltum
> 1 volume spar varnish
> 1 volume thinner (mineral)
> ¼ volume japan drier

The solution is heated to room temperature (70° F.) before application. After 48 hours of drying time, it is rubbed with rottenstone and allowed 24 more hours to dry before a light tufbacking with 600 wet-or-dry paper and a soapy solution. A coat of thinned orange shellac is then applied to the surface. Shellac must always be used to protect asphaltum as it dissolves rapidly when in contact with any material containing turpentine or thinner. The shellac is rubbed down with 0000 steel wool before the application of any design. The design is most frequently rendered in gold leaf. After the leaf is laid, the detail is immediately incised with a stylus, thus revealing the black-brown surface through the gold. After the gold has dried for 24 hours, the surface is ready for the final finishing. However, if an antique patina is desired, the surface is tinted with aniline antiquing fluid or raw umber or burnt umber oil color. In either case, the piece, when dry, receives the usual coats of varnish accompanied by intervening tufbacking, and finally a rubbing with rottenstone and lemon oil. If at any time an edge is rubbed through during the tufbacking, restoration can be done as follows. A fine cotton fabric pad is dipped in French varnish, rubbed out on paper, and then dipped in black aniline powder; when tacky, the pad is rubbed on the damaged edge, which is allowed to dry for half an hour, then if necessary, is again rubbed with the pad. If a higher gloss is desired, the piece is waxed.

## O'NEIL STUDIO LACQUER

Great pieces of European lacquer have modulations of color that do not exist in the flawless uniformity of fine Oriental pieces; there is a gentle quality, the result, perhaps, of an earnest desire to imitate the ware of the Orient but a lack of the necessary materials. European ingenuity and style brought forth a different beauty. The methods described below are the result of empirical experimentation.

### PREPARATION
To achieve the rich color of many European pieces, a base hue of japan color is mixed in a value two or more steps above middle value. Four to five coats are applied to the piece with an oxhair brush as smoothly as possible. The last two of these coats are thinned with flatting oil, and the whole piece is finally tufbacked with 600 wet-or-dry paper to a satin smoothness. The body of paint totally encases the structure of the piece. It is now coated with French varnish diluted 50 percent with alcohol. The French varnish coat must be so perfectly applied that it produces no roughness or noticeable thickness. After drying overnight the surface is rubbed gently with 0000 steel wool.

### PROCEDURE
A glaze of related color two steps deeper than middle value is mixed to the following recipe:

½ ounce japan color
2 ounces flatting oil
2 ounces undiluted clear gloss varnish
3 ounces thinner
2 to 6 drops japan drier

This is applied in any of the several ways described in the chapter on glazes. Several effects are possible. The glaze may be gently blended, or it may be given a more mottled effect with a natural cosmetic sponge and lightly patted over with soft tissue. The glaze coat requires a week to ten days of drying time. Two coats of thinned clear gloss varnish are applied. The second coat is tufbacked with 600 wet-or-dry paper.

An aniline glaze in a brilliant middle value of the body hue adds to the effect of richness and depth. It is made to this formula:

7 volumes alcohol (to dissolve aniline powders
separately before combining them)
3 volumes undiluted shellac (white or orange
depending on the color)
2 drops lemon oil to each 2 ounces of this
solution

The glaze is applied evenly in a thin over-all coat with a lightly loaded 2-inch oxhair chiseled varnish brush. Alternatively, a cotton bob may be used. The coat dries in an hour, but before it is hard dry, it is blended lightly with 0000 steel wool. Attention must be paid to the timing of the blending—neither too soon nor too late. Streaks in the film may be eliminated with steel wool when the surface has dried just to the point that particles of steel wool do not become embedded in the aniline. After the drying and blending, the color is deepened on the periphery of wide areas and at joinings—actually, wherever depth is needed to enhance form. This operation is performed with a 1-inch or 2-inch whisk brush (see drawing on next page). Color is applied in the deep areas and whisked to the light areas. The arm holding the brush rises from the surface in a gradual ascending arc, thus softening the stroke and blending the color into the light area. The ends of the whisking are further blended with 0000 steel wool at the proper moment (neither too soon nor too late). After a drying time of two hours, the surface is coated again either with an oxhair brush or a cotton bob dipped in an aniline glaze made to this formula:

1 volume denatured alcohol (to dissolve
aniline powder)
1 volume white shellac
3 drops lemon oil to each 2 ounces of this
solution

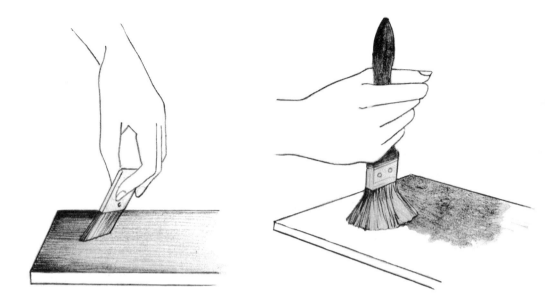

After 24 hours a further deepening on the periphery of areas and at joinings is achieved by pouncing with a lightly loaded 1-inch shellac brush. These operations are continued—with adequate intervals (3–4 hours) of drying time allowed—until a rich surface with depth and brilliance of color has come into being without obvious traces of the implements employed.

Varnish coats tinted with oil paints in a related hue must be applied before decoration or they will, unhappily, change its color. Now the field is ready for ornamentation, which may be rendered in leaf, in relief (see the chapter on burnishing), in casein (with polyethylene glue used as one half of the mixing fluid), or in japan color.

When the design has dried, a coat of thinned clear gloss varnish is applied before the antique patina is added. This patina is obtained by spattering or pouncing the surface with aniline solutions, thinned japan spattering fluid, or a thinned oil paint; whichever is used must be semi-transparent and related to the hue of the piece. As an alternative, the final coatings of varnish might be tinted with an oil earth color; these would then constitute the antique patina as well as the finishing varnish coats.

## LACQUER VARIANT

At one time in my professional career I had to transform some crude plaster cherubs into an elegant carved mineral. This challenge produced the finish which I call Lacquer Variant. Though it in no way resembles lacquer, it evolved from methods used in imitating lacquer.

### *PROCEDURE*

The piece is surfaced with four or five coats of base color which must be a middle or deep value. When these have dried and been smoothed, a brilliant aniline glaze of an analogous color is mixed as follows:

> 1 volume denatured alcohol (to dissolve
> aniline powder)
> 1 volume undiluted shellac

This glaze is applied by pouncing heavily with a 1-inch shellac brush. After an hour, the surface is rubbed with 0000 steel wool and an undiluted clear gloss varnish coat is applied and allowed to dry overnight. Then inexpensive dry pigment powder and wax are mixed to a light value which may be analogous or contrasting in hue. This mixture is pounced evenly with a stiff-bristle brush over the object. After it dries for half an hour, the high surfaces are buffed with a flannel pad until they retain only a slight film of the powder-and-wax mixture. A heavier deposit remains in the interstices. The result resembles a mineral polished to jewel-like brilliance.

## CONTEMPORARY LACQUER

The effort of understanding the older types of lacquer and the developing of facsimiles inevitably led to up-dated versions. The following finish is suggested for contemporary pieces or effects.

### *PROCEDURE*

The preliminary base coats are applied to a piece and tufbacked with 600 wet-or-dry paper. The surface is then coated with clear gloss varnish. After it has been allowed to dry, a brilliant aniline glaze is evenly applied. This having dried, a japan glaze in a lighter or darker value is brushed on in an even striation. After a week's drying time, the piece is finished with the requisite varnish coats rubbed down.

A lacquer finish of whatever type is very demanding in the exigencies of its technique, but it is one of the most rewarding in that it culminates in a masterpiece of jewel-like beauty.

# EUROPEAN LACQUER AND LACQUER VARIANTS

*Materials*

Water-soluble aniline powder
Alcohol-soluble aniline powders
White shellac (5-pound cut)
  or orange shellac
French varnish
Clear gloss varnish
Spar varnish
Denatured alcohol
Flat black paint
Burnt umber japan color
Raw umber japan color
Lampblack japan color
Other japan colors
Japan drier
Dry pigment colors
Casein colors
India ink
Asphaltum
Mineral spirits
Gold leaf
Rottenstone
Lemon oil
Flatting oil

Wax
Flat white paint
Turpentine
Artist's tube oil paints

*Tools*

Shellac brushes
Oxhair brushes
Varnish brush
Whisk brush (1″ or 2″)
Stiff-bristle brush
0000 steel wool
600 wet-or-dry paper
Stylus
Gilder's tamper
Fine-grained natural sponge

*Miscellaneous*

Unsized cheesecloth
Non-detergent soap flakes
Polyethylene glue
Soft tissues
Cotton bobs
Tube of heavy paper

# CASEIN

## VENETIAN GESSO FINISH

The delicately tinted gesso body of Venetian eighteenth-century furnishings is conceded to be one of the most pleasing surface finishes of its time. These pieces were rendered in a technique based on the one used for the panel paintings of the Italian Renaissance. William Odom suggests that in Italy much of the genius that glorified Renaissance panels was diverted to the embellishment of commodes, tables, and chairs in the eighteenth century. The gesso ground provided a velvety texture remarkably receptive to water color. The water-color medium, which was used for economy, was applied in manifold harmonies of color in exotic decorative fantasies, some rendered with naiveté, some with sophistication. Since the gesso body consists of many coats, its time-consuming, hence costly, method is ill-suited to the tempo of our day. A casein water paint, however, is a substitute which readily and rapidly creates a similar ground.

The coats of gesso on Italian furniture were originally used to conceal crude and hasty construction of inferior wood. Linen was first stretched over the joints of the frame and then the whole was covered with up to forty coats of gesso to conceal entirely the faulty structure. As other European countries sought to match the artistry and innovation of Italy's craftsmen, gesso which originated out of necessity was continued elsewhere because of the admirable end result. It prevailed throughout Europe until the end of the eighteenth century even in countries where the need to conceal construction did not exist. In Italy today, few modern covering types of paint are available, therefore the system of coating with gesso persists, though the exacting technique has succumbed to the pressure of today's commercialism. I have watched Italian craftsmen decorate gesso-coated pieces with a combination of water color and glue. The results are somewhat vulgarized replicas of the Venetian furniture rendered with lavish and imaginative painting in the eighteenth century.

# CASEIN—TODAY'S SUBSTITUTE FOR GESSO

The cold water paint which simulates the laudable older finish uses casein as the binding medium (the liquid which carries the pigment particles and holds them together). When this binder solidifies, it fastens the pigment permanently to the support material. We know from the earliest recorded history of artists' techniques that casein was used by the Egyptians, Greeks, and Romans for decorative painting. Through the ages it has been used both on exterior walls and on easel paintings.

To produce casein, skim milk is soured; the curd is separated from the whey, then is washed, dried, and ground. The resulting slightly yellowish granular powder is emulsified. Emulsions are made of oily and watery constituents, which usually separate. However, the curd of milk is a natural emulsion, and in time it becomes insoluble in water. This emulsion is the binder that was first used to make a casein paint in the early 1920s, the first true water-thinnable paint produced commercially. It dries to an extremely hard finish and has a number of advantages as a furniture coating. When it is used as an undercoating on the roughly carved period pieces available today, the crudity and carelessness of execution can be more rapidly veiled than with an oil base paint. Moreover, casein sets quickly and in normal conditions of temperature and humidity may be followed in an hour by another coating. Five coats of white casein will in most instances form an encompassing body which produces a reasonable facsimile of a gesso base. The paint is easily sanded and polished to a fine, smooth surface. It forms a luminous white base for washes of color, delicate with nuance or brilliant with exciting contrast. Because of the rapid-drying quality of the casein, a number of interesting textural surfaces can be achieved through the manipulation of diverse materials.

# CASEIN—PREPARATION

## *PRELIMINARY PREPARATION FOR CASEIN*

Any object must have thorough preparation before it is coated with casein. Raw wood—including that which has been stripped of any finish—and plaster each provide absorbent surfaces with which the casein film will bond effectively. Repairs are first made, cracks and holes filled, and carving checked for whiskers and roughness. Sharp edges are softened to eliminate any telltale newness; the effect of an antique gesso-encased piece is the desired final result.

## *APPLICATION OF PRIMER*

To insure the initial bonding of the casein with the surface, the piece is primed with a thin glue size. This is made by soaking a scant ⅓ rabbit-skin glue, sheets or granules, overnight in 14 ounces water. The glue absorbs the water and swells; the next day it is dissolved over gentle heat by placing the container in a pan of boiling water. Two ounces of this heavy glue solution are combined with 1 quart of boiling water. The resulting thin size is applied with a stiff-bristle brush, and the surface is left to dry overnight. The piece is then ready to be painted with casein.

## *FORMULA FOR CASEIN*

As commercial casein is intended for interior wall decoration, it requires certain modifications to make it a satisfactory medium for coating furniture. With help from a manufacturer, the following formula has been evolved and it has proved satisfactory:

> 1 quart white casein paste (called Deep White commercially)
> 2½ ounces casein emulsion (available at art supply stores)
> 6 ounces kaolin powder
> 3 drops pine oil
> ¼ teaspoon ox gall
> ¼ teaspoon Dowicide A crushed in ½ teaspoon water
> 12 ounces tap water or distilled water

Pine oil, ox gall, and Dowicide A are available at drugstore or chemist's.

Casein emulsion is easily attacked by bacteria, and when it decomposes there is a rank odor. Addition of the phenol solution—Dowicide A (a germicide)—prevents this to some degree. Kaolin powder (china clay) acts as an extender in the formula and reduces shrinkage as the mixture dries. Pine oil is a further odorant; it also prevents foaming in the mixture, which would dry in the form of ineradicable pinholes. Ox gall, a wetting agent, helps break the surface tension which creates bubbles. Storage of the casein medium under refrigeration helps to slow its decomposition.

A sash brush or a stiff-bristle 1-inch brush is used to mix the ingredients of the above formula. This brush is reserved for water-soluble media only, as are all brushes used for casein. Slow and gentle stirring reduces the aeration of the mixture.

The kaolin powder is first stirred into the white casein paste. To this is added the combined liquids: casein emulsion, pine oil, ox gall, Dowicide A, and water. When the mixture has been sufficiently stirred, it is strained through nylon hose into a glass jar with the help of the brush. The consistency of this paint should be that of heavy cream. If necessary, additional water is added. It is imperative that casein be stored in a screw-top glass jar as it would cause a metal container to decompose.

### CARE OF BRUSHES

All brushes used in casein painting are water-moistened and drawn through the fingers to remove any excess liquid before the initial loading with casein paint. After use they are immediately soaked in lukewarm water and washed. Casein must not be allowed to harden in the bristles as it becomes insoluble and destroys the brush.

## CASEIN—PROCEDURE

### APPLICATION OF CASEIN

The piece having been primed with the glue size, the entire underbody is coated with the white casein to imitate the gesso preparation of centuries-old furniture. The stiff-bristle brush is used to apply the paint. A heavier load than that used with japan paint is flowed on the surface and rapidly brushed out to an even film. The loaded brush is never wiped off against the edge of the jar. This reduces aeration of the liquid and the creation of pinholes. It is imperative that the coating be thin and even; a thick coat hardens first on the top surface and will subsequently crack as the wet casein beneath it dries. For the same reason special care is taken to avoid heavy deposits in the interstices of carving. One hour is required for complete drying when atmospheric conditions are equable—neither damp nor humid.

A second coat is applied, this time with the strokes running perpendicular to those of the first coat. The following coatings continue with strokes alternating between the horizontal and the vertical. Many thinly applied films of paint produce a superior surface. After each coat has been laid on, it can be smoothed out with a slightly dampened oxhair brush or one's fingers.

### SANDPAPER PROCEDURE

If the application is expert, the surface will need only a light sanding between every two coats. In past centuries the cuttlefish bone (*osso di seppia*) was used for sanding and, as I have seen, is used in Italy even now. Today, however, silicon carbide paper 220A does the job more easily. This sanding paper is costly, but the accumulated dust can be shaken out, and a single piece lasts through many operations. After the sanding, the surface is well dusted with absorbent cotton before the application of the next coat. As a general rule five coats of casein are sufficient to create the enveloping body of paint, which attains a bone-like smoothness when finely and painstakingly sanded.

### APPLICATION OF SEALER

*A solution of acrylic polymer emulsion diluted one-to-one with distilled water is applied to the casein body to seal it and prevent cracking when any further watery paint film is added.*

## CASEIN TINTS

Casein is a medium that invites experiment and ingenuity. Its properties of quick drying and easy application make it a joy to work with. Its versatility as a wash or covering coat enables one to build color upon color while retaining the individuality of each tone.

Commercial casein colors for tinting the white underbody may be purchased in artists' tubes or in half-pint jars. Once solidified, these colors cannot be softened, so it is wise to buy them in small quantity. It is essential to make dry tests for hue when mixing color in casein as these colors dry in a lighter value than they appear when wet. Casein color is combined to the hue desired. It is then thinned to a wash with the addition of this solution: ⅓ casein emulsion and ⅔ distilled water. To prevent the formation of a multitude of fine cracks, which are likely to occur after the surface has been moistened by the color wash, the one-to-one acrylic polymer emulsion solution is applied. This sealer is especially important when a series of tinting washes is brushed on. Casein pigment is opaque and discolors water quickly; therefore the water for cleaning brushes must be changed frequently.

Casein has a natural velvet-like mat surface that is especially beautiful. Whenever possible, the finishing film should be of casein to preserve this characteristic lean quality. The effects that can be produced on a casein ground are countless. The differences result from mutations of color or from the nature of the applicator. The methods of application which are described below may be used singly or in combination.

## APPLICATION OF TINTS

1. *The following method is most suitable for formal traditional pieces.* With an oxhair brush commensurate in size with the area to be coated, a casein wash is brushed on in the direct spontaneous manner used for water colors. Wash is a technical term used for paint that is sufficiently diluted with water to flow easily, and that can be carried over a considerable area with broad sweeps of the brush, leaving no indication of brush marks. The working surface may be dry or previously dampened with distilled water. In either instance the color wash is rapidly applied with free bold strokes which do not overlap; exposed white areas of the ground are an attractive characteristic of water-color technique. A mop brush may be used to absorb excessive pools of wash, but these can be kept to a minimum if the brush is not loaded too fully. After the first wash has dried, the color may be intensified or altered by subsequent applications. The chromatic value of the color should be somewhat exaggerated to allow for the neutralizing effect of any later antiquing medium.

2. *This method achieves a finish that can be used on contemporary or traditional pieces.* With a fine-textured natural sponge (for cosmetics), the color wash is applied to the casein surface over a dry or wet ground. Obviously, when a sponge, or similar tools, is used on a wet ground, the color becomes lighter in value than when such a tool is used over a dry surface. The color is applied as evenly as possible in a succession of pattings, the sponge proceeding forward and then doubling back over a small area at a time. While the surface is still wet, the dry end of the sponge is further used to soften and meld the toning.

3. *The following method is particularly compatible with early American or contemporary pieces.* The color medium is somewhat heavier in consistency than a wash and is applied over the white ground, with a stiff-

bristle brush in a striation. Each loading of the brush is followed by stroking out on clean white paper until a fine striation which does not expand trails from the bristle. This striation should be parallel and evenly disposed over the surface. Many light applications, slowly and carefully applied, produce the desired result.

4. *This finish lends itself to diverse types of furniture, pieces not necessarily traditional in style.* A mottled color effect is achieved by patting a paint film which has been applied with an oxhair brush. The paint mixture is of milky consistency. After it has been brushed over a small section of the surface, it is lightly patted immediately with any of these tools: a coarse-grained natural sponge, absorbent tissue, or squares of cheesecloth. They must be discarded or cleaned after the completion of each section. The brushed-on wash may be eliminated and these tools themselves may be used as applicators either on a dry surface or one previously dampened. The tool if wet produces a more delicate mutation of mottling than when used dry.

Among the other techniques and tools used in tinting casein are these:

Casein tinting color may be flowed on a surface with a brush *which is* immediately followed *by* a roller. The tinting can begin with a very thin solution of casein rolled on a surface with a rubber roller. While this film is wet, a second thin solution of casein in a differing value but a harmonizing hue is rolled on. This removes some part of the first color, leaving transparent areas. To intensify the effect, many coats of clear gloss varnish are applied and rubbed down. Analogous colors used in this manner are very successful.

Another method employs a lamb's wool roller saturated with color; this is rolled on a wet ground with great pressure, and the rolling needs to be repeated several times.

A twisted chamois rolled over an even wash for the length of the surface leaves an undulating trail that partially reveals the underlying color.

## *FRESCO POWDER TECHNIQUE*

Fresco powders are used as a tinting medium for casein, and perhaps this is the medium that best approximates the finish found on Venetian gesso furniture. The powder is mixed to a paste in hot distilled water; to 2 volumes of the paste, ½ volume acrylic polymer emulsion is added. The whole solution is thinned with distilled water and washed over the surface. Immediately, additional dry fresco powder is pounced discriminatingly on the wet ground, leaving the wash visible. Color of an analogous hue may be sprinkled through a flitter tube (see chapter on burnishing). When dry, the surface is sprayed with acrolite fixative to hold the powers.

# COMPLEX COLOR TECHNIQUES

Having experimented with the above methods of applying color to casein, and having realized the special delight of working with this fresh, clean medium, one may wish to progress to more complex color tintings. When differing and analogous color tones are built up in sequence they glow with a subtle luminosity. The following are combinations of color film, applied in various manners, which may succeed one another after the first has dried overnight. In some instances, a binding coat of the acrylic polymer emulsion medium (thinned shellac or mat varnish) may be applied between consecutive tonings.

### COLOR WASH

An analogous color wash, three or more steps removed from the base tint, may be brushed over the same or a different value.

As a variant, a hue closely related to the base tint (of heavier consistency for striating) but varying in either value or intensity is stroked over a previously striated surface. This will create an interesting mingling with an undulating luster.

Both methods combine to produce an opalescent effect somewhat akin to that of a Thai fabric woven with threads of two colors.

### SPATTERED COLOR

A thin solution of color contrasting in value but analogous in hue may be loosely spattered over the dried surface. Since this spattering will dissolve the initial color, it is gently patted with a pad of cheesecloth, or the initial color can be protected beforehand with the acrylic-polymer emulsion and distilled-water sealer.

### STIPPLED AND BLENDED COLOR

Semi-transparent color, lighter or darker in value than the base tint, may be stippled on the dry surface with a brush or a sponge, then softened and blended by patting with cheesecloth. Actually, this is a type of scumble (semi-transparent color applied over another color and blended to alter it.)

A related hue may also be scumbled immediately on a wet surface to produce greater fusion of the colors.

An opaque color can be stippled on with a stiff stencil brush and then blended with crisscross strokes of a dry 1-inch brush. These methods may be used on an unprotected surface or on a surface which has been sealed with the acrylic polymer emulsion solution.

## REVEALED COLOR—TINTS AND SEALER

The following methods for coloring the casein surface alternate tinted coats and binding coats, and result in partial revelation of each color. The first color application must dry for an hour before being sealed with an isolating coat, which also must be allowed to dry for an hour. Subsequent tints are added by using any of the applicators described above, one upon the other.

Over a sealed wash of color, a striated or a sponged application of a second color may be added, followed by a second isolating coat and a subsequent wash of a third color.

Over a sealed sponged coat, a sponged coat of another color may be applied in sections which are then blotted with cheesecloth or soft tissue.

Over a sealed deep wash of color, a thin covering coat of another color may be applied and allowed to dry. This coating is lightly sanded with 220A silicon carbide paper, and then is loosely spattered with a light value of either the first or second color, or with light values of both.

Over a sealed deep hue, a contrasting light hue may be washed; this must be patted immediately with cheesecloth to reveal the base color. This is followed by a light spattering with two related colors of brilliant intensity. When the piece is mat varnished and waxed, the result has a rich luster.

Over a sealed color wash, a wash of related color may be applied and spattered with clear water immediately. The second color will be loosened, and some part of it may be taken up with a blotter to reveal the first wash.

There are so many ways of tinting casein that the endless variations may seem confusing. The craftsman is therefore advised to test each one on a practice board before deciding which will serve his purpose best.

## DISTRESSED TINTED CASEIN

Sometimes it is interesting to distress furniture rendered in casein. Paint remover does not operate on this medium. However, any surface coating can be removed by dampening it and then blotting up the moistened color; this is done at points of wear. In addition, when a color coat has been sealed with flat varnish (of high wax content), the following color coat may be easily chipped off. A further variation is obtained by applying mat varnish after the second color coat. Before drying, the varnish is rubbed with a wet cheesecloth pad; this blends both colors harmoniously.

## TINTED GLAZE OVER WHITE GESSO

Because of the oil and water mixture in the emulsion binder, casein is compatible with an oil glaze. A transparent glaze of oil color, thinned with varnish for a glossy effect, is applied directly to the white casein body, thus retaining the luminosity of the white casein core.

If a glaze made with japan color (see formula in the chapter on glazes) is used, the casein surface is first sealed with French varnish. This is applied with an oxhair brush and blended in any of the manners described in the section on glazes.

For a glaze made with artists' oil paint, the following formula is suggested:

OIL GLAZE     ½ volume oil paint
5 volumes gloss varnish
3 volumes turpentine

Either the oil glaze or the japan glaze could effectively be applied over a decorative design executed in casein as *grisaille* (a monochromatic painting in tones of white, gray, and black).

A glaze using cadmium yellow light oil paint may be applied over a surface rendered in any of the various techniques in combination to produce the rich glowing depth of certain eighteenth-century Venetian pieces.

It is to be hoped that the many possible combinations of color, applied with the methods described, make clear the varied potentials of the casein medium, and that they will stimulate individual inventiveness.


# SURFACE TEXTURES

Casein offers many possibilities for varied textural effects and, owing to its quick-drying characteristic, interesting results can be achieved in a relatively brief period of time. Moreover, this material is readily manipulated and clean and easy to apply. After testing the finishes described below, one may wish to experiment further.

Textural finishes are rendered on wet casein—either the white base already achieved or one that has been tinted. Color is used in these finishes either as the last undercoat or as a surfacer over the white ground. Textured finishes look best on flat surfaces, such as frames for mirrors or pictures, screens, and panels of commodes and chests.


### *SAND*

Sand combines with casein paint to create a gritty textural surface. Obviously the proportion of sand is dictated by the brushing quality of the mixture. This coating, consisting of sand and color, goes over the white casein, and after drying is followed by a coat of mat varnish. A second coat of color, differing in value from the first, is added; when semi-dry, it is rubbed through with rough toweling to the particles of sand.

## FABRICS AND CARDBOARD

A number of textures are produced by pressing a final heavy coat of casein, tinted or white, with pieces of various materials. Only a portion of the surface to be so textured is coated at one time. The casein is allowed a few minutes to set and thicken. Its consistency must be just stiff enough that marks left by the superimposed material do not flow together and obliterate the pattern.

Burlap, coarse raw linen, or corrguated cardboard is used to impress the area of casein when it has reached the condition described above. The fabric or cardboard must first be sized with two coats of shellac on either side to stiffen the material and to prevent filaments from adhering to the casein. These materials are most easily maneuvered and provide the most decorative results when cut into specific shapes of convenient size, such as triangles, squares, parallelograms, and rectangles. These motifs are pressed onto the surface and lifted quickly to form a pattern of textured and plain areas for an ornamental effect. If the motifs are of burlap or raw linen, the additional pressure of a rubber roller makes their impression more distinct. The final coat of casein in which the material is impressed may be white or tinted; if tinted, the marks left by the impression will be white. When a combination of colors is desired, the final coat of smooth casein is tinted and sealed with mat varnish or thinned white shellac. Then the additional coat, the one intended to retain the impression of the material, is rendered in another color. Also, inexpensive dry powders and wax may be used to achieve the second color; these are mixed and pounced into the interstices created by the textural material.

## COMBS

Combs of metal, bone, or leather are used on a thick casein coat to imprint the surface with straight, serpentine, or diaper (diamond) patterns. Even the tines of a fork, or a razor blade nicked in several places, may be so used. Thick leather about 1″ wide may be cut to form a comb with teeth ¼″ deep. These teeth and the spaces between them need not be identical in width, but they should be in scale with the area to be textured. It must be remembered that only a portion of the surface can be tooled at one time. The same methods of color application are used here as in the textural finishes described before.

## BRUSHES AND SPONGES

The following two finishes need two thick coats of stiff casein before manipulation. Short, stiff-bristle brushes (scrub brush or toothbrush) create a roughened finish, which is effective in conjunction with alternating smooth stripings. A gentler texture is obtained with a coarse natural sponge; it is pounced over the area to be roughened when the casein has set to the point where it will retain an impression. When used for pouncing, the bristle or the sponge is held in a vertical position and rapidly moved over the area with a dabbing up-and-down motion.

The coloring may be treated as previously discussed. Alternatively, a mixture of powder pigment and wax may be pounced on after a protective coat of mat varnish or white shellac has sealed the surface. When the application of powder has set for twenty minutes, it is rubbed off with ooo steel wool.

# INCISED DECORATION

Whereas texturing is done on a slightly wet surface, graffito and linear intaglio are techniques used on a *dry* casein surface.

## GRAFFITO

Graffito is a type of decoration that has been used since the earliest efforts of primitive man to embellish his artifacts. It became formalized as a decorative technique when it was used by the Italians during the Renaissance. The word graffito derived from the Italian verb *sgraffiare*, meaning to scratch, and it became the accepted designation for this mode of embellishment.

A sharp metal tool such as sculptors use, or a #1 stylus, will scratch a design through a dry thin coat of color to reveal the white or a different color of the underlying surface; the latter must have been sealed with a protective coating before the application of the second color. As an alternative, the under-coat may be mixed in a thin solution of acrylic polymer emulsion and distilled water in equal quantities to render it insoluble. If intricate, the pattern is traced on the last color coat by means of a nongreasy transfer paper and a stylus or a pointed wooden instrument. The tool then goes over the line of the design to reveal the underlying white of the casein or the previously imposed color tint. Should the design be one of interlacing circles or curves, a compass is used directly to scratch the top surface.

Graffito is also rendered in a more complex manner. The inscribing tool is used to define a series of patterns, one over another, as coats of differing colors are added. Each coat of color is inscribed, then is bound with a thin film of the one-to-one medium of acrylic polymer emulsion and distilled water before the next color is applied. The principle is to reveal underlying color patterns through a surface of another color.

## *INTAGLIO*

For Italy's growing merchant class, which wished to emulate the luxury of the court, furniture having an incised casein or gesso surface was evolved as a substitute for more costly pieces with elaborate wood carvings in low relief. The new method of embellishment was a form of intaglio.

In the intaglio method the decorative pattern is outlined by a groove cut into the casein surface. Underlying the surface to be tooled are about thirty coats that have been added to the support. These coats are sanded at less frequent intervals than the coats for a casein base. This does not mean that the final surface should be less smooth, rather that care is taken to insure that the depth of the body is not consistently diminished by heavy sanding. The body built up to $\frac{1}{4}''$ allows the incision of a channel that is between $\frac{1}{32}''$ and $\frac{1}{16}''$ in depth, and $\frac{1}{32}''$ in breadth.

The design pattern is transferred to the surface with non-greasy transfer paper and a stylus. A portion of the design on the casein is wet with a #3 sable brush dipped in water. When the line of design has become somewhat damp, the metal stylus is used over it, forming a track for the incising tool.

In Italy each craftsman makes his own metal tool. In the United States satisfactory implements are unavailable; however we have found that the probing instruments of a dentist can be adapted for this purpose. They are cut off squarely just beyond the end of the shaft, before the curved or pointed end of the probe. The resulting tapered end is beveled on one side to a point, forming a (beveled) surface $\frac{3}{8}''$ long. The point is then blunted slightly on a carborundum.

After the stylus track is moistened, the tool is used to widen and deepen the track into a channel. The cut on the pattern side is vertical;

on the outside it is angled. All of the lines of the pattern are thus carved out. The result is a beveled grooving about $\frac{1}{32}''$ to $\frac{1}{16}''$ in depth which widens from nothing at the base to $\frac{1}{32}''$ in breadth on the top surface. To clarify: the channel surrounds each form of the pattern, with the beveled side, which reflects the shadow, always inclined on the outward periphery. Irregularities on either the perpendicular or angled side of the cut are smoothed with a moistened orangewood stick. This type of decoration may be used for an over-all pattern of repeated or varying shapes or more frequently to outline a cartouche (an ornamental framing border). Such embellishment may be emphasized with washes of color.

## TINTED INTAGLIO DECORATION

Color is used to heighten the decorative impact of intaglio pattern in various ways.

The ground surrounding incised decoration may be tinted with a color wash and the enclosed area tinted with a different color. The design may be gilded and the body of the piece rendered in color. Should the design create an over-all linear decoration, be it Baroque, Rococo, or Contemporary, the defining channels may first be colored. In this instance the color of the channels is sealed with a coat of varnish, then a different tint is applied to the entire piece. Any color catching in the intaglio is easily scraped out with a moistened orangewood stick.

Perhaps the only artist in the twentieth century to use these techniques in a decorative manner was Charles Prendergast, who combined incised line, leaf surfaces, and color in his delightful panels.

The beveled groove in any type of design may be colored with a raw umber casein wash for emphasis. If any part of a design has been rendered in leaf, that portion is shaded and antiqued with one of the earth color oils or with an antique aniline solution.

## DECORATIVE PAINTING ON CASEIN

### OPAQUE CASEIN COLOR

After the color wash has been applied to a casein object, it is ready for striping and decoration. If the ornament is to be rendered in opaque casein color, this is directly applied over the wash. If one lacks absolute technical assurance, an isolating coat is brushed on before the decoration as a guard against irretrievable error. This isolating coat may be mat varnish. The casein color used for decoration or on a lacquer or japan painted ground is, in this instance, combined with distilled water and a small amount of polyethylene glue to insure its adherence.

The brush method for opaque decoration begins with a broad free rendering in a color of medium value. Each brush stroke follows the form of the decorative motif. When the first application has dried, brush strokes with a color of deeper value are superimposed further to emphasize the form with detail and shadow. The whole is finally pointed up with white or off-white highlights and with accents of the darkest value.

A more subtle and delicate decorative effect may be achieved by first painting the entire design with white casein. The procedure is as follows. The design is traced on the tinted surface with a stylus and non-greasy transfer paper. Then the areas of design receive a thin application of white casein; after an hour of drying time, a second film of white casein is added; the design areas are now opaque. When the white has dried, casein color thinned to near transparency is laid on. The directions for the sequence of values of color applied are those given above for opaque decoration. In this case, however, the initial light wash counts as the highlight.

The carvings and moldings of eighteenth-century furniture are particularly appropriate for this method of tinting since the toning accentuates their form.

Casein is an excellent medium for decorative elements even on pieces which have been rendered in an oil base paint, for as long as the casein solutions contain polyethylene glue, they will adhere to the surface.


## GOUACHE

The depth and richness of a casein surface are emphasized when the medium for decorative color is gouache. Gouache differs from transparent water color in that the pigments are mixed with white. The opacity of gouache is generally enough to prevent the ground from reflecting through the paint. Like pastels, gouache has a delicate atmospheric quality. Unlike transparent water colors, it allows additions and changes to be easily made.

Gouache is applied over a design that has been repainted opaquely with white casein. Hues either delicately pastel or intensely brilliant are rendered over the white ground, not only exhibiting the ground but also enhancing the hue to greater brilliancy. The design might be rendered in full color followed by a series of washes of deeper or differing color applied to build up a rich depth of tone. Conversely, the design might be rendered monochromatically with a system of washes in a range of values finally intensified with deep lining color. Sepia, green, red, or blue were the tones generally selected for a monochromatic scheme. For this type of decoration, gouache should always be brushed on lightly and freely without reworking, somewhat as water color is used.

A cartouche with intaglio border was used most frequently on the drawers of a commode or the panels of breakfronts and secretaries. The cartouche served as an aperture through which the eye glimpsed the scene beyond. The area outside the border was rendered in the base hue of the entire piece. The border within the beveled channel was generally gilded. The portion enclosed by the cartouche was tinted in a contrasting color lighter in value and more neutral in hue than the body of the piece. This section was further ornamented with painted flowers and birds, a classical landscape, or a *chinoiserie*. Such enclosed design is most delightful when many thin transparent washes are used for the different elements of the decoration. These washes are applied to each separate element with broad yet delicate strokes defining the form.

*Shading Method.* The method used by the Chinese for shading color is a superior one, and proceeds as follows:

The portion of an element to remain unshaded is first covered with water. With another brush the shading color is flowed in on the unmoistened area, blending the two areas with gentle nuance. This Oriental trick eliminates hard dry edges of color and creates a finely graduated shading. Thus, the first tone is preserved as the highlighting tint and is followed by a series of shading washes in related color tones which graduate deeper until the modeling of the form is clearly brought forth.

To conclude the rendering, a heavier color in a dark value is applied with a small finely pointed #3 sable brush for any decorative detail and emphasis of deep shadow. The careful execution of these steps should approximate the delicate painting of the Chinese.


## ANTIQUE PATINA FOR CASEIN

Casein may be enhanced with the application of various antiquing media to build up patina.

1. Over a mat varnish, a thin casein solution in a becoming neutralized tint is used for antiquing. From a wax paper palette this solution is pounced or spattered on the surface with a short stiff-bristle stencil brush or a spatter brush. Shortly afterwards, it is patted lightly with a cheesecloth pad. The surface will be slightly stained. This neutral casein solution must be applied with deftness and control.

2. India ink watered to a gray tone may be spattered directly on an unprotected casein surface. It is blotted lightly with cheesecloth almost immediately. The blotting is gradual—first a light touch, followed minutes later by firm pressure. A fine web-like ring of the grayed ink mixture will remain; through this film the color of the piece will glow. The spatter of the thinned ink solution duplicates precisely the faded and casually spotted appearance of eighteenth-century furniture that I have had the pleasure of restoring.

3. Another way of reproducing this antique appearance begins with an application of the neutral casein solution over a protective coat of shellac. When the toning casein has dried, another coat of shellac is added. Next, a solution is made of 1 tablespoon of caustic soda (lye) and 1 pint of water. When the lye is being applied, rubber gloves with a finger cot reinforcing the index finger are worn. This solution when lightly spattered on the surface will burn through the shellac coats and the tinting coats to the white casein body. Since it will also cause animal bristle to disintegrate, a nylon bristle toothbrush is used for the spattering tool. The brush is dipped in the solution and shaken out once; then it is shaken on the surface to create the large irregular droplets characteristic of old Venetian furniture. A small area only is treated at one time. After a fractional waiting period, the surface is either wiped off or patted with a natural sponge wet with water; this halts the action of the lye. If the sponge is wiped over the area, the white casein ground is revealed through the color layer; but if the sponge is patted, a faint tint of color remains where the solution has touched the surface. To efface any remaining shellac, the piece is coated in 1 hour with a mat varnish.

4. A thin solution of antique aniline may be spattered loosely over an object painted with casein; the tone of the aniline should be pleasantly related to the base color. Upon drying, the piece is coated with mat varnish to retrieve its casein character.

All of the foregoing methods retain the dry, lean, powdery character of furniture finished in gesso or casein. In the eighteenth century, however, a casein finish was sometimes one with a satiny polish. Indeed, in France a tinted varnish was used as the final coat over delicate water color.


## FINAL PROTECTIVE FINISH

Casein ultimately dries to a permanent hard finish that is insoluble and therefore impervious to normal household damage. However, when a shellac film or an antiquing patina of any substance other than casein has been added, it is desirable to apply a final coating of mat varnish for the reasons already stated. Of these, rottenstone combined with wax is particularly becoming to the delicate colors attainable with casein. Of course, a wax finish used on a chair will rub off with the constant abrasion of physical contact. But if carnauba wax (derived from the leaves of the Brazilian palm tree) is used over varnished casein, the dry pigment will be encased strongly enough to withstand reasonable wear. Carnauba wax is also used directly on an unprotected casein surface and polishes to a beautiful luster.

A mat varnish having a high wax content will produce a delightful and almost porcelain-like finish on a casein piece rendered in brilliant and intense color. To ½ pint of this varnish, 1 tablespoon of flat white paint is added. Several applications of the mixture leave a white residue in crevices and a film over the brilliant color. The number of coats is determined by the degree to which one wishes to veil the color. When the final coat has dried, the piece is polished and buffed with a flannel cloth until it reaches the brilliance of porcelain.

Casein is a truly flexible medium—each time we have worked with it in the studio, new variations have been discovered and explored.

## CASEIN

*Materials*

Sand
Burlap
Coarse raw linen
Corrugated cardboard
Metal, bone, and leather combs
Rabbit-skin glue
Deep white casein paste
Kaolin powder
Ox gall
Dowicide A
Pine oil
Casein emulsion
Distilled water
India ink
Casein tinting colors in tubes

Gouache tubes
Carnauba wax
Turpentine
Protective mat varnish
Clear gloss varnish
Mat varnish of high wax content
French varnish
White shellac
Acrylic polymer emulsion
Acrolite fixative
Metal leaf
Fresco powders
Oil colors
Flat white paint

CASEIN: *Top left, sponge board; right, pounce-brush stipple.*
*Bottom left, rolled chamois; right, rubber roller.*

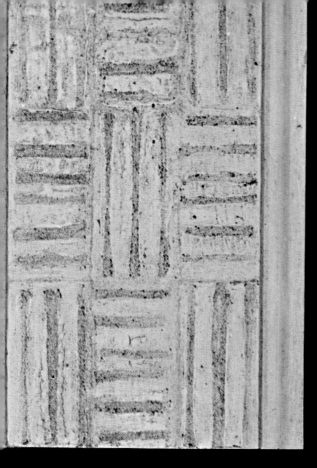

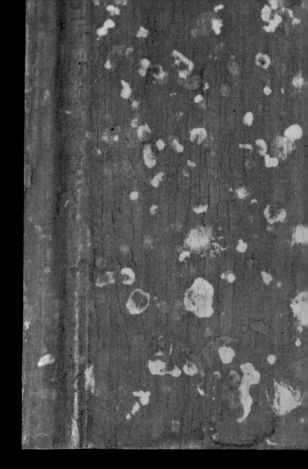

*Tools*
- 1″ stiff-bristle brush
- Oval sash brush
- Oxhair brush of size commensurate to piece
- ½″, 1″ stencil brush
- Nylon toothbrush
- Spatter brush
- Cosmetic sponge
- #3 and #6 sable brushes
- Mop brush
- Stylus
- Orangewood stick
- Incising tool
- Rubber roller
- Lamb's-wool roller
- 220A silicon carbide paper

*Miscellaneous*
- Glass screw-top jars
- Cheesecloth squares
- Blotter
- Absorbent tissues
- Foil and plastic container lids
- Nylon hose
- Absorbent cotton
- White paper
- Rough toweling
- Fork
- Razor blade
- Scrub brush
- Coarse natural sponge
- Non-greasy transfer paper
- Carborundum
- Compass
- Polyethylene glue
- Caustic soda (lye)
- Rubber gloves
- Finger guard

CASEIN: *Top left, corrugated checkerboard; right, wash-lye spatter. Bottom left, with cartouche; right, striation.*

# PART III

# Leafing, Gilding & Burnishing: Traditional Techniques

# INTRODUCTION

Gold, costly, romantic, and uniquely decorative, inflames the imagination. Its possession gives pleasure to king and commoner. Resistant to decay, gold was long associated with deathlessness—hence with the divine. Limited in supply, it has led to imitations. Extraordinarily malleable, it has enabled metalsmiths to render it in many decorative forms.

Gilding has been from time immemorial one of the most familiar forms of decoration and fantasy. The pharoahs, when gold was scarce and monumental offerings to the gods and to the dead were needed, substituted alloys or plated objects with heavy gold foil. Byzantine mosaics, medieval manuscripts, early Italian panel paintings, and similar religious works of art abundantly confirm the mystical connotation of gold. Inevitably, the conceit was established that a thin leaf of gold burnished to a mirror gloss was the magic metal.

The sumptuousness of this precious metal was achieved by using minute amounts, or at times by using an alloy that totally excluded gold. In court, cathedral, and home, the golden chair, the golden candle holder, and the golden mirror frame aroused admiration and gave a sense of affluence. Church and court were content to humor the pleasant fantasy that a coating of silver or gold transforms dross to precious ore. Owing to its intrinsic value and the devotion which it inspired, gold came to be regarded as a reflection of spiritual quality, an indication of worthiness of idea, and a symbol of power. Within the limitation of their means, lesser folk followed the court in acquiring the resplendent golden surfaces that give pleasure and lend distinction to the owner.

To become a master gilder in the past, the youthful novice entered a studio to serve his apprenticeship. The menial tasks were his—sweeping floors, cleaning tools, grinding color. For these privileges, the father of the youth paid the master. Eventually, the apprentice was allowed to apply gesso and to scrape it down in preparation for gilding. If the apprentice was not a son of the house, he was untaught and had only the opportunity to learn through participation and alert observation. Formulas and tools were jealously guarded and handed down from generation to generation. This explains the differences in the master gilders' formulas for gesso and in their techniques of application. After seven years the apprentice became a journeyman, and for the next three years was permitted to apply gold and to burnish. Becoming at long last himself a master, he was free to form his own studio and to be paid for his work.

Gilding as a decoration was lavished on furniture and accessories through the Baroque, Régence, Rococo, Directoire, and Empire periods. Gold on furnishings initially served as an expression of power. But as gilding became prevalent, it was used frequently as a relief from the dullness of wood. Lacquers sparkling with gold came to Europe through the East Indies trade and were so admired and prized that they brought on a positive fever for gilding. The following quotation from Lady Hartgord to the Countess of Pomfret in 1741 indicates that gilding was also a fashionable hobby:

> Within doors we amuse ourselves (at hours we
> are together) in gilding picture frames and
> other small things. This is so much in fashion
> with us at present that I believe if our patience
> and pockets would hold out, we should gild all
> the cornices, tables, chairs and stools about
> the house.

# MAT GILDING

## THE GROUNDS FOR BURNISHED AND MAT LEAF

The application of thin sheets of various metals, referred to as leaf, on a prepared surface is termed gilding. Precious leaf is gold or silver; it must be laid over a properly prepared ground of gesso and red clay size in order to be burnished (polished) to brilliance with an agate tool. During the Renaissance, gesso provided the white ground for panels which were to be painted and gilded. Gesso was also used to prepare furniture that would be painted and parcel-gilt (partly gilded). Leaf laid on any ground other than gesso produces a finish called mat; it gleams more softly and is lighter in color than burnished leaf. A distinguished effect emulating the ruddy brown gleam of antique burnished gold or the softer, gentle grace of antique mat leaf is achieved with a combination of wit, taste, and skilled technique. The desire to simulate the appearance of burnished gold urges the artisan to a wonderful cunning and artifice in his technique.

In the past a mat finish was obtained by laying the leaf on an oil size, but in the nineteenth century a new varnish size preparation came into being. The quick varnish size available today is, as its name suggests, fast-drying and convenient to use.

Past work with students demonstrates that an approach to the technique of gilding which begins with the simplest method of producing the glitter of gold is a delight and leads with ease to more complex steps. The use of two common alloys, aluminum and Dutch metal, which are heavier than precious leaf, develops a certain degree of tactile assurance in preparation for the moment of applying true gold. With the assumption that the reader is as unknowing as my students were on first learning to gild, I have aimed at presenting these instructions in simple and complete detail. The first and most essential directive is to read and understand all of the instructions before putting any one of the steps into practice. The process must be followed with earnestness and care. At times it may seem tedious, for progress proceeds at a snail's pace, yet if the beginner is patient long enough to acquire this new skill, he will have taken the first steps toward becoming a master gilder.

## MAT LEAF—PREPARATION

In preparing a perfect surface for leafing, all the care stressed in the beginning of this book is needed. Leaf, to gleam richly, must lie upon a satin bed. The smoother the surface, the brighter the luster of the metal.

Experience and discretion direct the choice of small objects for the first trials. If the learner does not insist on producing a usable and beautiful object right off and is content with the pleasure of acquiring technique, he best begins with inexpensive frames or with masonite cut into 8″ × 11″ sample boards.

### PRELIMINARY STEPS

General preparation for all objects has been thoroughly discussed in Part I, but a brief review is useful:

A previously painted or varnished piece is washed with alcohol, sanded with 220 garnet paper, and filled where necessary; the filled places are shellacked when dry.

A raw wood piece is filled and sanded with 220 garnet paper and shellacked.

A metal piece is stripped and coated with metal oil primer.

A plaster piece is coated with shellac twice, to stop the plaster from being absorptive.

If partial leaf decoration is desired, the entire piece is first painted in the color of one's choice. The piece after its final sanding is ready for further steps preparatory to leafing. It is interesting to note that eighteenth-century French chairs and sofas were often decorated with color and leaf—parcel-gilt—as were commodes and secretaries. In many instances not only they but smaller objects as well were lacquered before the additional embellishment of leaf. Later, during the Directoire and the English Regency periods, a black surface frequently provided the base for gold decoration in classic motifs.

## TRADITIONAL BOLE

Study of antique leaf will reveal at points of wear a foundation of varying tones of red, yellow ochre, or gray. This is the bole—a variety of clay—which was used as a size under the leaf to facilitate polishing. A knowledge of the range of color to be found in bole is imperative so that a hue can be selected which contributes to the general tonal scheme of the piece. The locale from which the clay was extracted determined its color, and it was possible by using a mixture of clays or by adding pigment to alter the original hue. As one observes old pieces it is well to remember that some variations in the color of the bole were caused over the years by sun and damp, by soil and use. Therefore, it would not be contrary to tradition to choose a color for the undercoat that harmonizes with the general scheme of decoration.

## SIMULATED BOLE—JAPAN

The glow of red bole comes through the transparent leaf, warming the tone of the gold as well as inducing a higher brilliance when the leaf is polished. The undercoat to be used in our procedure is not the traditional clay but a paint that resembles it. This red japan bole is preferred as a base for mat leafing with any substance that simulates gold.

## JAPAN BOLE FORMULAS

RED JAPAN BOLE     2 volumes red red-orange japan color
1 volume burnt sienna japan color
2 volumes flat white paint
½ volume turpentine
¼ volume flatting oil (soybean oil)

The mixture is strained through nylon hose. After the first application, additional flatting oil is used, when necessary, for thinning the medium for subsequent coats. Endless variations are possible by modifying the volume of the colors as well as their value and intensity.

In cases where mat leaf was laid in combination with burnished leaf, yellow ochre clay bole was used as a size for the mat areas in order to guide the gilder. Occasionally it may be discerned even under burnished leaf where it was used, because its color made holidays (skips in the gilding) less visible. Yellow ochre is charming when revealed through silver leaf, and is particularly so through silver gilt (gold-tinted silver).

YELLOW OCHRE     2 volumes French yellow ochre japan color
JAPAN BOLE     ½ volume chrome yellow light, light japan
color
½ volume flat white paint
½ volume turpentine
¼ volume flatting oil (soybean oil)

This mixture is strained. Additional flatting oil for thinning is added if required for subsequent coats.

Gray bole, because of its hue, reduces the visual impact of holidays in silver leafing. However, blue pigment added to the bole makes a more becoming undercoat for aluminum and silver.

BLUE JAPAN BOLE     ½ volume blue blue-green medium japan
color
½ volume Prussian blue japan color
¼ volume chrome yellow-orange japan color
8 volumes flat white paint
½ volume turpentine
¼ volume flatting oil (soybean oil)

The mixture is strained. Additional flatting oil is used when necessary for thinning subsequent coats.

Japan bole in any of the described hues provides an excellent surface for leafing. It is necessary for all objects except small items, such as bibelots, frames, and painted pieces on which decorative designs in leaf are to be placed, or pieces on which only the moldings are to be gilded. In these instances a casein paint is recommended because of its fast drying.

# JAPAN BOLE—PROCEDURE

As the object is about to become a gleaming example of the goldsmith's art, a fantasy of solid gold, there must be a body of paint which completely encases all evidence of structural elements as well as the nature of the original material. Accordingly, four to five coats of japan bole will be applied to the prepared piece.

### APPLICATION OF BOLE TO FLAT SURFACE

An oxhair brush of convenient size facilitates the smoothest coating. First the surface is tack-clothed. Then a fairly ample application of the bole is brushed out rapidly with the grain, and is finally stroked, without pressure, to minimize the bristle markings. This coat and each successive one must dry overnight before being tufbacked with 400 wet-or-dry paper and a non-detergent soapy solution to eliminate brush marks. As skill develops, tufbacking after every other coat is sufficient.

### APPLICATION OF BOLE TO CARVED SURFACE

For a carved object, a stiff-bristle brush is used to push the paint into the interstices and depths of the carving; any excess is then brushed out to avoid losing detail. Fewer coats, three perhaps, are necessary, as only the few smooth top surfaces can be tufbacked.

### PREPARATION OF SURFACE FOR SIZE

Next the paint body is sealed to provide a surface where porosity is evenly controlled; this insures that the gold size subsequently applied will dry at an even rate. The sealer is prepared as follows:

> 1 volume orange shellac (5-pound cut)
> 1 volume isobutyl or denatured alcohol

Isobutyl alcohol has a slower evaporation time than denatured alcohol, thus making the application of the shellac easier.

Orange shellac enhances red and yellow ochre bole. White shellac, made to the same formula, but with *denatured* alcohol, is preferable on blue bole.

For a flat surface, the best applicator is a "bob," a 3-inch pad of absorbent cotton encased in fine linen or cotton fabric and fastened at the top with a rubber band. The bob is modestly loaded from a shallow-rimmed receptacle containing the shellac mixture. Coverage begins at the center of a surface and proceeds with a light stroke to the right edge, followed swiftly by a stroke from the center to the left edge. This method spreads the inevitable puddle which forms at the first touch of the applicator on the surface. On either side of the initial application, strokes from center to sides continue until the load on the bob has lessened, at which point, and with increasing pressure, successive strokes from edge to edge cover the remaining surface. If it is necessary to reload the bob, the initial procedure must be repeated. Shellac has to be applied swiftly and dexterously to keep

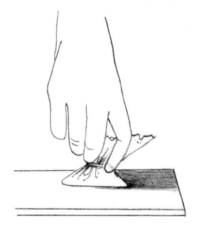

the working edges wet. There must be no retracing of a stroke and no overlapping, as shellac sets up (dries) so rapidly that gummy edges might form. Should there be holidays or overlaps, the surface is cautiously smoothed with ooo steel wool at the end of the hour required for drying shellac. If necessary, a second covering coat is applied. Final smoothing of the shellac coating is done with ooo steel wool and soapy water, so lightly that the shellac coat is not harmed.

The application of shellac with a brush follows the same stroking procedure. A brush, its size determined by the area to be covered, may also be used on flat surfaces. It should be remembered that after it has been dipped, the brush is pressed out within the container, rather than across the top edge, to avoid air bubbles.

For a carved piece, a 1-inch shellac brush, handled in accordance with the pouncing method, is most suitable for reaching the varying levels of the interstices. It is very lightly loaded to prevent the bubbles that are likely to result from pouncing in the crevices. Here it is obvious that only the top surfaces can be smoothed with ooo steel wool.

## CASEIN BOLE

On some occasions a medium other than japan paint is useful for reproducing the bole color. It is casein paint, water-soluble and quick-drying. Casein is an ideal medium for raised decorative elements, such as moldings and carvings, on larger painted pieces (parcel-gilt), and for flat gilded designs to be used on a painted ground.

With a #6 sable brush (first dipped in water), one coat of casein is smoothly applied over the unprotected, and therefore porous, flat paint base; this is allowed to dry for one hour. It is then smoothed with 280 garnet paper and shellacked. One hour later the section may be gilded, thus condensing the entire process to a day's time at most. Casein may of course be mixed with other casein colors to any of the hues previously suggested, with water used this time as a thinning agent.

Two coats of shellac seal the casein coverage on carved pieces, but no less than three are applied to flat surfaces. These are patted with a soapy solution and polished with ooo steel wool very lightly (else the water-soluble casein may be removed). Preparation is now complete—a satin-like base stands ready for leafing.

## SIZE

The carefully rendered japan or casein bole surface makes a fine smooth cushion for the application of leaf. The bole having been shellacked is now thinly coated with size (a siccative to which the leaf will cling). Size is made with a varnish base. There are two types: oil size and quick size.

### OIL SIZE

Many gilders recommend an oil size which, colored with chrome yellow medium, renders the areas sized more visible and any holidays of leafing less so. It reaches tack in 12 to 18 hours and holds it for 8 hours. The oil size of the fourteenth century (introduced to Italy by northern artists) included a drier, which was required because of the humidity of that southern climate. Some say that leaf laid with oil size has superior luster. This is not necessarily so. Leaf laid at precisely the right moment of tack (degree of readiness to receive the leaf) on a seat of quick size, more expedient than oil size, will gleam brilliantly. Moreover there is no danger as there is with slow size that oil will sweat through and disfigure the leaf and "check" any coating which is applied over it. It is conceded, of course, that for leafing a hall, or large areas such as those at Lincoln Center, oil size is essential.

### QUICK SIZE
Quick size contains a drier which hastens the tacky state. When thinned with a few drops of turpentine, it permits a very light coating which reaches tack condition even more rapidly. Size loses its adhesive grip when thinned too much. A small amount of oil paint—enough to tint but not to overbalance the density of the size—may be added to make the size more visible against the background. Gilder's quick size should be purchased in 4-ounce cans (¼ pint) since it congeals rapidly in larger containers. To prevent the liquid from jelling to an unusable consistency, a few drops of turpentine are added after each using and the can is tightly closed.


## SIZE—PROCEDURE

A piece must be wiped with a tack cloth immediately before sizing to eliminate all dust.


### SURFACE APPLICATION
Application of size to a flat surface is most readily accomplished with a bob having a fine silk cover or with an oxhair brush of suitable proportion. The object is to cover the surface with the thinnest possible film. A stiff-bristle brush is essential for carvings in order to reach deep into the interstices. A small #6 sable brush, lightly loaded, is used for moldings or applied design. After the surface has been covered, it is worked over again, without additional size on the brush, in order to avoid skips. If the surface is flat, this re-stroking is best done first with, then against, and finally with the grain—the same technique used in varnishing. For carved pieces, a thrice-over stippling and pouncing without re-loading the brush insures a complete light and even coverage. Obviously, small areas of decorative design do not require this treatment.


### APPLICATION ON DESIGN
Before the sizing of a design area, the entire surface is lightly powdered with talc as a precaution against any excess leaf adhering to some spot out-

side the design. To facilitate the sizing of design areas, a pinpoint of Indian red oil paint should be added to the size. A #6 pointed sable brush is used to size the design area. After loading, the brush is stroked out on a piece of paper so that the applied covering will be the thinnest possible film. It is advisable to fill in a design area by working from the top down, and from center to edge of each form within the area, rather than to outline and fill in. The latter method is apt to run, making the edge uneven, or it may leave an encircling ridge. Since *the look of inlay is the ultimate aim,* not only must the edges of the sizing be sharp and clean, but also there must be no perceptible difference of level between the embellishment and the surface. The pattern, gleaming richly, is an integral part of the unbroken surface. As one looks across the surface at eye level, the shine and color of the tinted size will indicate where skips have occurred and re-sizing is needed.

The purpose of such a careful technique of sizing is twofold: first, to insure a thin, level coating of size, which, drying evenly to the tack point, avoids scattered wet areas that might "drown" the leaf; second, to eliminate holidays, so tiresome to repair.

Any craftsman must assess his own speed in the actual laying of leaf and determine accordingly the extent of the area that he is able to size at one time. As technique improves, the area can be increased.

### *ORDER OF SIZE APPLICATION*

Zones of size should be disposed thoughtfully on objects too large to be leafed at one time in their entirety. To avoid scattering bits of leaf on adjacent areas sized and not yet tacky, it is desirable to size only one part with a certain time lapse before sizing adjoining sections. An upright object is sized in sections from the bottom up; a four-sided object, on non-adjacent sides; a box, first on the inside closing edges, then on the sides, and last on the top. It is necessary to set small objects and frames on blocks or cans to facilitate full coverage of the lower edges.

### *TEST FOR READINESS OF SIZE*

Size is most satisfactorily applied in a room as dust-free as possible, and having a dry, even temperature; damp, cold, and humidity affect drying time. Under the best conditions, a half hour to an hour's time brings the size to a "whistling tack." This gilder's term designates the slight click made when a knuckle placed on the drying size is lifted. However, this sound is apt to occur too soon. The optimum moment is reached when a slight sensation of pull is felt by the knuckle but not the faintest mark is left on the surface. At this stage the result of leafing will be rewardingly brilliant. Leaf laid too soon will drown in the size and become cloudy, murky, and rough; it must be removed with turpentine, and then "all's to be done again."

### CORRECTION OF HOLIDAYS

The holidays that are bound to occur must, on completion of the leafing, be carefully re-sized very thinly to just beyond the edges of the gap. This size must come to an even drier tack than that for the initial leafing in order that the patches may be so well rubbed in as to be imperceptible. The tack must dry to the point where the condensation of breath exhaled upon both size and leaf is sufficient to moisten both, thus assuring adhesion.

## MAT GILDING WITH GOLD POWDERS

Gold powders used discreetly over a carefully prepared base and subsequently antiqued with skill can effect a convincing facsimile of gold. Actually these are bronze powders—metal flakes made from copper-zinc or copper-tin alloys; bronze lining powders are the finest in texture. There are a number of shades available but only three are suitable for this purpose:

*Pale Gold*: a soft light shade, useful in imitation of the faded gold of the Renaissance.

*French Gold*: a deep warm shade, resembling the tone used in the seventeenth and eighteenth centuries by the Venetians and the French.

*Rich Gold*: a strong brassy shade, used in the Directoire period, and most successfully applied on a black ground.

So-called silver powders are unusable—they are lusterless and dark, being based on aluminum pigment.

All powders quickly lose their brilliance and therefore must be protected and heavily antiqued to retain any illusion of gold. Only if applied over a proper ground as directed in the preceding paragraphs will the result be successful.

MAT GILDING: *Top left, mat gold and sand;*
*right, black ground etched through gold.*
*Bottom left, Renaissance finish; right, relief design.*

## GOLD POWDERS—PROCEDURE

Size is applied and allowed to reach the tacky stage already described. With a bob covered with velvet, or a velvet finger casing, dipped in gold powder, the entire surface is rubbed; excess powder is brushed off with a piece of absorbent cotton or a gilder's tamper (a soft fine oxhair brush). This kind of application insures the thinnest possible coating of powder, with neither the brush strokes nor the grainy build-up which are the hallmark of a painted rather than gilded surface.

To produce the first antique effect, by revealing the bole in a manner which simulates age and wear, a cotton swab dipped in alcohol and well dried out is used. It lifts the powder at corners, high grounds, and edges. This removal occurs so easily that there is some danger of losing the powder altogether. To control this rapid action, a binding coat of thinned orange shellac may be applied after twenty-four hours drying time and rubbed through when dry with ooo steel wool and soapy water. Pressure must be used against the grain, rather than with it, to reveal the bole discreetly. If the procedure with the cotton swab is used, the surface is coated with shellac after the bole is revealed. When the shellac has dried, the piece is ready for the heavy antique patina, which is essential to achieve the illusion of gold.

Powders can be used to advantage on moldings, frames, metal chairs, and grille railings. I have rendered this gold powder technique on moldings in a showroom where a gilder was engaged in water-gilding the glass doors. To my astonishment he was totally deceived, and praised my gilding! I thought it kinder not to disillusion him.

## DECORATION WITH LEAF AND POWDERS

There is a non-greasy transfer paper available in many colors which is ideal for transferring a design. A white-coated transfer paper serves best on metallic surfaces; it is placed on the gilded surface with the white-powdered side down; the design, on tracing paper, is placed over it. Strips of tracing paper acting as bridges are secured with masking tape, at one end to the design and at the other to an unleafed portion of the object. (Masking tape must never be placed directly on a leafed surface; otherwise, when removed,

*Mat Gilding with Oriental ink brushwork*

it will inevitably tear away the thin metal.) The design is traced firmly with a metal stylus, for the outline must be clean-cut and precise. It is wise to take the precaution of lifting one end of the transfer paper to ascertain that the design is completely traced. After the design has been laid on the leaf, any transfer lines that have not been concealed are carefully removed with an eraser or vinegar and water.

A design is also applied in this manner on a wood or painted ground that is to be decorated with leaf or powder. It is advisable, after transferring the design and shellacking it, to talc the entire ground lightly. The talc can then be sized over, but it will prevent metallic powders and leaf from sticking beyond the boundaries of the design. If, as a matter of precaution, the surfaces were coated with one of the shellacs, errors made during the decorating process are removable with a cotton swab moistened with mineral spirits, or an eraser stick may be used on more stubborn spots. Any extraneous light film of gold powder that may remain somewhere on the surface is easily washed off with soapy water next day after the size has dried. Leafed decoration is protected after 24 hours with thinned white shellac gently applied with an oxhair brush. White shellac is also used when the three shades of gold powder are combined in one area, otherwise the differences between them are lost. To attain a crackled effect of age, a clear gilding lacquer is brushed over the shellac.

Elaborate use of powders was made on the beautiful English trays created at Pontypool. The edges of the metallic powders on these trays were shaded and softened with charcoal powder, which was applied with a charcoal stump, chamois, velvet bob, or a feather end. Powders blended and shaded were used on the English ware called Japan or Bantam, which was most popular during the seventeenth century, and on American stenciled trays and Hitchcock chairs.

Powders can be used to advantage in numerous ways. While some tack remains, they can be brushed into the elusive depths of an otherwise leafed carving. Should a tiny fault appear when leafing is completed, it can be masked by a dexterous touch with a fine brush dipped first in orange shellac and then in powder. This trick should be employed with discretion, as powder near any leaf looks dull and murky.

## RESTORATION WITH GOLD POWDERS

Powders may also be used to "touch up" antiques; in this case they are combined with the five japan earth colors—yellow ochre, raw sienna, raw umber, burnt umber, and burnt sienna. They are prepared as follows: First a teaspoon of quick size is mixed with ¼ teaspoon of gold powder; this makes a glowing mixture superior to any containing bronzing liquid. Brown striations on the surface indicate too much size and too little powder (such a ratio, however, is used for very fine line decoration). A card file showing the earth colors sufficient to tint but not overwhelm the gold makes a convenient reference. Six 1-inch squares are drawn on each card: the first square is painted with one of the gold powders, followed by five variations tinted with the earth colors. A drop of flatting oil binds the japan color with the gilt mixture. This series enables the artisan to determine the tone for a small touch-up on antique gold pieces, or to simulate the shades used on old French and Italian tole.

Powders tinted thus with earth colors are often the only way of restoring a fine antique piece without damaging its patina. I found this to be so in the restoration of a pair of Empire dolphin-tailed satyr benches as well as in the reproduction of two copies. A palette of earth colors, flat white, and pale gold powder, applied as meticulously as if painting a miniature, was required to restore and yet retain the ravages of time, and to simulate the creamy gesso with hints of bole and faint tinges of browned and worn gold. The result was so amazingly successful that the upholsterer had to look underneath at the webbing to distinguish the new from the old.

## MAT GILDING WITH COMMON METALS

There is beside the true leaf gold, another
kind in use, called Dutch gold, which is copper
gilt, and beaten into leaves like the genuine.
It is much cheaper, and has, when good, greatly
the effect of the true at the time of its being
laid on the ground; but with any access of
moisture, it loses its color and turns green in
spots, and indeed in all cases its beauty is
soon impaired, unless well secured by lacquer or
varnish. It is nevertheless serviceable for
coarser gilding where large masses are wanted,
especially where it is to be seen by artificial
light, as in the case of theatre, and if well
varnished, will there in a great measure answer
the end of the genuine kinds.

*The Handmaid to the Arts*
1764   Robert Dossie

As the Renaissance receded, and as the number of master gilders dwindled, various alloys which in some way resembled the precious leafs, and which could be manipulated more easily, came into use. These were and are inexpensive, and their lavish use need not disturb the novice. Called the "common" metals to distinguish them from the "precious," they have their own rich and individual qualities, and moreover, may be tinted skillfully to a facsimile of gold and silver leaf.

I recommend the progression from powder to the common metal leafs before work is attempted with gold or silver leaf. The exceptional thinness of precious leaf requires special skill which is best developed through work with other metals.

The first of these, an alloy of copper (90% copper, 10% zinc), is today called "Dutch metal" or "gold metal." In the eighteenth century it was termed "Dutch gold."

Another common metal is aluminum (first beaten into sheets for leafing at the end of the nineteenth century), which, although non-tarnishing, is of a darker hue than silver. It may be used to give the effect of pewter, of heavily antiqued silver, or of tinted French or Venetian silver.

Both Dutch metal and aluminum are cut into 5½-inch squares made up in books of 25 sheets, with a tissue between each leaf. Twenty books make a package and will cover a surface of 86 square feet. Because the sheets are heavier than silver or gold leaf, they are quite easy to handle.

## COMMON METALS—PROCEDURE

### FLAT SURFACES

The object to be leafed is placed on a box lid or a piece of clean paper. Next the heavy outer pages and the spine of the book of leaf are removed with scissors; then the sheets are cut, while protected by the tissue, to strips or squares scaled to the areas to be laid. The pieces should be large enough to allow for initial errors. With talc brushed on the fingers (a precaution against tactile adhesion which would fragment the leaf), the sheet is taken up with its covering tissue on top and, held between the index fingers and the thumbs of both hands at the top edge, is placed on the tacky surface (see drawing opposite).

The leaf is then pressed down on the sized surface and, still covered, is firmly smoothed out with the fingers. Only now is the tissue removed. Proceeding from left to right, leaf follows leaf, each overlapping the pre-

ceding one by ⅛″; the overlaps must all be in the same direction horizontally as well as vertically. The process is repeated until the surface is
covered. Small faults are ignored as they can be remedied with "skewings"
(the remaining particles of leaf resulting from the overlaps). To "skew" is
to brush the particles off in the direction of the overlaps with a gilder's
tamper, a 1-inch fine oxhair chiseled brush. It is most important that these

instructions be followed to the letter lest the edges of leaf be pulled away
at the joinings. Being careful to prevent the tamper from touching exposed
spots that retain the size (for this would smear the leaf already laid), the
skewings are brushed to the faults and firmly pressed in with the tamper

or finger. Areas larger than ⅜″ should not be covered in this manner with skewings or the patch will acquire a cloudy appearance. For larger holidays, the leaf is cut to measure and laid on. The gilder must be sure that the leaf is firmly secured everywhere. Provided that no portion coated with size remains uncovered, the tamper used in a circular movement totally removes the fine residue of the overlaps. Next day, when the size is fully dry and there is no danger of smearing over the leaf and marring its brilliance, the surface is polished gently with a ball of fine absorbent cotton.

Any residual skewings on the box lid or clean paper placed under the object have been kept free of foreign particles; they are brushed into a container for future use.

Squares of leaf may be laid on larger surfaces—chests, screens, and table tops—to form decorative patterns of checkered, staggered, or diagonal rows from a centered diamond or square. Before sizing, guidelines are ruled in with a white Conté pastel pencil.

## CARVED SURFACES

Procedure for leafing a carved piece depends on the different problems posed by its interstices and undercuttings. If the carving is in the round, a section of the circumference is completely covered from the bottom up to prevent skewings from scattering downward on areas not yet tacky. If the carving is in low relief or is pierced, one section at a time is leafed as follows: One layer of leaf is placed on the area with just enough pressure to secure it, then the tissue is removed; a second layer is now placed on top of the first one; finally skewings are firmly pushed, wherever necessary, into the leafed carving with a tamper which has been dipped in the skewing box. One need not fear contact of the tamper with size, since the second layer of leaf and the skewings fill in all the breaks caused by the multi-level surface. To fill exceedingly tiny recesses, however, it is sometimes necessary to use a cotton bud dipped in skewings and firmly pressed into the recesses. A final brisk brushing with a gilder's tamper gives the work a gleam on its rounded surfaces. Carving is difficult—first to size, then to leaf. The beginner should not be dismayed by faults—even a master does not avoid them! When faults are impossible to reach, that is the moment for gold powder to come to the rescue. It may be brushed in with a tamper. If the holiday is in an inconspicuous recess and has escaped sizing, it can be repaired with a matching gold powder on a small brush first dipped in shellac. French gold powder blends with Dutch metal and gold leaf; rich gold powder, with French silver gilt and lemon gold.

Far be it from the frugal European to lavish gold and silver where it was not seen. The deep inner curves of a pierced carving, the peripheral curves of relief, the backs of small chests, the underside of bracket shelves, and other unseen areas, were painted in yellow ochre. Indeed in the late eighteenth century, yellow ochre was sometimes used in modest rooms as a substitute for golden moldings to bring out the line of furniture and panels.

### *EXPOSURE OF BOLE*

After the leafed objects have set awhile (two or three hours), the first step toward creating the illusion of antiquity is taken by revealing the bole. This may be done on the same day or on the following, the difference being that at the later time more manual pressure is exerted to rub through the leaf; on the first experience, the next day is better. With a cotton bud, or a piece of fine silk, dipped in denatured alcohol (the solvent least damaging to the leaf), the corners, edges, high rounds, and other areas of possible wear are rubbed through to the bole.

The end result must be determined before the bole is revealed. Careful observation of museum pieces laid with leaf will be of immense help in this and further processes of antiquing. Very old gold often has faint worn areas dispersed throughout. If the leaf has been laid evenly, a decorative delineation is effected by working the bole through from the edges toward the center of each sheet, revealing the pattern established in the laying. When this "aging" is completed, all traces of the alcohol stain are washed off with soap and water.

All common leaf—aluminum, Dutch metal, and copper leaf—are applied by the previously discussed method. There are various methods of tinting and antiquing which transform these substitute metals to such a degree that even the knowledgeable find them hard to distinguish from the precious ones. These procedures will be described farther on.

# MAT GILDING WITH PRECIOUS METALS

### *MANUFACTURE OF LEAF*

Pure gold, called 24-carat, is alloyed with silver and copper to become 23-carat. An ingot of this, 1″ wide and ⅛″ thick, can be beaten into leaves that are 3⅜″ square and 1/250,000 of an inch thick. This leaf, rendered to a thinness impossible with any other metal, is so fragile that it powders at a touch. It is more delicate than that used in ancient Egypt (which in thickness resembled foil), and it is one quarter of the thickness of the leaf used during the Renaissance. Today leaf is often hammered by machine. In previous ages the manufacture of leaf was a lengthy and arduous hand process, and it is interesting to examine how it was done in the eighteenth century, when the art of decoration reached its zenith. The bar of gold was first rolled into a thin sheet; then rolled even thinner into foil, which was cut into squares. These were placed between larger yellow papers, and the lot was known as a "cutch." Banded with parchment and placed on a polished granite block, the cutch was beaten with a special broad hammer (weighing up to 18 pounds) until the leaf attained the size of the papers. The beater then extracted the gold leaf and placed it between 4-inch squares of skin containing no moisture or grease. These skins formed the "shoder."

The shoder was clamped on leather-cushioned board and beaten until the gold spread beyond the edges; this excess was termed the "shruff." The leaves were taken from the skins of the shoder, cut into quarters, and placed between 1,000–1,100 "gold beaters' skins" (segments of membrane from the intestines of oxen). These skins formed the "gold molds" 5½" square. Bound with parchment bands, they, too, were beaten, with a series of hammers weighing from 8 to 12 pounds, until the shruff again emerged. At last the fine leaves were lifted with delicate pincers, were cut one by one with the "gold cutters" into 3⅜-inch squares, and were placed between papers dusted with red clay (powder obtained from red oxide of iron) in books containing 25 leaves. Today twenty such books form a pack, 1/60 of a pound of gold.

A book of leaf skillfully laid covers 1½ square feet; a pack, 30 square feet.

Double-weight gold leaf is available, and is closer to the weight used in the Renaissance; it is more costly, of course, but somewhat easier to handle. There is also transfer gold, or patent gold, which is leaf pressed to the tissue of the book. This is useful against the treachery of wind during outdoor gilding. Otherwise it is not recommended, as the gold is apt to cling to the sheets, leaving gaps in the gilding. However, transfer gold in ribbons ⅛" to 3¾" wide and 67' long is efficient for outlining architectural moldings; this is applied with a gilding wheel.

Then there are the tints of gold, each mixed with varying percentages of silver alloy. Pure gold itself is almost inert chemically and consequently will not tarnish. Hence the smaller the carat content of gold in a tint, the greater the chance of tarnishing. Lemon gold is 18½ carats; pale gold is 16 carats; white gold is 12 carats.

Silver is prepared in the same way as gold, though not beaten to as thin a leaf, and it is cut to the same 3⅜-inch squares. If kept too long, it is apt to tarnish in the book. Palladium leaf looks somewhat murky when compared with silver leaf but is the most permanent white metal and will not tarnish.

The beginner's greatest hazard in handling gold is his own nervousness, caused by the fragility of the leaf and increased by an exaggerated awe of its value. Discipline and practice will help in mastering the technique and lead to an increased economy of labor and material. The novice at laying precious leaf is advised to begin with silver, using exactly the method employed for gold.

## GILDER'S IMPLEMENTS

The following equipment is needed: a klinker, a gilder's knife, a gilder's tip, and a tamper.

*Klinker.* Leaf clings and catches on any slightly damp or greasy surface; therefore, in laying it out, a gilder's cushion known as a "klinker" is used. A klinker is a panel of wood 6″ x 10″ covered on one side with a chamois, or with the reverse side of calf, over a cotton padding. Raised up around the back end is a 2-inch shield of buckram to protect the leaf from air

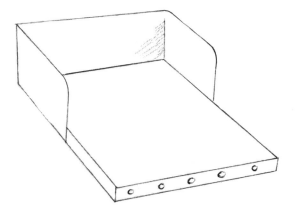

currents. A master's klinker has, in addition, a leather loop on the underside to enable him to hold the pad as a palette in his left hand, as well as a leather strap which holds the gilder's knife. French chalk should be thoroughly worked into the leather of the cushion with the flat of the gilding knife or with rouge paper from an old book of leaf. Rouge paper is especially good for rubbing on the cushion to keep it grease-free.

*Gilder's Knife.* This tool is longer than a dinner knife and its straight tip is cut diagonally. In the studio we have found the so-called blunt edge to be quite sharp enough for dividing rather than cutting the leaf. It is most important to polish the knife well with rouge paper so that the leaf does not cling to it and thus tatter. Scissors are useless for cutting leaf as they cause the delicate sheets of metal to become welded together, making the difficulty of picking up each piece even greater.

*Gilder's Tip.* A tool for laying leaf is a gilder's tip, which came into use in the seventeenth century. This thin flat brush is made by fastening badger or camel's hair between two pieces of 4-inch cardboard. A ⅛″ thick strip of wood glued to the top of the cardboard makes handling easier. The brush may also be cut in half lengthwise and taped, readying it for use on small pieces of leaf. To smooth the bristles, the tip is placed against a flat surface and under the left hand. It is then pulled out from under the firmly placed hand, turned over, and the operation is repeated.

Gilders are in the habit of brushing the tip on their hair and face to acquire a thin coating of oil that will affix the leaf to the tip. I prefer to use a little petroleum jelly rubbed well into the inside of the left wrist. The ends of the tip are brushed back and forth across the wrist in such a way that the flat sides do not become coated—a necessary precaution because leaf is so volatile it might fly up and cling to the sides of the tip and thus be wasted. It should be noted at this point that wool and rayon are not worn during the gilding process because of the static electricity they create.

## PRECIOUS LEAF—PROCEDURE

### DISPOSITION OF LEAF ON KLINKER

To begin, the spine of the book of leaf is cut off with a scissors, the outer pages removed, and the top tissue slid off. The pack is now flipped over on the front of the klinker, and then all but the bottom leaf of the gold is removed with the knife and fingers and placed to the side of the klinker. (When the initial fear of handling leaf has subsided, a number of sheets may be shaken out on the back of the cushion.) The leaf is now in position

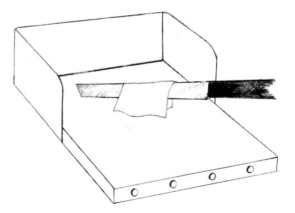

to be moved to the front of the klinker. A gentle tap of the knife on the flat of the klinker will stir the leaf so that the broad side of the knife can be inserted under it. The leaf is then lifted from the cushion, and is given a slight shake to straighten it. The knife turns in the gilder's hand to roll the leaf underside up onto the front of the cutting surface. Should the leaf be rumpled, a gentle breath with pursed lips, as if one were saying "pō," directed at the center of the sheet will flatten it. The entire process can be summed up as: lift, roll, blow. No unthinking movement must disturb the calm necessary for the leaf to lie smoothly, ready for cutting. Should the leaf be "contrary," the gilder's knife must be used to control it.

## DIVISION OF LEAF

The leaf is now cut in sizes suitable for covering the object—strips, halves, or quarters, whichever is easiest to handle. The edge of the blade is laid firmly across the leaf where the division is to be made and lightly pushed

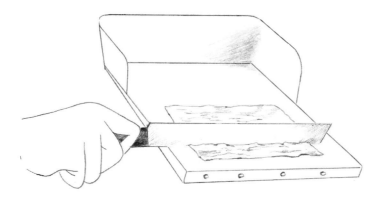

forward a little beyond the leaf and then drawn straight back with even pressure and without lifting until completely off the cushion. To repeat: the knife is not raised until it is well away from the leaf or it frays the edges. It is absolutely essential that the cut be drawn clean beyond the edge of the leaf.

## DISPOSITION OF LEAF ON OBJECT

To lift the leaf, the tip is held directly over the nearest ¼″ of the leaf on the klinker, which has been placed to the left on the table. With a quick downward pressure at right angles to the leaf (a staccato motion similar to testing a hot iron), the tip touches the leaf, instantly lifts it about 3″ high,

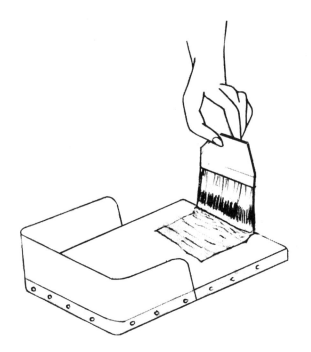

and carries it gently to the tacky surface (moving from left to right if the gilder is right-handed). The leaf is deposited and the tip drawn off in a continuous arc. Should the tip not hold the leaf firmly, the petroleum jelly is insufficient. Should the leaf tear when parting from the tip, there is too much oil. Executed skillfully, the movement consists of: pounce, lift, lay, and draw off—in an unbroken curve from pad to object and away. The petroleum jelly holds the leaf securely, and if the carrying movement is kept low and steady, the leaf reaches the object in perfect position for deposit. If the transfer is disturbed by an erratic draft, a carefully directed puff will float the leaf behind the tip. After the leaf has been deposited, a gentle tap on its corners with one corner of the bristle end of the tip secures the leaf until skewing. The tip must never touch a sized area, as any size contaminating the surface of leaf will blur and disfigure its brilliant appearance. After use, the tip is carefully wiped with a cotton cloth and closed in the pages of a book in order to keep the hairs straight. From this point on, mat leafing in precious metal follows the procedure of mat leafing in common metal. Overlapping, skewing, and polishing are precisely the same.

The movements of the gilder, like those of any skilled craftsman, are beautiful—disciplined as they are by centuries of experience to the quickest, simplest, most direct relation of tool, material, and object. When the technique described becomes automatic for the learner, he will feel the easy efficiency and harmonious perfection of the manual skill of gilding.

## FINISHES FOR MAT LEAF

Many finishes are possible but only after a protective coat of the proper shellac has been applied to the leaf. This coating seals the metal against tarnishing unless the object is exposed to salt sea air, in which case the further protection of varnish is necessary. Thinned orange shellac, because of its warm tone, is preferable for French gold powder, Dutch metal, and true gold.

Aluminum and silver leaf retain their light color under a coat of thinned French varnish, the clearest and most refined of the shellacs. As it deteriorates even more rapidly than the other shellacs, it must be purchased in small quantities and thinned with an equal amount of isobutyl or denatured alcohol. For application on the common metals and silver leaf, a shellac brush or a bob is used. To avoid damage on gold powders and true gold, an oxhair brush with its softer bristle is preferable. To achieve a crazed (minutely cracked) surface on leaf, a coat of clear gilding lacquer is applied over a surface previously lightly rubbed with denatured alcohol.

Uncoated pure gold leaf not used in combination with other metals may be waxed with carnauba or beeswax and polished without any intervening process unless browning is desired.


## MAT GILDING

*Materials*

400 wet-or-dry paper
000 steel wool
220 garnet paper
280 garnet paper
Quick size (gilder's)
Flat white paint
Japan colors
  raw sienna
  raw umber
  burnt umber
  red red-orange
  burnt sienna
  French yellow ochre
  chrome yellow light, light
  blue blue-green, medium
  chrome yellow orange
  Prussian blue

Indian red oil paint
Casein paint colors
Orange shellac
Denatured alcohol
White shellac
French varnish
Common leaf (Dutch
  metal, aluminum,
  copper, etc.)
Precious leaf: gold, silver,
  and tints of gold (gold
  alloyed with silver)
Bronzing (gold) powders
Flatting oil
Turpentine
Carnauba wax
Clear metal lacquer

*Tools*
  Stylus
  Gilder's tamper
  Gilder's knife
  Gilder's tip
  Klinker (gilder's pad)
  7/8″ to 2″ oxhair brush
  1″ stiff-bristle brush
  #6 sable brush

*Miscellaneous*
  Absorbent cotton
  Fine cotton or linen fabric
  Fine silk fabric
  Velvet fabric

Non-detergent soap flakes
Lids
Low containers
Petroleum jelly
Talc
White Conté pastel pencil
French chalk
Non-greasy transfer paper
Masking tape
Tracing paper
Nylon hose
Tack cloth
Cotton tips
File cards
Scissors

# ANTIQUE PATINA
# FOR LEAF

## MANY METHODS, MANY MEDIUMS

The gilding is finally complete; the object glitters as if newly minted. Indeed its shining surface is almost too showy, for we have come to admire the gentler patinas of the antique, the tarnish of silver, the brown of old gold. Pieces with some slight damage of age, areas of wear that reveal the bole beneath the gold, seem to look less commercial. There are many ways of achieving a soft luster and a gentle patina. A Renaissance method might be selected, one used, say, by the seventeenth-century Venetians or by the eighteenth-century French. The subdued tarnished antiquity of Dutch and German silver, the silver tinted to the lemon gilt admired by the French, or the bronzy gold esteemed by the Venetians—each antique effect has its own appeal.

These patinas are obtained through the use of a wide range of mediums. And a particular type of leaf is not limited to a particular style of antiquing. Thus silver can be yellowed, blackened, or tarnished, or again it may be tinted to resemble gold. In the thirteenth and fourteenth centuries, a varnish called *auripetrum* tinged with transparent yellow was spread over tinfoil and metal to produce a fine gold color, beautifully clean and lustrous.

With the use of a modern technique, gold may be browned and so encrusted that when a few golden glints are revealed they assume the brilliance of burnished metal in contrast with the heavy antiquing. Many of the mediums may be combined with others to produce surprising effects.

## EXPERIMENT BEFORE CHOICE

The reader should study this whole section before selecting the method to be used. Indeed, since so many methods are described here, he will find that experiments on a series of panels or small boxes will help him to narrow down the choice for a particular surface or carving. On such practice surfaces some problems will be met and solved and a degree of skill achieved.

## ANTIQUING MEDIUMS

Certain mediums used for antiquing painted areas are discussed here again when they may be used effectively on leaf; in accordance with the manner of coloring, it is possible to gray, yellow, or blacken silver, and to brown gold. A wide range of effects that simulate the alterations of time and use is achieved but without the messy and smeared appearance of newly applied antiquing.

## DRY COLORS

### *POWDERS AND WAX*
Inexpensive dry powders, sold by the pound, are combined to a smooth paste with colorless wax having a high turpentine content. The amount of powder determines the strength of the color (approximately 1 volume pigment to ½ volume wax). Too great a proportion of powder makes a grainy mixture; too much wax, a greasy, colorless mixture. Only a test with a brush on newspaper reveals whether the proportion is correct. If kept for a period of time, the paste is stored in an airtight tin. Before reuse, the

tin is placed in a pan of water and heated. However, the mixture is not used in a liquid state, but only after it has cooled into paste. It is used most effectively on leafed carvings or multiple moldings, which have of course been protected. In either case the interstices hold the waxy medium.

When the earth powders—raw umber, burnt umber, raw sienna, burnt sienna, gray, and rottenstone—are combined with wax, the mixture is applied over a protective coating as a dulling or yellowing agent for silver or as a browning agent for gold.

### POWDER AND WHITE SHELLAC

Dry powder—one of the umbers—is mixed with white shellac, then is pounced on a leafed surface which has been bound with diluted clear varnish (60% varnish, 40% turpentine). The shellac-powder coating dries rapidly. It is blended with steel wool before hard dry. This medium is used to brown the leaf.

### ASPHALTUM

Over a leafed surface which has been shellacked, a coat of asphaltum thinned with mineral spirits is applied. After ten minutes it is rubbed off with rottenstone and ooo steel wool. This medium is also used to brown the leaf.

## JAPAN ANTIQUING FLUID

Japan color (and flat white paint, if needed) is combined with colorless mat varnish (3 volumes paint to 1 volume varnish). The mixture is strained before use. Then a small amount is spooned out on a wax paper palette and lightly pounced over a protected flat surface. (If the mixture is stored afterward for a long period, its surface should first be coated with turpentine.) The japan medium may also be combined with colorless wax having a high turpentine content, care being taken not to weaken the color by adding too much wax. This mixture is used for pouncing on leaf which has been previously protected with shellac. A heavily pounced surface on leaf can be blended with ooo steel wool to reveal glints of bright metal. This effects the look of ancient encrusted leaf—an interesting patina on flat surfaces.

## JAPAN SPATTERING FLUID

For use on leaf, this medium is made in a fairly thin solution as follows:

1 volume japan color
3 volumes mat varnish
4 volumes turpentine

An interesting patina results from either spattering or pouncing this semi-transparent medium on a flat leafed surface. Irregular clustered spatter, especially enhancing to gilded surfaces, is achieved by knocking the spatter brush on a wooden block or a brush handle or vice versa. This flings the spatter over a greater area and in larger drops. There must be some practice on newspaper to determine whether the spray falls ahead, to the side, or in back of the block. As a strong blow is necessary to effect large loose form, the spatter may land as much as 12″ behind the block. To avoid a dulling smear, the spray must be almost dry before the pouncing.

Blotting can be substituted for pouncing. In this case, the large and ample spatter is covered with a sheet of absorbent newspaper. This is either pressed lightly with the finger on the obviously dampened portions, or tentatively and lightly pounced with the brush. When the paper is removed, any remaining heavy portions of unabsorbed paint are blotted with little pieces of paper. If a dual tonality is desired, the spattered surface after drying is coated with thinned shellac, then spattered with the second color.

For all methods, wax paper is used as a palette. The medium is spooned out and the brush is loaded directly from the paper. To avoid overloading, the pouncing brush is tested on newspaper before application to the leaf. All mediums when dry are blended safely with ooo steel wool, as the patina has been applied over a protective coating of shellac. Inadvertent errors are ignored until completely dry, when they can be easily corrected.

## ASSORTED ANTIQUING PROCEDURES AND EFFECTS

"Noble" describes the antiquing effect of the Renaissance finish, one becoming to carved objects and frames. On gold it is mellow and soft; on aluminum and silver it assumes a yellowed tarnished look. The mixture, made of wax and raw umber japan antiquing fluid, is evenly pounced over the surface. The pouncing is performed lightly and with care lest heavy deposits of the medium remain in the interstices of the carving. The surface is piled at once with rottenstone. Any residue may be reused, so the powder is prodigally applied. Rottenstone acts here in two roles: it is a polishing agent and, being of a warm gray color, it also simulates the dust of past ages. In approximately half an hour, when the wax medium has dried, the raised surfaces and edges are briskly buffed with a wad of soft absorbent newspaper heavily and blackly printed. Some of the rottenstone is retained, especially in the crevices of the carving. The buffing brings up the gold, at the same time leaving on its surface a residue of black ink from the newspaper. The red bole is revealed on the high surfaces.

Rottenstone may be applied over any of the leaf finishes, either dusted over wax which has been pounced on, or mixed in a wax paste which, too, is pounced on the object. Rottenstone is universally effective on metallic surfaces when used to simulate dust, and it might well be the final touch of artifice over any antiquing medium.

The various golds are enhanced when raw umber or burnt umber are used as the pigment in either the japan antiquing or the japan spattering fluid. On aluminum and silver leaf, raw umber japan spattering fluid creates the effect of slightly yellowed silver. They are mellowed to the tint of Dutch silver by a thinned solution of black japan spattering fluid.

For emulating the luster of pewter, a spattering fluid is made to this formula:

> ½ volume raw umber japan color
> ½ volume burnt sienna japan color
> ½ volume lampblack japan color
> 4 volumes flat white paint
> 3 volumes mat varnish
> 4 volumes turpentine

To glaze and tone lightly any of the leafs, oil paint in the earth tones—raw umber, burnt umber, raw sienna, burnt sienna—is combined with turpentine, gloss varnish, and a drop of japan drier. Varicolored tints occasionally appear on French and Italian eighteenth-century gilded objects; over silver, a red purple-pink (alizarin crimson) and a pale green (thalo green, a short form of pthalocyanine); over gold, a true green, which is warmed by the golden hue. These early tints were prepared in glaze form through the addition of varnish and thinner. Any leaf that is to receive oil glaze is previously protected by shellac.

To turn silver to gold (*auripetrum*), picric acid added to thinned shellac is still used occasionally. Over this, gloss varnish must be applied to hold the yellow color.

For tinting gold a ruddy color, a mixture of ¼ teaspoon dragon's blood (resin from the Malayan palm tree) and 1 teaspoon varnish is used.

After a tinted finish has dried and the surface has been protected, it may be further antiqued.

# CASEIN ANTIQUING MEDIUM

Casein antiquing medium creates a variety of patinas on leaf. One of them is called "Antique Mirror Finish." It is made by combining 1 teaspoon raw umber casein with ½ pint water. The medium is pounced on the surface, which in this case is unprotected by shellac. It is necessary to use a great deal of the liquid, as the glossy metallic surface is loath to receive it. The pools of solution are increased by laying the fully loaded pounce brush alongside and "feeding" them more liquid. A sufficient amount finally crawls into irregular large forms, leaving some of the leaf untouched; and it remains on the surface for a long period—until the water content evaporates and only the casein film is left. To hasten drying, the water may be absorbed from the center of the amorphous pattern with a blotter, great care being taken not to disturb the edges. Over this dry film, a coat of thinned orange shellac or French varnish is applied. A fascinating patina results. It is particularly effective on aluminum or silver leaf, for the metallic areas that have resisted the antiquing seem to gain an additional mirror-like reflection.

Casein is also used as a coat over any deeply carved gilded or silvered piece—frame, sconce, bracket, console, or chair—provided that such a piece has been treated with an isolating coat of thinned shellac. White casein is sparingly tinted with raw umber, French yellow ochre, and lemon yellow to a pale rottenstone color. In a covering coat, the casein tint is then applied to the leaf. When the casein has surface dried, it is immediately rubbed against the grain with turkish toweling, burlap, or a toothbrush; the rubbing partially reveals the gold on the raised surfaces, avoids that in the recesses. If portions of the casein become too dry to rub through, they are lightly redampened by allowing a wet cloth to rest on them for a few moments. They must, however, be allowed to dry a little before the rubbing proceeds. They are then scrubbed with a toothbrush in a rotary motion. The final result allows the leaf to glimmer faintly through the casein.

When the rubbing is complete, the surface is ready for further tinting

and antiquing. First, a section is pounced with wax by means of a pounce brush or stencil brush of suitable size. Then it is sprinkled with dry color. This is done by dipping a tip of cheesecloth in the powder and gently tapping the finger that holds it over the waxed portion (see drawing opposite). Several colors may be used—raw umber, French yellow ochre, Turkey red; the wax obviously acts as a binder. When the wax is well dried, the piece is buffed with a soft wad of newspaper, which leaves traces of ink behind.

## TARNISHING

Any leaf containing an alloy will, of course, tarnish. This type of surface alteration is often beautiful, and can be induced with chemicals. In using any of the following methods, one will find that a design which contrasts areas of brilliant metal with areas of tarnish gives the happiest result.

### *DUTCH METAL TARNISH*

Sodium sulfide tarnishes Dutch metal, but only when this leaf is unprotected by shellac or varnish. The tarnishing solution is made by dissolving a pea-size amount of sodium sulfide crystals in 2 ounces of water. To be effective, the solution must rest on the leaf in a puddle at least ⅛″ in depth. The process of oxidation proceeds with a change of hue from orange to magenta to silvery green-blue (the preferred color) and finally to rusty black, the ultimate stage of burning. The process is stopped before the black stage by gently absorbing the fluid with fresh cotton. Having sustained some

degree of burning, the leaf is now even more fragile, so extreme care is taken to avoid lifting or breaking it while blotting the solution.

## *APPLICATION OF TARNISHING AGENT*

The following devices are used:

1) A 2″ × 6″ strip of absorbent cotton. The ends of the cotton may be graduated or cut unevenly to create an irregular pattern. One end of the cotton is dipped in the solution and slapped over the surface. A portion of the leaf surface should remain untouched for the most effective result.

2) A sheet of absorbent cotton wrapped around a roller and immersed in solution. This is rolled lightly on a surface, and is used especially for large panels.

3) A cotton bud. This is used to tarnish the interstices of carvings.

4) A jet sprayer or an insect sprayer. Solution applied with these produces a less traditional effect.

5) Spatter brush. A spattering of clear varnish precedes the tarnishing. The varnish is applied by knocking the spatter brush against a wooden

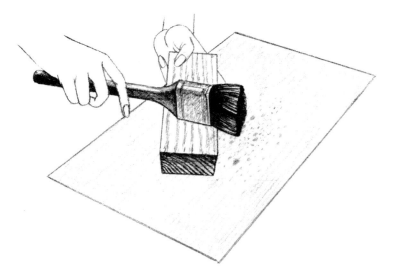

block and is allowed to dry overnight. In this way, a dappling of metal is reserved before the object is covered with the oxidizing solution. The resultant effect is tinged with a Far Eastern flavor.

Dutch metal, completely tarnished, serves as an ideal ground for a credible facsimile of excavated bronze with its green patina (*verte antique*). After the tarnishing liquid dries on the leaf overnight, a coat of clear varnish is applied to prevent further tarnishing. Then dry powders or fresco powders are combined to a suitable verdigris color. With a mortar and pestle, the color is mixed first with a little non-detergent soapy water, which acts as a binder, then with beer, which is added to dilute the paste to a creamy solution. After the varnish has dried, the color solution is applied to the leaf with a pounce brush; when this in turn has dried, it is sprayed with a pastel fixative. The leaf is then given three more coats of varnish, and at the last is treated with wax or with rottenstone and wax. All tarnished surfaces must be coated with at least two coats of thinned gloss varnish to prevent further oxidation.

### TARNISH FOR SILVER AND SILVER ALLOYS

A pea-size nugget of liver sulfate (potassium sulfate) is dissolved in 2 ounces of water. This solution is applied in the methods described for sodium sulfide but with even greater care because of the extreme fragility of silver leaf. The color transitions are like those seen in an oil slick on a rainy day— yellow-orange to opalescent blue. Here, too, gentle blotting stops the action before the black stage is reached. To reiterate, all leaf tarnished by any chemical is sealed the following day so that the air in conjunction with the chemical agent does not continue the oxidation. The ugly shine that is bound to result is reduced by tufbacking and a light, unbuffed waxing.

### FACSIMILE OF PITTED SILVER

To facsimile pitted silver, the Italians apply a solution of copper nitrate. It is made by combining ½ volume copper nitrate dissolved in 1 volume distilled water with ½ volume sal ammoniac (ammonium chloride) dissolved in 1 volume distilled water. When the mixtures are completely dissolved, they are combined and 30 volumes of distilled water are added. The amount of distilled water determines the depth of the graying of the silver. When the solution is brushed haphazardly over a silver surface, the effect of graying tarnish is charmingly evident.

### AURIPETRUM FINISH

For a finish that resembles *auripetrum*, the following solution is made: A pea-size nugget of picric acid dissolved in ½ ounce of alcohol is combined with ½ ounce of undiluted white shellac. This is applied to the surface with an oxhair brush (which must be immediately cleaned with alcohol). After the coating has dried for an hour, it is brushed with thinned clear varnish, followed by another coat in 24 hours, and is subsequently rubbed down with 600 wet-or-dry paper and a soapy solution.

# TINTING

### ANILINE POWDERS

Aniline powders, which are alcohol-soluble, are used for toning gold, silver, and the common metals. They are dye powders, derived from the distillation of coal. As these dyes are volatile, their color must be combined with shellac, and when dry, their fugitive color locked up with clear varnish. Many craftsmen, because of these factors, reject their use categorically.

My initial use of aniline powders occurred as a result of restoration. On an armoire, the still extant Venetian gold was bronzy, owing to the coating of old heavily browned shellac—dirty and thickly crusted. A segment when cleaned revealed a basic silver leaf. By mixing various anilines, I was able to achieve the original marvelous cruddy patina. When a dozen Louis XV *fauteuils* from the salon of Franz Josef were restored with burnished gold, the new leaf was so much lighter that it was glaringly obvious. In this instance, oil glazes destroyed the brilliant metallic quality, and a blend of aniline and shellac sparingly applied faintly browned the gold and made the restoration imperceptible. These experiences led to further experiments with useful results.

### ANILINE SOLUTIONS—PREPARATION

Aniline powders are powerful and one grain of powder left on the mixing table can unhappily permeate everything. They must be used sparingly and carefully. An eighth of a teaspoon of powder provides a pint of solution. The amount of powder, however, may be varied, depending on the density of hue that is needed. The powders used in the following mixtures are those soluble in denatured alcohol. Each powder is dissolved separately in alcohol —only then are the solutions combined to the desired color. Tests of the combination are made on wax paper, and only while the anilines are wet can the color be ascertained; the moment the test spot is dry, all that remains is ashen in hue. When the alcohol mixture reaches the desired color and is strained into a glass jar, 5-pound cut shellac, undiluted (white or orange, depending on the color), is added in equal quantity. The mixture is now ready for use. As the alcohol content evaporates each time the jar is opened, care should be taken to maintain the proper proportion.

Wax paper with a small amount of solution spooned out on it makes the most efficient palette. A container of denatured alcohol should be at hand to dilute the solution from time to time, as exposure causes it to coagulate to a shellacky gum. During application, the usual difficulties of overlapping shellac may be encountered.

## *ANILINE SOLUTIONS–PROCEDURE*
Methods of applying aniline color solution include the following:

The solution is applied with a slightly loaded shellac brush which has been previously brushed out on the palette.

The solution is pounced on with a lightly loaded shellac brush. This is constantly turned and back-tracked to avoid spottiness as it covers the leaf.

The solution is applied with a fine linen or cotton bob in a thin coating —the procedure identical with that used for shellac; or it is padded on with the back-tracking of the pounce method.

The solution is spattered and then lightly pounced. Each coverage is allowed to dry 15 minutes in order to avoid shellac gum build-ups. A finger cot is desirable for personal protection when spattering. This method gradually builds a heavy crusty antique surface. After the series of color spatters has dried, a very light fine spatter of denatured alcohol followed immediately by one, or at most two, firm bangs with a short handled pounce brush will lift the aniline here and there to reveal brilliant glints of leaf creating the illusion of ancient burnished gold. This effect may also be achieved by pouncing a short stiff brush, dipped in denatured alcohol, on a cloth placed over the dry aniline surface. The cloth is removed and the surface pounced again with a dry brush to break through to the gold.

On carved surfaces coated with aniline solution, the tops and edges may be tipped off with a brush, or silk that has been dipped in denatured alcohol. If a very heavy aniline coats the carved surface, it is partially pounced off with alcohol, or heavily spattered with alcohol and blotted with a brush. Shellac rings on an intricate surface are eliminated with the pounce brush. The leaf is tinted and heavy deposits remain in the interstices. When this is waxed and dusted with rottenstone, the resulting patina is very fine.

Should an accident occur—an oversized spatter, a drop from the brush or fingerguard—it is safest to let the error become semi-dry before gently pouncing out the offensive gummy edges which form. At times an alcohol-dipped cotton bud is helpful in shading out an error. Cotton adhering to shellac is a danger, so extra care is urged.

A soft antique effect results from thinning the solution with 50% additional denatured alcohol and toning the surface with a series of large, irregular, thin spatters. These are not pounced, and there must be drying intervals between spatters as the dissolving action of so much alcohol can create unattractive rings on a semi-dry coating.

### ANILINE FORMULAS

The formulas which follow may vary in quantity of powder and choice of white or orange shellac since the dry aniline powders are seldom stable in color. Every opportunity to study true antique leaf should be taken before attempting to recreate them with aniline medium.

> BLACK ANILINE    Nigrozine black
>                           Orange shellac

Nigrozine black dissolves slowly, and in the studio it is well to keep some in denatured alcohol solution available for mixing. A half pint of this liquid is combined with the same amount of orange shellac (5-pound cut) to make a black aniline solution. This used heavily on aluminum and silver gives the effect of corroded silver. When a much-diluted nigrozine black is combined with white shellac and used lightly over the leaf, it produces a soft eighteenth-century luster.

> ANTIQUE ANILINE    Dark golden oak
>         COOL        Nigrozine black
>                           Orange shellac

This solution and the one following are primarily for browning gold. They may either be used under japan antiquing fluid instead of orange shellac to produce a heavier patina, or be spattered over japan antiquing fluid to create another layer of depth. The cool aniline is becoming to gold, silver, and aluminum, to which it adds a pale glow. For this purpose it is sometimes further neutralized with additional black aniline.

> ANTIQUE ANILINE    Dark golden oak
>         WARM       Nigrozine black
>                           Mahogany medium
>                           Orange shellac

This solution, which browns the leaf, is only recommended on gold or Dutch metal.

### ANILINE FORMULAS FOR ALUMINUM AND SILVER

The following formulas are used only on silver and aluminum leaf, transforming them to shades of gold. They were frequently employed in the eighteenth century to produce what were termed *ors variés*. Although they indeed do create the illusion of gold, part of their charm for the discerning eye lies in the hint of silver here and there.

| | |
|---|---|
| FRENCH SILVER GILT | Yellow maple |
| | Dark golden oak |
| | White shellac |
| | |
| FRENCH SILVER GILT ANTIQUE | Yellow maple |
| | Dark golden oak |
| | Nigrozine black |
| | White shellac |

Vermeil—meaning "metals yellowed by lacquer"—is simulated with French Silver Gilt aniline, which magically turns silver to a brilliant lemon gold. The deep bronze of seventeenth-century Venetian gold is achieved with the aniline solution bearing its name.

| | |
|---|---|
| VENETIAN GOLD | Yellow maple |
| | Mahogany medium |
| | Orange shellac |

French Silver Gilt is neutralized and further deepened by the addition of French Silver Gilt Antique. Warm Antique aniline solution does the same for Venetian Gold.

All aniline applications are blended with ooo steel wool. Then they are protected with thinned clear varnish, which for the most part prevents the color from disappearing into thin air. The pieces are finally rubbed down and waxed.


# DECORATIVE ELEMENTS USED WITH LEAF

Decoration on a leafed background may be rendered with japan colors, a medium employed on many of the Oriental decorative papers. The design is preferably one of fantasy. It should be initially rendered in a light value of the hue chosen; then shaded with a thin transparency of a medium value, either in the same hue or in an analogous one; and finally accented with fine brushwork in a very dark value.

Another means of elaboration, often seen on Oriental lacquer, consists of fine brush lines, used to render detail and fantasy. India ink is suitable for this work. Should it crawl upon the metallic surface, a few drops of Non-crawl, available in art stores, can be added to the ink. A rottenstone, or a thin emulsion of non-detergent soap and water, rubbed over the surface before inking serves the same purpose. The surface to which color decoration or ink design is added is antiqued before the application of the design.

In a reversal of the ornamentation described above, gold leaf is laid over a fine black lacquer surface. A design is immediately traced on the gold, and the black is etched through with a stylus.

A low relief pattern is possible for a surface that is to be mat gilded. A design is traced on the bole surface and painted in with polyethylene glue. Sand is sprinkled over it. When the glue is dry, any surplus sand is brushed off. If the design is not sufficiently coated, more glue is brushed on and the process repeated. When dry, the whole is sized and leafed. The result is a low textural relief. Another low relief of this type is made with a mixture of damar varnish, kaolin powder and yellow ochre powder pigment. This must be shellacked before the sizing and leafing.

A gilded object is successfully brought to its most pleasing appearance as a result of many small steps, each one of which is executed carefully and skillfully with a governing desire for perfection. Patience is essential throughout the processes. Any desire to rush impulsively through the steps described will result in a travesty of the eighteenth-century ideal. Drying periods must be faithfully observed; the processes of toning and antiquing must be gradual. If these rules are observed, the reward is great. An object of beauty will have been wrought which will give pleasure to all who behold it. Moreover, having mastered these techniques, one can translate them into an individual and contemporary expression.

## ANTIQUE PATINA FOR LEAF

*Materials*

000 steel wool
Dry powders
  raw umber
  burnt sienna
  raw sienna
  French yellow ochre
  Turkey red
  rottenstone
  black
Flat white paint
600 wet-or-dry paper
Asphaltum
Mineral spirits

Turpentine
Mat varnish with high wax content
Wax with high turpentine content
Carnauba wax
Copper nitrate
Ammonium chloride
Dragon's blood
Japan colors
  earth colors
  lampblack
Orange and white shellac (5-pound cut)

Alcohol solvent
French varnish
Aniline powders
   nigrozine black
   dark golden oak
   mahogany medium
   yellow maple
Casein colors
   raw umber
   French yellow ochre
   lemon yellow
   white
Clear gloss varnish
Oil colors
   raw umber
   burnt umber
   raw sienna
   burnt sienna
   alizarin crimson
   thalo green
Fresco powders

*Tools*
Shellac brush
Oxhair brush
1″ stiff-bristle brush
Pounce brush
Spatter brush
Stencil brush
Stylus

*Miscellaneous*
Wax paper
Newspaper
Sodium sulfide crystals
Potassium sulfate
Picric acid
Spoon
Wooden block
Japan drier
Turkish toweling
Burlap
Cheesecloth
Absorbent cotton
Roller
Cotton buds
Jet or insect sprayer
Non-detergent soap flakes
Beer
Mortar and pestle
Pastel fixative
Distilled water
Glass jars
Fine cotton or linen bobs
Finger guard
India ink
Non-crawl
Polyethylene glue
Sand
Damar varnish
Kaolin powder

# BURNISHING

## APPEARANCE OF BURNISHED GOLD

The Italian verb *brunire*, "to make glossy," is the source of our verb "to burnish." This word is used to describe the polishing of gold and silver leaf with a tool. Precious leaf which is to be burnished is applied on a gesso ground with the technique known as water gilding, and before the burnishing it is frosty and light in color. After the burnishing, the gold has greater brilliance and its tonal value is deeper and browner than that of mat gold; in these respects the leaf has become similar in appearance to polished ore. Because of its delicacy, true leaf adapts to every irregularity of the surface. Accordingly, a mirror gleam is achieved by burnishing gold upon a bed of glassy smoothness. If the surface is rough and craggy, the gleam is broken up into multiple reflections, and as a result the leaf is pale and dull. However, a slight undulation of the surface melded by the burnisher increases the planes of reflection, creating more angles to catch the light, and in so doing, emphasizes the gold's mirror-like quality and brilliance.

## GESSO

Gilding over gesso originated in Italy. It was later brought to France, and eventually to England. Gesso is a combination of gilder's whiting and an aqueous binder, glue. Many thin coats of gesso form the smooth resilient ground for burnished leaf. Good gesso is not chalky, but has an eggshell gloss as hard as ivory. It is without imperfections, pinholes, or foreign matter. Whiting is an inert pigment, a calcium carbonate which occurs as a form of soft white rock built up from the remains of a sea organism. This natural chalk is crushed and ground in water. The second grade in fineness of the particles is gilder's whiting. The glue used with it is made of animal cartilage and skin. These are soaked in water, then boiled in fresh water; the solution is strained, set to jell, and subsequently sliced and dried.

## GESSO—PREPARATION

### *RABBIT-SKIN GLUE SIZE*

A surface to be prepared for gesso must be an absolutely clean one, with all irregularities filled and sanded. A sizing solution of thin glue is applied to this surface to provide tooth for the following coats of gesso. The size must be able to move with these coats. Accordingly, it must not contain so much glue in proportion to water that its shrinkage will not correspond with the shrinkage of the gesso coats, otherwise they will contract and separate from the support.

The right size to use contains rabbit-skin glue, which comes in granules or sheets. The sheets weigh approximately 2 ounces; for use, they should be placed in toweling and crushed with a hammer. Standard Size is prepared from the granules as follows:

> STANDARD SIZE    Scant ⅓ cup rabbit-skin glue granules
> 14 ounces water

The granules are soaked overnight in a can containing the water. The next day the can is placed in hot water over heat until the contents dissolve. From Standard Size, a thin size solution is made.

> THIN SIZE SOLUTION    1 ounce Standard Size
> 1 quart boiling water

(Any portion of these sizes not immediately required may be reserved in a screw-top jar and refrigerated. Because of the animal matter, size molds unless kept cold.) The Thin Size Solution is applied as a bonding coat to the surface, which, after overnight drying, is ready for the application of gesso.

## TRADITIONAL GESSO

The recipes for traditional gesso are complex and delicately balanced—any variation in the properties of the materials is sufficient to mar success. For anyone requiring a traditional gesso formula, the one described in *The Practice of Tempera Painting*, by Daniel V. Thompson, Jr., is recommended. In the studio the formulas mentioned so far have proved to be hazardous and too complex. An easier formula, one quite satisfactory for beginners, is presented below.

## O'NEIL STUDIO GESSO

| GESSO MIXTURE | 2 ounces polyethylene glue |
| | 2 ounces distilled water |
| | 5 ounces gilder's whiting |
| | 4 ounces kaolin powder |

The glue is combined with the water. Into this is sifted the gilder's whiting, which has been combined with the kaolin powder. This mixture is stirred with a stiff-bristle brush, or sash tool, slowly and gently moved around the sides and bottom of the container in order to avoid forming air bubbles. The gesso is strained through nylon hose held by a rubber band on a wide-mouthed screw-top jar, the brush being used to push it through gently. After straining, the brush is rinsed and used to stir the gesso once more. If there are bubbles, the gesso mixture is allowed to stand for an hour until they have subsided. A few drops of grain alcohol speed this process.

Cold gesso such as this need not be refrigerated; it keeps for many months. Should a surface crust form, the gesso must be strained anew. Should it thicken so that application is clumsy, it can be diluted with water. So long as the glue-whiting ratio is maintained, the formula works.

Many thin coatings are preferable to a few heavy coatings whose top surface hardens before the under part and thus produces cracks. To insure thinness, water is added to the gesso for each successive coat after the first coat. The importance of thinning should not be underestimated. Since water evaporates as gesso stands, the proportion of glue naturally tends to increase; and if gesso with a concentration of glue is applied over a coat having less glue content, crazing results.

Gesso is applied in a room where the temperature is moderate so that drying will be even. If the temperature were low, the materials would be difficult to work with, and the gesso slow to dry. Direct heat, sun, drafts, and a fan must be avoided, as any of these makes the drying uneven.

All brushes used for gesso must be reserved for water-soluble materials only.

## GESSO—PROCEDURE

### INTELAGGIO

After the coat of Thin Size Solution dries overnight on the surface, the *intelaggio* is applied. The *intelaggio* is a piece of old linen or damask (not so worn as to have lost its strength) which is used to conceal joints or to even a surface. For joints, the fabric is cut in strips of suitable size. For flat areas, it is cut to be just short of the periphery. The pieces are soaked in the thin glue size solution, then are pressed down over the joints or surface, with the fiber of the fabric aligned with the grain of the wood. The fabric is smoothed out with the finger from the center to the edges. It must dry

for at least 48 hours. If there are nailheads which cannot be countersunk they are covered with metal foil before the *intelaggio* is placed; this prevents them from rusting through.

### APPLICATION OF GESSO

Gesso is applied with a stiff-bristle brush that has been wet and wrung out between the fingers. The brush is fully loaded. Application is rapid, the gesso lightly stroked on—first in one direction and then at a right angle. Any drips, laps, or roll-overs are smoothed out with moistened brush, cloth, or finger.

Each coat of gesso is applied at right angles to the preceding one as soon as it has just dried mat. Gesso when first brushed on is naturally shiny with wetness. As it begins to set, the surface dulls. It is at this point that the next coat goes on. At the very least, five coats are necessary as a cushion for burnishing. The smoothness and evenness of application determine the number of coats. If a greater thickness is needed for an incised design, a "tap" coat expedites progress. It is made in the following way.

## *TAP COAT*

The surface is tapped with a full brush, held perpendicularly, which begins at the near edge and pushes out to the far edge, always advancing. This

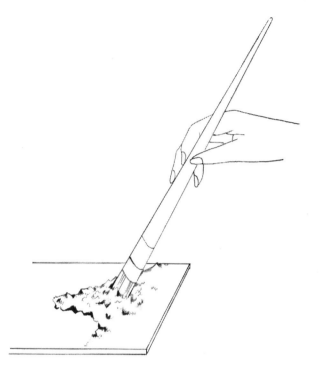

creates a thick stipple which is filled by the second coat—a full coverage flowed on rather than tapped on. The succeeding coats of gesso are thinned to avoid cracking and chipping. An alternative to the tap coat is a sponged-on coat, the sponge used in the same way as the brush to accelerate building. Eighteenth-century apprentices applied no fewer than forty coats to a surface.

## *APPLICATION ON CARVED PIECES*

On carved pieces, the gesso coats are thinly applied so that the indentations and recesses are not filled. A thick coat would blur the detail; moreover, too heavy a deposit in the interstices would dry on top, only to crack as the depths dried out. If the interstices inadvertently become filled, a gouge is used to work out the excess; as these depths cannot be burnished in any case, smoothness is not essential. The tops of the carved ornaments receive an extra build-up of gesso. As the edges of the build-up dry, they are smoothed out and around with a wet brush. First the top is brushed over.

Then the brush is squeezed out, and the process is repeated. Excess water can be taken up with the brush, and the tops smoothed over with the hand.

### POLISH OF GESSO

The object is now ready to be sanded and polished. In some of the early studios a 2- to 3-inch piece of glass was used in a crisscross motion to scrape flat surfaces. Italian artisans often used a cuttlefish bone (*ossa di seppia*) on its layered side for smoothing. In the studio we have found a piece of cork covered with wet cheesecloth an excellent first smoothing implement. It is moved in a circular motion over the surface, rubbing lightly to avoid removing too much at first, particular attention being given to corners and edges. The final sanding is done with silicon carbide paper 220A twisted into a cone for hard-to-reach curves and hollows. It is necessary to tilt the piece in diverse angles in order to search out the light reflections indicating flaws in the polished surface. A fine powdering of charcoal rubbed over a gessoed surface lingers in any indentation; this, too, shows where additional pressure is needed. After the final sanding, a lightly dampened piece of China silk is good for polishing the surface; it is wrapped around the index finger to smooth the rounded portions of carving. To produce a porcelain-like surface, a dry piece of China silk is used as a final polisher.

The gesso is now cleaned with cotton which has been dampened in a solution consisting of 4 parts grain alcohol and 1 part distilled water. The object is now ready for additional sizing.

# TYPES OF SIZE AND ORDER OF APPLICATION TO GESSO

To size—when the gilder uses this expression—means to provide a seat for the leaf; in the case of burnished leaf a cushion resilient enough to give a little under the burnisher. This polishing implement must move easily and smoothly over the gold to produce a brilliant luster.

*The cushion began with the gesso. To this must be added various other sizes: bole and commercial quick size for any areas to be rendered with mat leaf; bole, glue size, and mordant for the object, or any part of it, to be embellished with burnished leaf.*

Just as traditional recipes for gesso were jealously guarded, so were recipes for bole, glue size, and mordant (literally "something that bites," and by analogy something that catches hold of the gold). Along with burnishing tools, these recipes constituted the chief inheritance of each generation of gilders.

## BOLE—DESCRIPTION

The first size applied to the gesso is the gilder's clay size called "bole," a word derived from the Greek *bolos*, meaning clod or lump. Bole is a soft, unctuous type of clay containing iron oxide; it is found in deposits throughout Europe, in colors that range from light pink to deep purple-red and include yellow ochre and gray. It is fat and soapy, smooth as wax, and capable of receiving a high polish. During the Renaissance, there was a preference for Armenian bole, which was available in dry lumps almost orange in color (as it is today) and having a transparent quality. The craftsman ground his own bole and prepared it in a paste. Today bole is sold in an opaque paste—slightly purple-red, ochre, or gray. These hues may be further modified by the addition of fine-grade pigment.

## EFFECTS OF YELLOW BOLE AND RED BOLE

Some gilders prefer to use yellow ochre bole under gold leaf because, thanks to its neutral color, any faults or holidays are less easily discerned. Red bole glows through the transparent gold, warming its color and adding a pleasant note to the leaf as it ages. Preferably, if the gessoed object is to be embellished with both mat and burnished gold, a thin coat of gesso tinted with yellow ochre clay bole is applied to all areas. As an alternative, two coats of yellow ochre clay bole, made to the recipe given immediately below, may be substituted. A gradual color transition is thus made from the white of the gesso to the yellow ochre and then to the red clay bole.

## BOLE—PREPARATION

Every master gilder has his own recipe for bole and his own procedure for the whole process of water gilding. Each gilder would, of course, insist that his own method was the best. After experimentation, the craftsman may wish to vary the following methods. The following instructions for bole are like the rules of a Cordon Bleu chef—without exact measurements. They have never yet failed, but the proportions indicated below serve only as a guide.

BOLE RECIPE     Approximately 4 volumes of Standard Size are warmed and set aside. Then approximately 3 volumes of warm distilled water are stirred into 4 volumes of commercial paste clay size (bole) until the mixture reaches the consistency of light cream and flows freely. Next, a portion of the warm glue stock is added in small amounts until the mixture stiffens like whipped cream and stands in a peak. The remaining glue stock is then added freely until the mixture returns to the light-cream state. (This method is precisely the one for making mayonnaise, in which case oil is added drop by drop till the emulsion stands, whereupon it is thinned with additional oil. If the mixture does not reach the intermediary point of stiffness, neither proper mayonnaise nor proper bole is finally achieved.)

For reassurance, the mixture may be tested on the thumb nail; if it dries without cracking and responds to burnishing with the agate, the ratio of glue is correct. As long as this ratio of glue to bole is maintained, the mixture can now be thinned with water; it should be thinned to the consistency of skimmed milk. The bole is now strained through nylon hose.

During application, bole should be kept warm—never hot—in a metal container placed in a pan of hot water. Intense heat would create pinholes. A fine brown camel hair brush with a nylon quill (#6) fitted into a long handle, previously wet and wiped out with the fingers, is the best applicator. The gessoed article is wiped with a damp linen cloth before the first coat of bole—dust motes, which would blemish the gilding, must be removed.

## BOLE–PROCEDURE

The brush is modestly loaded, then is wiped off on the back of the hand—not the edge of the can—to avoid air holes. With the flat of the brush, the bole is brushed thinly over the surface with as little pressure as possible;

the aim is a smooth coat free from drips or ridges. No effort is made to cover in a single coat. Any attempt to stroke out or rectify errors, to touch up holidays, or to move the bole in any way, results in disaster. Defects are to be disregarded as they can be remedied by the succeeding coat. Bole requires no more than 15 minutes for drying before the next coat is applied. On flat surfaces, the two coats of yellow ochre are succeeded by six to eight thin coats of red bole. On carvings, only four to five coats of red are needed, with one or two additional dollops on the high planes. In the depths of the carvings, the two coats of yellow ochre bole are enough; it is impossible to burnish there, and slight faults in the gilding will be less obvious over the yellow.

The effort throughout this preparation is for a coating as smooth and even as possible. When the last coat has dried, the bole is polished with a half-inch round stencil brush of pure white bristle. The bristles are held close with masking tape wrapped around them, leaving ¼ inch of bristle free. A rotary motion is used over the surface for a preliminary polishing of the bole. Now the surface is polished with burnishers reserved for this purpose only. An agate used as a bole polisher roughens to the point where it is not fit for polishing leaf; therefore, several agates are needed.

The bole is now ready for the additional sizes. If both burnished leaf and mat leaf are to be used on the object, the order of rendering them must be decided. For a beginner, it is perhaps easier first to complete the burnished leaf and lacquer it and then to apply the mat leaf. However, since the latter is a simpler process and has been described in detail in a previous chapter, it will be discussed next.

## MAT LEAF AREAS—FINAL PREPARATION AND PROCEDURE

Areas of the bole to be mat leafed are now coated with orange shellac. If the shellac appears to sink in, a second coat is applied, thus assuring an even surface. A small brush dipped in shellac is used to outline lightly the areas to be mat leafed; a larger brush is used to fill them in. The work must be free from drips or overlaps, which show through leaf and mar its beauty. Since shellac must not touch the parts to be burnished, a cotton bud or cloth is dipped in alcohol and run over such parts as a precaution. When the shellac is dry, the mat areas are coated with quick size, and this, too, is carefully kept away from the areas to be burnished. If a slip occurs, benzine will remove it.

After a very thin coating of the quick size has reached a dry tack, the mat leaf is laid and allowed to dry overnight. It may then be aged, if desired, with a very thin application of antique aniline solution. Whether the mat leaf is antiqued or not, a border ($\frac{1}{16}$″) of rubber cement thinned with its solvent serves to protect the even edge of the mat portion from the burnished leaf about to be laid. Later, when the burnished portion is complete, this cement border is easily removed.

## BURNISHED LEAF AREAS—FINAL PREPARATIONS AND PROCEDURE

The following three steps must be taken before precious leaf to be burnished is laid on the object.

### 1. GLUE SIZE
A coat of thin glue size is applied; it reduces the hazards encountered in the actual laying of the leaf. One volume Standard Size and 2 volumes water are combined. The mixture is warmed, as usual, over hot water; then two coats of it are brushed over the bole with a suitable drying interval. At last the object is ready for gilding.

### 2. WATER MORDANT
In water gilding, a water mordant is used to hold the leaf. It is prepared in this way: $\frac{1}{2}$ sheet of gelatin broken into bits (or 28 #1 gelatin capsules) is soaked in 2 ounces of water for $\frac{1}{2}$ hour. The mixture is heated over hot water until it melts, then is cooled in the refrigerator until it becomes a loose—not a firm—gelatin. One teaspoon of this is dissolved in 1 pint of warm distilled water to which 1 ounce of grain alcohol has been added. The mixture is refrigerated and is best used when ice cold.

### 3. PREPARATION OF TOOLS
Water gilding requires two special implements. The gilder's tip is prepared by wrapping masking tape around the bristles, about $\frac{3}{4}$″ above the end; this holds the hairs in place. A piece of plywood $\frac{1}{32}$″ thick may be glued to the cardboard holder to make it easier to grasp.

Camel brushes are used to make the gilder's pencil. These brushes are generally made with quill ferrules. Therefore, a ⅜" camel tamper can be slipped on the stem of a ½" round camel brush and can be fastened with wire or tape.

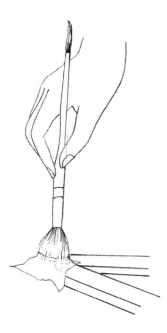

## PROCEDURE FOR LAYING LEAF

As the water gilding begins, it is well to be ambidextrous so that the mordant can be applied with the pencil in the left hand while the tip is held in the right. With the larger end of the pencil, an area slightly larger than the piece of leaf to be laid is flooded evenly with mordant from the top down. The leaf is already picked up on the gilder's tip and is held parallel to the surface. When the leaf is lowered directly over the flooded section, the mordant literally seizes the gold. The tip carrying the gold responds quickly to the magnetic wetness. An instant staccato movement, like one's instinctive reaction to being burned, is all that is required to deposit the gold. The movement is low and parallel. The tip is not raised until the gold is seized by the mordant, or the leaf will be broken. The tip must not touch the mordant, or the gold will cling to the bristles. Practice will perfect this seemingly difficult operation; in addition, the following details about procedure must be mastered.

It is essential that the mordant flow under the gold from top to bottom as this helps the wrinkles of the leaf to flatten out. There is a slight pause between the flooding of the surface and the laying of the gold. During this pause the glue size beneath the mordant becomes tacky and the mordant itself evaporates just enough not to drown or burn the gold.

After a few trials the gilder learns the correct pause. My students have found a count of 3 just right to insure the deposit of the leaf at the proper moment. If the delay is a little too long, warm breath blown on the surface will sometimes revive the tack. This condensation of breath is also used when small skips, or holidays, need covering. Gold is laid on flat areas evenly from left to right, and from top to bottom. The flats of carvings are covered first, the raised portions last. As each successive piece is laid, the edge of the one already laid is wet with the mordant so that the overlap adheres evenly and cleanly. These laps are sometimes faintly perceptible in the gold background of Italian thirteenth- and fourteenth-century paintings; they are also evident on Chinese and Japanese screens.

The alcohol in the mordant is included to speed the evaporation, but if it touches the top of the leaf, it burns the surface and spoils it for burnishing. Therefore, the tamping down of the leaf with the dry end of the gilder's pencil (done to insure total contact of the leaf with the boled surface) is delayed until the exact instant when the water mordant dries to tack. Students have found that a slow count of 6 is the correct interval between laying the gold and tamping it. (Twelfth- and thirteenth-century gilders used a rabbit's foot for a tamper.)

## SECOND APPLICATION OF LEAF

The gold leaf of the twelfth and thirteenth centuries was heavier than ours. The average weight of modern gold leaf is 0.20 troy grain, which is very thin. The leaf used for glass gilding has fewer pinholes and is a little more costly though of the same weight. Gold leaf is also available in a double weight, 0.40 troy grain. A double leafing of the thin weight is necessary to produce a fine surface. In addition to eliminating faults, it provides practice. It is possible at the first instant to lay double leaves or to fold over a leaf on the gilder's pad with a gilder's knife, and thus apply the double layer to the surface at the first instant. This achievement, however, is hazardous until experience develops skill to a sufficiently rapid speed to allow both layers to be floated simultaneously on the mordant.

Beginners are advised to use the two-stage process—releafing three to four hours after the first leafing. The second leafing must completely cover the surface, as any area touched by the mordant and not releafed fails, of course, to respond to burnishing. If the gold leaf does not adhere, there is a chance that glue size may have been totally washed away by the mordant. In such case, another coat of glue size is applied before the second leafing. A fault, called a "dry lay," is corrected after the double leafing. Small patches do not require much wetting. In fact, professional gilders often use a touch of saliva. The fault may be dampened by breathing upon it, or it may be moistened by a cotton bud dipped in the mordant, after which a skewing is deposited with the tip or a cotton bud.

When the gilder becomes expert and has learned to deposit the leaf at precisely the right moment, the two coats of glue size may be omitted as they will no longer be necessary.

After two hours of normal drying, the gilded surface is ready for burnishing. Any leaf applied as a corrective over a previously gilded surface may be burnished within an hour. The surface is ready when it responds to the tap of the burnisher with a clear click.

## BURNISHING THE LEAF

### AGATES—PREPARATION

In the thirteenth and fourteenth centuries, the burnishing tool was a hematite (an iron ore) or the tooth of a canine. Today a polished agate mounted on a long wooden handle is used. A tapered, rounded form is better for flat surfaces, a curved hook form for rounded moldings. Old

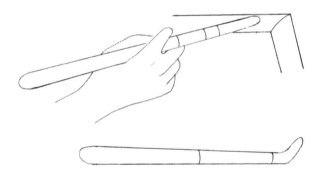

burnishers smoothed and polished by use are highly desirable but hard to come by. A new burnisher must be broken in by polishing it with a chamois or felt impregnated with a little linseed oil and rottenstone. New or old, the tool must always be warmed by friction with these materials before it is used.

### AGATES—PROCEDURE

The first burnishing proceeds cautiously over the surface with a gentle rotary motion and a little pressure. Any roughness or wetness will be discovered; these areas must be avoided until dry. The burnishing continues, now with a somewhat firmer pressure evenly stroked in *one* direction. Should the gold feel gritty and lift under the burnisher, warm breath on the area will condense to allow another piece to be laid. Such a patch is immediately burnished. With increased pressure and a change of direction, the burnisher is again worked over the surface. The operation is repeated at intervals with regular strokes, but each time in a different direction, until the surface is evenly polished. If the golden surface becomes too dry to burnish, it is covered with a dry cloth, over which a second cloth well wrung out but damp is placed.

A few days later, when the gesso and size are hard dry, a final burnishing brings up the brilliant gloss that is the reward of all the preceding care and travail. On carvings, only the high points and top surfaces are given this brilliant polish. The flat and recessed areas are generally left mat. This contrast emphasizes the gleam of the raised portions. If faults or dry laps appear at this late stage, they are corrected by releafing, and then the final polishing is resumed.

# ANTIQUING BURNISHED LEAF

A burnished surface of either gold leaf or palladium can be left just as it is—neither of these metals will tarnish. However if an antique tone is desired, either one may be tinted with any of the aniline solutions. If other solutions are used, the leaf is first protected with a mixture of 2 volumes of clear metal lacquer diluted with 1 volume of lacquer thinner—this dries in 15 minutes. Silver, lemon gold, and pale gold must have a coating of lacquer or French varnish to prevent them from tarnishing.

# LEAFED SURFACES—DECORATION

### PASTIGLIA

*Pastiglia*, a low relief of arabesques, scrolls, diapers and other geometrics executed in gesso, was used by the Venetians to embellish the expansive surfaces of *cassoni, credenze*, and screens. At its inception this decoration was intended as a replacement for wood carvings, which were considerably more costly. Like certain other conceits of this craft, it soon attained its own status as an extension of the artist's virtuosity, with less regard for similitude of the original intent than as an expression of artistry. As imitation of wood carving ceased to be a function of *pastiglia*, it sometimes deteriorated and was rendered quite crudely. The degree of refinement was dependent on the desire of the craftsman and was influenced as well by the scale of the piece. For the most part *pastiglia* was finished with a metallic surface on either a leafed, a lacquered, or a delicately tinted gesso ground. The latter ground is prepared to completion in gesso. Priming coats of thinned shellac are applied on the back of such a panel to equalize the tension on both faces.

## GILDED PASTIGLIA ON TINTED GESSO

If color is desired as a background, the thin glue size solution is first coated over the gesso. Then the color coat is prepared. One volume of fine artist's pigment (finely ground with a mortar and pestle) is mixed with 1 volume of hot distilled water to a cream consistency and allowed to cool. Two volumes of the pigment cream are then combined with ½ to 1 volume of polyethylene glue. This is strained and applied thinly to the surface in four or five coatings. These color coats are applied with a well-loaded stiff bristle brush (first wet and wrung out). The stroke goes in one direction only, avoiding rebrushing or lapping. To create a smoother surface, the brush is cleaned after every stroke. The surface may be further smoothed with a wet finger. Each coat dries for one hour, then is sanded with 220A silicon carbide paper. The final coat is sanded with 280 garnet paper that has its grit cut. To cut grit, two pieces of 280 garnet paper are rubbed together.

The next step is to transfer the projected design to the surface. When this has been done, the design is coated with the thin glue size solution and then painted in with two thin coats of gesso. On each segment of the design, a center line of gesso is built up, with a sable brush, to the desired height of the relief. The right angles on either side of this center line are filled out with gesso, which slopes to the periphery of the design in a convex curve. Modeling of elements within the form may be indicated by extra building. The form is shaped and modeled constantly as the filling proceeds. The completed relief is higher than desired to allow a margin for tooling, carving, and refining. Discarded dental tools with their ends beveled to a rounded point, a ⅛-inch carving chisel, and orangewood sticks provide an adequate assortment of instruments. A light moistening of the gesso, followed by partial drying, facilitates the carving. The relief is ready for the bole size.

## GILDED PASTIGLIA ON LACQUER

Should a raised gesso design be desired on a lacquer ground, the tinted varnish coats (see chapter on lacquer) are built up short of the final two varnishing coats (these final coats, of *clear* gloss varnish, will be applied after the raised design is completed). The design for the gesso relief is transferred to the surface; is abraded with 280 garnet paper; and then is coated with the thinned glue size solution before the gesso is applied.

When the gesso design has been completed, leafing and burnishing follow, and lastly tinting and antiquing.

## ORIENTAL RELIEF ON LACQUER

Gesso relief done by English and French craftsmen was lower than that of the Venetians. The Orientals admired a high, almost sculptural relief. This is most beautiful when the dominant elements are in various tones of burnished silver and gold. Such a design when accompanied by areas of mat leaf, flitters, and decorative detail of fine gold lines was a tour de force of the Oriental craftsman. The Europeans evidenced their admiration through imitation. Despite their Oriental subject matter, the translation has a heavy western accent. The physiognomy of the pseudo-eastern people is delineated with the native features of the European craftsman who executed them. Without the delicate, detailed precision of the Eastern craftsman, the expression, ranging from sophistication to naiveté, from the elegant to the crudely grotesque, is charming and imaginative. This union of East and West was termed *chinoiserie*, an offspring which evolved its own character and was admired for its individuality, its airs, and its graces.

To render such a decoration on a lacquered ground, the raised elements are first outlined on the surface. These areas are then scratched and abraded to provide tooth for a coating of the thinned glue size solution. Following this, two covering coats of gesso are applied and, in the same way as for *pastiglia*, the form is built up—curving from the high center line to the flat surface. To increase the illusion of three-dimensional space, which is one of the charms of raised work, the remote elements are raised to a lesser degree than those nearer, which increase in relief until those in the foreground surmount all. Within the planes of each motif there is further differentiation: in the levels of the folds of a garment, the overlaps of leaves, or the projections of a rock. When the general levels are established, the detail of the design is painted on with a wash of red bole. Now that points of projection and form have been denoted, they are built up with heavier gesso, which should drop from the brush on any point to be brought forward. Carving and shaping of lower portions of the relief proceed along with the raising of the higher portions. When the figures or objects in relief have been raised sufficiently, they are refined with the tools, smoothed with silicon carbide paper 220A, and then brushed over with a wet sable brush. Now the work is ready for its coats of bole size.

# APPLICATION OF LEAF, FLITTERS, AND GILT LINING

The coats of bole size are applied carefully to avoid blurring the detail; these are followed by coats of glue size. The background is powdered with talc to prevent any gilt from adhering where it is not wanted. The gilding is rendered with water mordant and finally burnished. When the burnishing is brought to its full brilliance, a coat of gilding lacquer is applied to the completed areas, and the surrounding ground is carefully cleaned with a cotton bud dampened with witch hazel, or with an eraser stick or a little rottenstone. Antiquing and shading with burnt or raw umber oil colors further emphasize the form. Fine lines of India ink, added with a #3 sable brush, designate details and patterns that emphasize the planes of the raised work.

Now the mat areas are sealed with thinned shellac, and any of the gold alloys are laid on with quick size. The detail here may be rendered in India ink, or fine detail may be drawn with a stylus which scratches through the leaf to reveal the ground hue. If the tool is used immediately, one's breath provides the moisture for it to penetrate the leaf. Otherwise, the tool must be dipped in mineral spirits and used more cautiously. Mat leaf is best antiqued with one of the aniline solutions.

## *FLITTERS*

Flitters, charcoal, or gold powders may be applied to some parts of the design, most aptly to mountains, boulders, rocks, and clouds. Application of the powders and charcoal to sized areas is done with a velvet bob or finger from a palette of velvet. The flitters require a sieve. Stiff paper is rolled into a tube, 4″ long with a diameter of from ½″ to ¾″, and is pasted firmly. A fine mesh of cheesecloth, which acts as the sieve, is glued over one end. The

other end is cut off at a 45-degree angle. Into this tube the flitters, fragments of gold, are poured, and a gentle tapping sprinkles them through the meshed end onto the sized area. Any outlying scatterings are swept with a tamper to the top and sides of the sized areas, thus deepening the edges of the motif and emphasizing shadow and form. After the first application has dried, the area may be re-sized and additional flitters of silver or differing gold tones applied.

## GILT LINING

Final detail and line design in gold are added with a #3 sable brush dipped in the following mixture:

FINE-LINE MEDIUM — 1 volume gum arabic dissolved in 2 volumes hot water is combined with 1 volume gold bronze powder. To the mixture is added ¼ volume honey, which contributes to the elasticity of the medium. Water is used on the brush, but *sparingly* so that the gold is not made thin and weak. The line should flow freely, with variation in width further to emphasize form. This mixture builds up as it is applied, adding another dimension.

In the twelfth and thirteenth centuries, lining was done with real gold. The metal was ground with salt, which was then washed away. The resulting gold powder was mixed with water-soluble gum arabic (derivative of acacia bush) and honey. Gold leaf, too, was mixed with honey, and when dry was ground in a mortar and mixed with gum ammoniac; the product was termed "shell gold" since the craftsmen of that day stored it in mussel shells. Shell gold can be purchased today; however, the suggested formula is much less costly and gives the lining a light build-up that is very effective.

When the decoration on a lacquered ground is finally complete and has dried, two finishing coats of clear varnish are applied and rubbed down with rottenstone and lemon oil.

# INCISED DESIGN, COLOR, AND GOLD GRAFFITI

Another type of decoration involving burnished gold is that used by the artists of the thirteenth and fourteenth centuries on frescoes, panels, and triptychs: a combination of incised design, tooled decoration on burnished gold, and some painted surface through which burnished decorative motifs are revealed. The ground for this is built up to a depth which allows an

ANTIQUE PATINAS FOR LEAF: *Top left, Chinese bronze (Dutch metal and distemper); right, aluminum leaf with japan spatter. Bottom left, gold leaf with bole exposed; right, Italian, acid on silver.*

incised channel about 1/32″ deep. The procedure for the incised line has been described in the chapter on casein. Here, however, the channel is not beveled, rather is a straight-sided groove. After the design has been transferred and the channel put in, the surface is boled and polished, water-gilded and burnished. Some portions may be mat gold. On areas of burnished leaf to be painted, a protection of clear metal lacquer is applied, or a coating of a rabbit-skin glue solution (1 ounce glue stock to 1 pint water), called *imprimatura*, is flowed on. This sinks into the surface, filling it to some extent rather than creating a film.

A color coat for the burnished gold requires artist's fine pigment ground with a mortar and pestle. This is combined with oil paint of the same hue. One volume of oil paint is mixed with 1 volume of turpentine to a smooth consistency. It is always easiest to thin oil paint by adding the turpentine little by little. When this has been mixed, 1 volume of artist's fine pigment is stirred in.

If the color is to be painted over lacquered burnished gold, the gold is first washed with non-detergent soap flakes and water; this will prevent the color from crawling. When the color coat has surface-dried, the burnished gold is "pulled through" in a graffiti design with a stylus. Larger decorative motifs, or an over-all design, may be traced on the color, and the gold revealed by working the design through the paint with a #1 stylus.

## TOOLED DESIGN

In the fourteenth century, the artist emphasized the brilliance of burnished gold by tooling it with steel or bronze punches with smooth points in a decorative series of rings or other small forms. Today a common 20D nail may be shaped to a point or chisel-end with fine files and an oiled sharpening stone (carborundum stone). These, tapestry needles, chasing and matting tools, dapping punches and burs—the last four used by silversmiths —are excellent instruments. They are impressed on the burnished gold with a wooden mallet or chasing hammer.

The hammer strikes the tool, tapping quickly and evenly across the surface in a pattern (see drawing on next page). Punching produces many small areas that reflect the light. The glow of unbroken gold is changed into a

BURNISHING: *Top left, burnished-gold graffiti; right, tooled burnished gold. Bottom left, raised burnished design and mat leaf; right, pastiglia.*

sparkle as minute brown depths contrast with the brilliance of the lighter burnished areas.

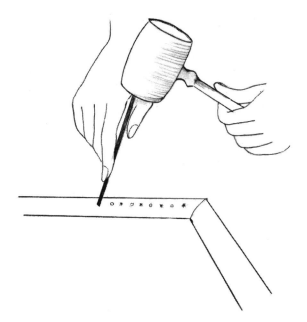

The techniques described in this chapter are exacting, time-consuming, and complex. The satisfaction, however, that will be derived from exquisite technique is commensurate with the discipline demanded. The beauty of the object thus rendered outwits the ravages of time.

## BURNISHING

*Materials*

Precious leaf (silver, deep gold, pale gold, lemon gold, white gold, palladium)
Gilder's whiting
Distilled water
Rabbit-skin glue (granules or sheets)
Polyethylene glue
Kaolin powder

Old linen or damask (for *intelaggio*)
Charcoal powder
Bronze powder
Yellow ochre clay bole (commercial paste clay size)
Red clay bole (commercial paste clay size)
Orange shellac
Grain alcohol

Benzine
Witch hazel
Alcohol solvent
Linseed oil
Rottenstone
Fine artist's pigment
Oil paints
India ink
Gum arabic
Honey
Clear gloss varnish
Isinglass
Gelatin (sheets or #1 capsules)
Clear metal lacquer
Lacquer thinner

$\frac{1}{8}$" carving chisel
#1 stylus
220A silicon carbide paper
280 garnet paper
Mortar and pestle
Chasing hammer
Chasing tools
20D nails
Files
Carborundum
Dapping punches
Matting tools
Burs
Tapestry needles

*Tools*
Several agate burnishers
Stiff-bristle brush
Sash brush
Natural sponge
$\frac{1}{2}$" round stencil brush with white bristles
Small gouging tool
#3 and #6 sable brushes
Shellac brushes
Gilder's pencil (1"–$\frac{1}{2}$" round camel-hair brush with wooden handle and nylon-quill-ended $\frac{3}{8}$" camel-hair tamper attached to stem end)
Klinker (gilder's pad)
Gilder's knife
Gilder's tip
Dental tools
Orangewood sticks

*Miscellaneous*
Cotton buds
Screw-top jars
Cork
Cheesecloth
Nylon hose
China silk
Rubber cement
Rubber cement thinner
Masking tape
Velvet
Tin cans
Scissors
Plywood strip
Metal foil
Chamois
Felt
Transfer paper
Talc
**Non-detergent soap flakes**

# PART IV

# *The Great Impersonators: Faux Finishes*

# INTRODUCTION

The use of paint to simulate marble, semi-precious stones, and exotic woods goes back as far as the ancient Egyptians and Chinese. When rendered by craftsmen in ages past, painted imitations became a stylized and decorative fantasy of the real. Human artistry surpassed nature in uninhibited flights of fancy. Today we call these "fantasies," or *"faux* (the French adjective for false) finishes." Fantasy finishes differentiate human artifice from nature's creations. The painted device is an exaggeration, an idealization, yet a symbol of the real.

The fantasies transplanted from the East found a favorable climate in Italy, whence they flowered all over Europe. In the sixteenth century after Vasco da Gama rounded the Cape of Good Hope, Venetian trade declined. The merchants cleared the goods from the first floors of their palazzi, invested their wealth in banking and real estate, and found themselves at leisure. In the surrounding countryside, they proceeded to build villas, furnishing them lavishly and decorating walls and ceilings with frescoes, just as they had done in their palaces in Venice. To make rooms seem more spacious and to enrich the architectural detail in the great villas built by Palladio and his followers, *trompe l'oeil* was used. With equal wit, the Venetians employed the virtuosity of the artist's atelier to embellish the furnishings of their homes. The theatricality of the Venetians demanded a whole series of fantasies—a play with paint to imitate porphyry, marble, tortoise shell, lapis lazuli, malachite, and exotic woods. Skilled artisans reproduced these materials with such ebullient fancy that their painted renderings had a charm often valued as much or more than that of natural materials. Individuality increased this charm. There was a spontaneity and imagination expressed in the manner of a virile sketch. The simpler Italian furniture had an innocent liveliness, as did the work of the provincial French of this period. Such fantasies were not too perfect, too rich, too royal, to awake widespread human response.

Italy's fine artists had first employed these fantasies, using them to create illusionistic architectural elements in painting. Then the artisans took over the idea, and used it to great effect. The columns of *faux* porphyry in the Pitti Palace in Florence, the architectural details of *faux marbre* in the Borghese Palace in Rome, in Fontainebleau, and Versailles, to enumerate only a few, are outstanding examples.

Luigi Barzini states with astute perception in *The Italians*:

> Inevitably Italians are tempted to applaud more
> those performances which stray dangerously
> farthest from reality, those which make
> do with the scantiest of materials, those
> which do not even pretend to imitate existing
> models and still manage to be effective,
> convincing, stirring or entertaining. Take
> imitation marble. Since the earliest days
> local craftsmen have been unique in their
> ability to counterfeit the real thing. Half
> the marble one sees in churches or patrician
> *palazzi* is in fact but smooth plaster deceptively
> painted. It is not necessarily always cheaper
> than the real thing: at times it can be infinitely
> more expensive and inconvenient. Of all the
> imitation marbles, Italians appreciate more those
> which really imitate nothing at all, but create
> a combination of colours which never existed
> in nature. What is specially prized is the daring
> of their makers, their Promethean challenge to God.

Painted fantasies were so esteemed that there was rivalry concerning their origin. The French contended that the exorbitant cost of importing the natural semi-precious material from the Venetians had aroused their parsimony and that they therefore had originated the painted fantasies. The Italians, on the other hand, maintained that the inferior materials they were forced to use—a result of their impoverished condition in the eighteenth century—had forced them to inventiveness when luxurious and elaborate furnishings were in demand and that, in fact, they had been the originators.

From Europe the techniques went forth to America, where they were translated with naiveté on furnishings and walls of modest country houses but with some awareness and sophistication on the furnishings and paneling of colonial mansions. By the nineteenth century these arts declined; they became a travesty of ideals, by now remote as the graining and marbleizing became increasingly crude. Ludicrous reminiscences have since turned up in apartment lobbies, on woodwork, and even to this day on elevator interiors.

Faux finishes fall into two categories: the naive and the sophisticated. The naive and free rendering of the fantasies appeared most often on country pieces and in *boiseries* executed by the itinerant artisan or the home craftsman; such works are therefore termed provincial. Characteristics of this type are an exaggerated scale and a reiteration of the design form executed with spontaneity and vigor. On the other hand, the sophisticated fantasies were exercises conceived with wit and executed with style and subtle minutiae; they may be termed *trompe l'oeil*. Here the finished effect is an embellished and fanciful creation that outstrips reality.

Both expressions should create a question in the beholder's mind, a question so unanswerable that he must touch the object to ascertain whether or not it is what it professes to be. Both expressions share creative merit and today give us more delight than the natural materials they parrot. An astonishing reality with an additional imaginative fillip is requisite for these painted simulations. They are meant to delight the beholder at once with their similarity and their departure from the real. These are *fantasy finishes*.

The motive behind the rendering is to express fantasy in terms of design. Design organizes space, space is divided by form, and form is used to manifest rhythm—overlapping, continuous, or broken. This rhythm has a basic uniformity but at the same time is capable of infinite variations. The form creates balance or strain. Lines divide and relate. The total design is a complete interaction of these. The statement of the fantasy will be a transformation in the terms of paint, which cannot copy the physical properties of the model. The expression of fantasy should be an equivalent impression rather than a literal one.

# BAMBOO

## THE INFLUENCES OF BAMBOO ON EUROPEAN DESIGN

Bamboo, a delicate and decorative tree, had strong influences on European design from the seventeenth century onward. This chapter discusses several bamboo fantasy finishes, some of them invented long ago and some in recent decades.

The flourishing China trade brought home to Europeans the exotic creations of the Orient. Among these were articles constructed of bamboo. For centuries in the East, bamboo had been a most challenging subject for the painter and had been used for structural and decorative elements by the builder. At first the kings and princes of the West were the favored few who collected and enjoyed the phantasmagoria of the Orient. Toward the end of the seventeenth century, the courts took up the vogue, and in time it became fashionable for the *haut monde* not only to purchase these wares but also to attempt to emulate them. In the eighteenth century, Oriental goods were avidly sought by an ever-increasing public. Taking advantage of this demand, cabinetmakers carved and turned wood to resemble bamboo sections. Tables, chairs, beds—a galaxy of furniture—were supported and framed with imitation bamboo. In 1770, the factory of Robert Adam produced turned bamboo which was sometimes painted. The trend carried over to household accessories; both silver and the ceramics of Josiah Wedg-wood carried the bamboo motif. Later, under Queen Victoria, the fashion for bamboo was revived, but this time true bamboo was used, covered with gilt or crowded with a tortured burned design.

A delightful painted version of bamboo was popular in the eighteenth century; depending on the modulation of color, it was rendered in either a subtle or a vigorous style. Both styles are charming for mirror or picture frames, for moldings on doors and woodwork, for cabinets and commodes, and for chair frames and table legs. Just as bamboo was used long ago as a light relief in rooms of heavy mahogany furniture, it is still used happily today.

# DESCRIPTION OF NATURAL BAMBOO AND MALE AND FEMALE FANTASIES

Before a bamboo fantasy is created, natural bamboo must be studied. The innate decorative quality of the stalk makes it easy to perceive the elements that led an imaginative craftsman of long ago to conceive the fantasies of female and male bamboo.

Bamboo consists of sections, which at their place of joining have bands that are called knots. Beginning at these knots and extending vertically into each section are spines which are splits curving from the knot to a point. On either side of the knots are slightly ovoid circles—eyes—with darker dots in their center. All three of these features are exaggerated and stylized in painted female bamboo.

Circling the length of each section between the knots of natural bamboo are fine age lines at differing intervals; these, exaggerated and stylized, characterize the fantasy of male bamboo. The surprising variation of nature itself leads to innumerable inventions; color in painted bamboo, for in-stance, may be as unrelated to the natural as the imagination can conceive.

# FEMALE BAMBOO

### *PREPARATION*
Should these instructions be applied to wood-turned bamboo, in the round or in the form of moldings, the usual preparations for base coat painting and tufbacking should be followed. If, however, the object is made of natural bamboo, it is washed well with alcohol to remove the oil from its surface,

and is then given a coat of thinned shellac before the flat paint is applied. Either a color scheme of great contrast or a muted scheme of closely related hues may be used for female bamboo. If the rendering is to be on a light background, two additional colors are necessary: a dark contrast for the knots, spines, and dots; a vivid hue in a medium value for the eyes. For a dark ground, one light contrasting hue for rendering knots, spines, and eyes suffices. In this case, the dots in the eyes may be rendered in the background hue. An especially delightful effect is created when the eyes on female bamboo are rendered in gold or silver leaf.

After it has been tufbacked with 400 wet-or-dry paper and a soapy solution, the base hue is protected with a coat of thinned shellac. It is now ready for decoration.

### PROCEDURE

The knots or rings between the sections of bamboo are painted first, with a #3 sable brush pressed to its widest. The painted stripe extends $\frac{1}{16}''$ beyond the ring, going up over the lips of the turned sections. The spines are rendered in the same color. They are dispersed irregularly around the knot—two to three being used if the bamboo is in the round. The spines, attractively scaled in relation to the section, extend in varying lengths, but never measure more than one-third of the total section. Each spine begins as two lines $\frac{1}{4}''$ apart; these curve from the knot to a point about $\frac{3}{4}''$ beyond it; then they merge into a single line and taper to the fineness of a hair. The curved triangular-like area at the beginning of the spine may be filled in or left open. Eyes singly or in twos are plotted with a piece of chalk at

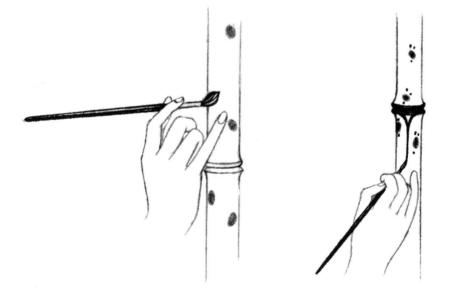

irregular intervals throughout each section; acting as a rhythmic continuation of the pattern, they are so placed that they relate to the spines but are never contiguous. The eyes, somewhat rounded but slightly oval, are applied with a #6 sable brush loaded fully, pressed directly down on its point, and then lifted away. It is important to scale them so that the decorative accent of intense color is striking. Female bamboo is most lively when the spacing of spines and eyes varies and is not repetitive. After the paint has dried, the dark dots in the color of the knots and spines are placed slightly off-center in the eye with a #3 sable brush. Two, three, or more dots—irregular in size, unaligned, and varied in spacing—are clustered in a haphazard manner around each eye. These secondary dots direct the rhythmic pattern throughout the length of the section. The paint dries overnight; a binder of mat varnish with a high wax content is brushed on and allowed to dry for 24 hours before the antiquing. Either japan antiquing medium, or dry powder and wax, is stroked on with a dry brush, forming a slight, interrupted striation that further accentuates the grain of the wood. The striation extends lengthwise along a section, but stops ½″ short of the

knot at either end, thus avoiding the heavy deposits which would occur if the stroke passed over the knots. Alternatively, the antiquing may be pounced on. It should be noted that both of these antiquing methods call for the medium to be pounced or spattered at the knots of turned bamboo. The antiquing is lightly blended with ooo steel wool and 220 garnet paper.

Then medium-sized drops of spattering fluid are sparsely sprayed around each knot. The spattered area extends about 1½″ away from the knot, thus leaving the center area only lightly covered. After a drying period of a week, the bamboo is coated with a protective mat varnish and is waxed and polished.

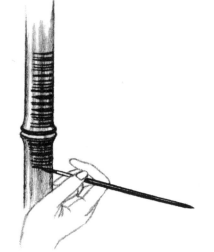

## MALE BAMBOO

### *PREPARATION*

If male bamboo is rendered in hues of strong contrast in value and color, it has a vivid, contemporary look. If done in close values and analogous colors, its effect is antique. The surface is painted with the usual four coats, tufbacked with 400 wet-or-dry paper, then sealed with thinned shellac.

### *PROCEDURE*

The knots for male bamboo are left in the base hue. This sets them off from the intervening areas, where a series of contrasting rings of different widths with varying spaces between them are painted. A #3 sable brush held perpendicular to the surface is used to make these stripes. The rendering is made easier by the application of short strokes across a section which continue the length of it on one side. The object is then turned and the rings are completed on the other side. The pressure of the brush reduces or increases the width of these rings, which varies from 1/16″ to 1/4″. Spaces of 1/16″ to 1/8″ are left between them. After the paint has dried, it is protected with thinned shellac or mat varnish. A loose and sparse spattering is now applied at the knots; this may be either of a dark contrasting color or of a somber neutral tone related to the hues in which the bamboo has been rendered. When the spatter has dried for 48 hours, a thinned gloss varnish or a protective mat varnish is applied, depending on whether a strong contrast or an understated effect is the goal.

# STYLIZED BAMBOO

### PREPARATION
This type of bamboo fantasy, which originated in Paris in the twentieth century, is for use on turned bamboo. It may be rendered on a color ground or on a ground leafed with aluminum or Dutch metal. The base, if painted, is prepared in the usual manner with four or five coats, tufbacked finally with 400 wet-or-dry paper and a soapy solution. Either of these base preparations is sealed with thinned shellac.

### PROCEDURE
In this conceit the characteristics of female bamboo are rendered uniformly. Each section is a repeat pattern—spines are exactly duplicated. Comparable spines from section to section are on the same line. The spines within a section need not be of the same length; nor need the spines in all the sections be of the same length; nor need they be evenly separated. But whatever the pattern of spine placement is in one section, it must be exactly followed in all the others. The ascending spines do not abut at the knot with the descending spines. The eyes are arranged in a pattern which is repeated exactly in each section. A single dot is placed somewhat off-center in each eye. The surrounding dots are eliminated. The entire pattern is rendered with clarity, precision, and sharp emphasis. If this fantasy is rendered on metal leaf, the decoration is allowed to dry; then the piece is toned with antique aniline, which is spattered and pounced. The object is then coated with 2 coats of thinned gloss varnish and waxed to a high polish. When stylized bamboo is rendered in color, a protective binder of thinned shellac or French varnish is applied, and then a thin solution of japan spattering fluid in a related hue is pounced on. When dry, the piece is varnished and polished.

# EIGHTEENTH-CENTURY LACQUER BAMBOO

## PREPARATION

The base hue for this bamboo consists of:

> ½ volume burnt umber japan color
> 1 volume vermilion japan color
> ⅛ volume flat white paint

The base coats are tufbacked with 600 wet-or-dry paper and a soapy solution and are then protected with thinned shellac. An Indian red oil glaze is applied over all. This coat is protected with varnish, followed by a pouncing with mahogany-red aniline glaze.

## PROCEDURE

Knots are rendered in burnt sienna japan color. Dots and eyes in varying circular forms are painted in burnt sienna japan color lightened to a middle

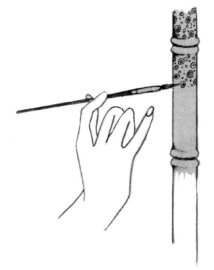

value with flat white. The dark value is burnt umber japan color, and orange-red is a second middle value. All values must contrast with the base hue. There are no spines; the eyes and dots cover each section. They range from ⅟₁₆″ to ¼″, depending, of course, on the size of the

FAUX BAMBOO, *left to right: Lacquer; conceit; "female"; antique faux bois; with leaf spray; "male"; variation.*

bamboo turning. These are interspersed with spirals to the right and reversed to the left, and with concentric circles of different sizes each having a dot in the center. When dry, the piece is completed with the usual coats of thinned gloss varnish required for lacquer.

The type of eye described here for lacquer bamboo is also very effective when rendered in multi-color on a leafed ground.

## THREE BAMBOO VARIATIONS

The bamboo finish lends itself to innumerable variations. Each time it has been taught in my studio, new decorative concepts have evolved. Painted specimens from the eighteenth and nineteenth centuries often provide inspiration.

One variant is a *faux bois* rendering of bamboo. Over a base coat of medium value, which has been tufbacked and then protected with an isolating coat of thinned shellac, a heavy glaze of a lighter value is brushed on. The glaze is combed with a metal or leather implement having teeth that vary in width and spacing. Each member of the piece is rotated during the combing, which is done in a tremulous zig-zag to form an interesting pattern.

In another variation, a dark brown base (tufbacked and protected) is rendered with black knots. On each side of a knot, oval eyes, pointed at the end, going toward the center of the section, are leafed in gold. Black dots are spotted into the golden eyes. This version is varnished or antiqued.

A third variation is rendered with delicately painted sprays, each consisting of three bamboo leaves on a stem, which extend into the sections from the knots. Two or three of these are placed at each knot. The space between them is filled with fine lines of varying colors separated by colored dots.

Only a few of the existing fantasies derived from bamboo are listed here. It is hoped that study of the live tree, so delicate and decorative, will act as a stimulus to original creative fantasies.

PORPHYRY: *Top left, with inlay; right, granite.*
*Bottom left, purple; right, French.*

## BAMBOO

*Materials*
  Japan colors
  Shellac
  Mat varnish with high
    wax content
  Protective mat varnish
  Dry powder colors
  Wax
  Clear gloss varnish
  Aniline powders
  Alcohol solvent
  Indian red oil paint
  Flat white paint
  Gold leaf
  Dutch metal leaf
  Silver leaf
  Aluminum leaf
  Japan drier
  Turpentine

*Tools*
  #3 and #6 sable brushes
  Oxhair brush
  Pounce brush
  Shellac brush
  Spatter brush
  Varnish brush
  400 wet-or-dry paper
  600 wet-or-dry paper
  000 steel wool
  Metal or leather comb
  220 garnet paper

*Miscellaneous*
  Non-detergent soap flakes
  Chalk

# PORPHYRY

## DESCRIPTION

Porphyries are like a frozen rock aggregate, having detached crystals of some mineral—commonly feldspar (fool's gold)—embedded in the finer-grained groundmass of igneous rock. Usually the dark minerals form first and the later-growing feldspar grains fill in the voids.

The word porphyry derived from the Greek word *porphyritēs*, meaning purple, and was used to designate a red red-purple stone which is hard and takes a high polish. This stone was used by the Greeks and Romans for columns. Its color and its polish made it the stone of emperors: Hadrian's sarcophagus was made of porphyry; so, too, was Napoleon's in Les Invalides.

Today the name is used to designate a great number of stones of similar composition but varied color. These stones cut well, and with their fine grain and beautiful shadings, with their aptitude for polish and their glints of feldspar, are highly esteemed for the decorative arts. Red porphyry came primarily from Egypt. From Greece came an antique green variety, containing feldspar and a few grains of black augite. The porphyry of Sweden and Norway is brown, veined with quartz, and flecked with pink, reddish, and greenish particles. France also has deposits of porphyry—violet and light green—containing particles of feldspar, black augite, and iron.

These varied species, so rich in shade and tone, inspired the Italian craftsmen to a painted fantasy. In the Pitti Palace in Florence, for example, is a fine column, dominantly red-brown in color, rendered on a golden surface with raw umber, burnt sienna, ochre, and yellow-green.

In the eighteenth century, porphyry was admired as a material for desk and table tops, ornamental bases, and inlay. Porphyry painted in fantasy lends importance to otherwise ordinary objects. It can be rendered in a close grain with a high polish, or, more coarsely, as a rough, granular surface.

## PORPHYRY—PREPARATION

The illusion of stone is created by spattering an object with many fine particles of paint, layer upon layer, in contrasting hues. No single application of paint spatter is designed to cover the surface entirely. Through their sharp contrast, the final set of applied colors together accomplish the ultimate magical transformation to rock.

The spatters are applied over one of two surface materials, depending on whether the finish is to resemble polished porphyry or rough stone.

1) The polished effect is created on a Dutch metal base, small reserved flecks of which assume the look of the feldspar particles. The usual japan bole preparation precedés the laying of the Dutch metal. When dry, the leaf is reserved with thinned orange shellac.

2) For the base of granite-like porphyry, a preparation with a light value of gray-beige is made to this formula:

6 volumes flat white paint
1 volume raw umber japan color
1 volume French yellow ochre japan color

Two coats of this mixture applied to the surface, and sanded when dry with 220 garnet paper, are sufficient.

### SPATTERS

For any shade of porphyry except the red red-purple Egyptian variety, the following system of colors and values is prepared. First a dominant hue is selected in a color which will be most apparent in the completed porphyry; then three different, contrasting hues are chosen. Six spattering mediums are made with them.

1. Dominant hue, light value
2. Dominant hue, middle value
3. Dominant hue, dark value
4. First contrasting hue, light value
5. Second contrasting hue, middle value
6. Third contrasting hue, dark value

The formula for each of the mediums is:

1 volume japan paint (flat white tinted with desired japan colors)
3 volumes turpentine (or sufficient amount to achieve skim-milk consistency)
10% japan drier (if japan color is used alone)

## SPATTERING TECHNIQUE

Porphyry sometimes contains drifts or larger crystals of one of the elements in its composition. These are achieved by smartly rapping the long side of a spattering brush on a wooden block as it is swung over the surface.

The majority of the particles, however, are finely spattered. The forefinger passes up or down the brush, releasing a few bristles at a time, then lifts off the brush and repeats the operation. In this way the spatter is controlled and directed. Jerking of the finger produces spotty and heavy deposits. Should such occur, they are easily scraped off, when dry, with a razor. Each spattering of a different color offers an opportunity for evening the tonality of the surface.

# SIMPLE PORPHYRY (WITHOUT INLAY) — PROCEDURE

Over the prepared leafed or painted base, the spatters are applied in the following order; it is not necessary to allow drying time between them:

1) Middle value of the dominant hue. Coverage—90% (not all) of the surface.

2) Light value of the first contrasting hue. Coverage—70%.

3) Dark value of the dominant hue. Coverage—60%.

4) Middle value of the second contrasting hue. Coverage—50%.

5) Light value of the dominant hue. Coverage—40%.

6) Dark value of the third contrasting hue; rendered over the wooden block to create drifts. Coverage—40%.

To create a livelier texture of drifts and crystals ranging from ¼″ to 1½″ in size, spatters 4, 5, and 6 are thinned with additional turpentine, and are applied by knocking the brush against the wooden block as described earlier.

The accent spatters, so critical to the final result, by their sharp contrast emphasize the beauty of the preceding spatters. If the porphyry is rendered on the gray-beige surface, a thin solution of rich gold powder mixed with quick size and turpentine is sparsely spattered. The proportions are:

> ¼ volume rich gold powder
> 1 volume quick size
> ¼ volume turpentine

(Obviously this gold spatter is omitted over a Dutch metal base.) It is followed by a spattering of black India ink which covers not more than 10% of the surface. Then comes a light powdering of thin white paint, which, acting like a magic wand, completes the transformation to stone.

When the surface has dried for two or three days, it is finished with protective mat varnish if a rough, granite-like texture is desired. For the more elegant, highly polished finish, coats of clear gloss varnish sufficient to level the surface are applied, with drying intervals of 24 hours. Every other coat of varnish is tufbacked with 600 wet-or-dry paper and a soapy solution.

# PORPHYRY WITH GEOMETRIC INLAY— PROCEDURE

On flat surfaces, the porphyry fantasy is particularly handsome when combined with a simulated inlay. For such an inlay the following materials are required. A pattern for an inlaid design of three colors is made on tracing paper. The forms to be rendered in each color are cut out of brown wrapping paper, or paper of a similar thickness; then each one is properly numbered 1, 2, and 3. Each group of forms is fastened to the surface at intervals between the spatters with surgical adhesive (of the type used for eyelashes).

The following instructions indicate the intervals at which such an inlay is masked off. The masking occurs after each two spatters in order that the color of each portion be strong in contrast to the tone of the porphyry ground. It is obvious that the color of the second spatter in each pair has the stronger influence on each portion of the inlay.

In the inlay, the first color will be rendered with one pair of spatters, $a + b$; the second with $c + d$ over $a + b$; the third with $e + f$ over $a + b + c + d$. When two of these spatters have been repeated and the accents have been added, the background for the design will be a composite of ten spatters.

1.  The entire surface is spattered with $a, b$.

    *a)* Middle value of the dominant hue.
    Coverage—90% (not all) of surface.

    *b)* Light value of the first contrasting hue.
    Coverage—70%.

2.  After above dry overnight, the pattern is outlined on the surface.

3.  The cutouts for the first inlay color are glued to the surface. These now mask areas of $a, b$.

4.  Entire surface is spattered with $c, d$, but the paint is concentrated at the edges of the masks to create a sharp distinction between the inlay and the background.

    *c)* Dark value of the dominant hue.
    Coverage—60%.

    *d)* Middle value of the second contrasting hue.
    Coverage—50%.

5.   After above dry overnight, areas for the second set of masks are out-lined on surface.

6.   Cutouts for the second color are glued to surface.

7.   Entire surface is spattered with *e, f*. A portion of this may be rendered by knocking the brush on a wooden block to create large crystals of color.

   *e)* Light value of the dominant hue.
        Coverage—40%.

   *f)* Dark value of the third contrasting hue.
        Coverage—40%.

8.   After above dry overnight, areas for the third set of masks are outlined on surface.

9.   Cutouts for the third color are glued to surface. (All forms have now been attached.)

10.   Entire surface is spattered with *g, h*.

   *g)* Either the dark value (*c*) or the middle
        value (*a*) of the dominant hue is used again.
        Coverage—40%.

   *h)* If *c* has just been repeated, this final
        spatter is *f*. But if *a* has just been used,
        this final spatter can be either *f* or *d*.
        Coverage—40%.

11.   Spatters *g* and *h* dry overnight. The three sets of masks are then care-fully removed. It is evident that each of the three types of inlay is pre-dominantly in one of the contrast colors, and that at this stage the background for the design is a composite of all four pairs of spatters.

12.   The accent spatters and the final varnish coats with tufbacking are the same as for Simple Porphyry. So, too, is the method for creating large drifts and crystals.

# EGYPTIAN PORPHYRY: INLAY ON DUTCH METAL—PROCEDURE

The red red-purple porphyry of the Egyptians and the Romans is most successfully simulated on a Dutch metal surface, glints of which will mimic the stone's characteristic sparkle. The spattering fluids mixed for this rendering follow a somewhat different system from that used previously. Here the contrasting hues are for the most part *related* to the dominant hue. The following instructions include the recipes for the colors of Royal Egyptian porphyry. These colors are to be used in the standard porphyry spatter formula: 1 volume japan color, 3 volumes turpentine, 10% japan drier if required.

*a*) Middle value of the dominant hue (red red-purple):

> 1 volume red red-orange japan color
> ½ volume burnt sienna japan color
> 1 volume flat white paint
> Coverage—90%

*b*) Light value of the first contrasting hue:

> 2 volumes flat white paint
> ¼ volume burnt sienna japan color
> Coverage—70%

When the above pair of spatters has dried overnight, the first part of the pattern is traced on the surface and the masking pieces are attached with surgical adhesive.

*c*) Dark value of the dominant hue:

> 2 volumes purple japan color
> 1 volume red-purple japan color
> Coverage—60%

*d*) Middle value of the second contrasting hue:

> 1 volume flat white paint
> ½ volume red red-orange japan color
> ¼ volume raw sienna japan color
> Coverage—50%

When the above pair of spatters has dried overnight, the second part of the pattern is traced on the surface and masked.

*e*) Light value of the dominant hue:

> 2 volumes flat white paint
> ¼ volume red red-purple japan color
> Coverage—40%

*f*) Dark value of the third contrasting hue:

> ½ volume flat white paint
> 1 volume blue-green dark japan color
> Coverage—40%

After the above pair of spatters has dried, the last part of the pattern is traced on and masked.

*g*) Dark value of the dominant hue (same as *c*):

> Coverage—40%

*h*) Light value of the first contrasting hue (same as *b*):

> Coverage—40%

When these spatters have dried, the three sets of masks are removed. A light spattering of India ink follows. The porphyry is then completed with a spatter made of:

> 2 volumes flat white paint
> ¼ volume red red-orange japan color

This is applied by the brush-and-block method, which deposits drops resembling large crystals. Egyptian porphyry is always finished with sufficient clear gloss varnish coats to achieve a highly polished surface.


# ENGLISH AND FRENCH PORPHYRY

In the nineteenth century, English porphyry was rendered in a simple manner with distemper paint (*see* chapter on *faux bois*). Combinations of only three spatter colors were used: (1) Venetian red, vermilion, and black; or (2) a light brown and black spattered over a brown-red ground.

French porphyry used a slightly different palette. An equal spatter of red red-purple combined with black was used over a brown-red ground and completed with a loose spatter of pale pink. Spattering was done by drawing a brush across a palette knife.

This fantasy further develops the technique of spattering, which was first described in the chapter on antiquing, and a variation of which was discussed in the chapter on gilding. It is obvious that porphyry is a versatile finish and can be adapted in numerous ways for use on contemporary furniture.

## PORPHYRY

*Materials*
Dutch metal leaf
Alcohol solvent
Orange shellac
Turpentine
Quick size
Protective mat varnish
Clear gloss varnish
Japan colors
  red red-orange
  burnt sienna
  purple
  red-purple
  raw sienna
  red red-purple
  blue-green dark
  raw umber
  French yellow ochre
  lampblack
India ink

Flat white paint
Rich gold bronzing powder
Japan drier

*Tools*
Shellac brush
220 garnet paper
Spatter brush
Wooden block
600 wet-or-dry paper
Varnish brush

*Miscellaneous*
Non-detergent soap flakes
Tracing paper
Transfer paper
Wrapping paper
Surgical adhesive (glue)
Razor

# FAUX MARBRE

## PAST USES OF SIMULATED MARBLE

One of the most ingenious painted fantasies is that inspired by marble. *Faux marbre*, as it came to be called, made an early appearance, for it occurs on Mycenean pottery dating to 2200 B.C. Later, despite a plentiful supply of real marble, it appeared on Roman columns, where it was rendered in a combination of colored plasters. In addition, there survives from the seventh century A.D. a description of how stone was prepared with white lead oil paint before veins of marble were added with a mixture of pigment and oil.

Both the French and the Italians used *faux marbre* wherever structure defied the use of actual marble; thus it was used for curved and vaulted ceilings, window shutters, and doors of salons that were otherwise paneled with actual marble. Examples are found in the Borghese Palace in Rome, the Palladian villas in the Venetian countryside, and at Fontainebleau and Versailles. The Neoclassic period in France and England employed *faux marbre* on small tables in an attempt to simulate the marble-and-bronze tables found in Pompeii. Ornamental pedestals in Adam houses were painted to resemble marble and porphyry. Marble was combined with satin-wood in the classicism of Sheraton. In the reconstruction of the Brighton Pavilion during the 1820s, *faux marbre* was used lavishly in decoration.

The Europeans ingeniously used *faux marbre* for woodwork, baseboards, intricate panels, and borders in both churches and the dwellings of the wealthy; less frequently for the tops of commodes and consoles. The patron's taste for *faux marbre* was a tribute to the craftsman's talent. They both enjoyed this subtle trickery with paint—this *double entendre*—which on the one hand satisfied the patron's need for elegance and, on the other, the artist's need for fantasy. People in the provinces whiled away the winter months with their own naive rendering of *faux marbre* on objects that could not possibly be made of the real thing.

## FORMATION OF MARBLE

Marble is a metamorphic rock resulting from the action of heat or pressure on limestone. This action produces an aggregate of calcite crystals—pure white, colored, or black. The term marble also designates certain non-crystalline stones that are ornamental and capable of a high polish. Marbles are beds of rock that are veined by metallic or other substances running in the direction of the strata. These various substances spread themselves on the limestone, penetrating the surface and becoming interspersed within the strata. The transparency of marble allows the veins and substances deep within the rock to be dimly perceptible, while those nearer the surface present a sharper appearance. Marble which consists of layers piled one upon another contains petrified fossils embedded in the matrix. The flow of marble was caused by an upturning of the layers in such a way that they separated like leaves of a quire of paper bent into an arch. The fissures so created were filled by various materials during the metamorphic changes.

## TYPES OF MARBLE USED FOR FAUX MARBRE

The patterns in these marbles should serve only as inspirations.

*Lumachella*—made up of fossilized shell fragments, and showing small circles in regular order.

*Fossiliferous*—containing fossil remains.

*Variegated*—made up of patches and veinings of various colors, with the veining in the majority.

*Brèche*, or *Breccia*—having angular fragments of various colors.

*Serpentine*—having sinuous veins; includes most of the dark green marbles.

*Conglomerate*—composed of rounded fragments clustered together.

*Unicolored*—without veinings and with even color tone.

*Broccatello*—resembling brocade.

## EXPERIMENTS WITH FLOW AND DRIFT OF COLORS

In a nineteenth-century treatise on *faux marbre*, it is suggested that rivulets of water running on a tilted surface, turning in varying directions, sometimes coming together to form a thick stream, then spreading out again but always traveling in the same direction, approximate the way in which the accessory minerals and other substances spread within the stone. The same thing happens when colors and turpentine are floated on a base of thin wet paint. Additional turpentine propels the colors together, so that sometimes they blend with each other, or spreads them apart, so that they sometimes blend with the base paint. Everything appears to be traveling to the same point by different roads.

The flow and drift of marble is always strongly evident, and the craftsman wishing to simulate it will find the following experiment instructive. A large baking tin is filled with several inches of water. Into this are put two or three spoonfuls of either oil colors thinned with turpentine, or japan colors thinned with flatting oil. These are stirred on top of the water, then a sheet of paper either is placed on the surface or is slid under the color. The paper is carefully lifted out and allowed to dry. It will be observed that the colors mingle and flow, interspersed by veinings. This is how Italian and French marbleized book papers are made.

It is so important to understand how the drifts and floats in marble occur that yet another demonstration should be made. Three or four blobs of two different paint colors are dropped on paper, some close together, others far apart; another piece of paper is placed over these and weighted with a heavy object. When the weight is removed and the papers separated, the spread of the paint is equivalent to the effect of the pressure of the earth on the foreign matter in limestone.

Contemporary taste seems to favor simulated marble in a palette totally unrelated to any of the natural marbles. Nevertheless, the observer must be intrigued—must be tempted to ascertain by touch whether a surface *is* marble or not; hence its form and flow must be based on a study of actual marble. In rendering *faux marbre*, the form and size of the surface must be considered. Design and scale, rhythmic line and balance, these are requisites for a harmonious and varied pattern. The rendering must be free and bold. The larger the area, the larger and softer are the floated portions and the veining.

## "FLOATING" MARBLE—POSITIVE METHODS

Marbles, as we have indicated, are distinguished by a wide range of characteristics. There is one type which we shall call "floating," where the drifts of foreign matter spread themselves in varying values of color.

When the patterns of *faux marbre* are created by the direct application of paint to surfaces, the method is termed positive. This method includes flooding the surface with the base color and, while the paint is still wet, laying other colors on. Another positive method is laying the thin floating colors on a dry surface and inducing them to flow with a spattering of mineral spirits.

## "FLOATING" MARBLE—PREPARATION

### THE BASE
The area to be rendered in floating *faux marbre* is prepared with three coats of the background color. When dry, it is tufbacked with 400 wet-or-dry paper and a soapy solution. If the base coat has been rendered in enamel or semi-gloss paint, the surface is now ready for marbleizing. But if a flat base has been used, the surface is now protected with a thinned shellac solution so that later any unpleasing portions of the float may be safely removed.

A variety of tools is needed to render floating *faux marbre* on either a wet ground or a dry ground.

### TOOLS FOR THE APPLICATION OF FLOATING PAINT

One stiff-bristle brush clipped at intervals along the ferrule to produce distinct clumps of bristles; these groups vary in width

Two oxhair brushes (½″ and ¼″)

Six 8-inch lengths of cotton twine tied in the center to form a tassel

Several 6-inch squares of cheesecloth

Several 12-inch squares of cheesecloth

Turkey feathers, one of which may be clipped along the quill to afford unequal fronds of feather

One coarse natural sponge

### TOOLS FOR MOTTLING AND BLENDING

Bager or camel hair whisk
Natural sponge
Crumpled newspaper
Crumpled tissue paper
Chamois
Absorbent cotton
Cheesecloth

Before marbleizing an area, it is wise to try out the entire set of tools on the wet surface of a sample board purely to learn the effects that can be achieved with them.

The craftsman's aim is to create the impression of marble, not exact duplication of some specific type. He will be helped in this if study of natural marble has familiarized him with the various forms. Moreover, by floating and mingling wet paint he will achieve natural and varied effects that could not be obtained with the most painstaking and studied use of the brush.


# PROCEDURE FOR FLOATING THE COLORS ON A WET GROUND

All tools should be at hand and ready for use when the marbling process begins, and a specimen of marble should be available for inspiration. Floating japan colors are thinned with a solution of equal parts of flatting oil

*Faux-marbre top, distressed base*

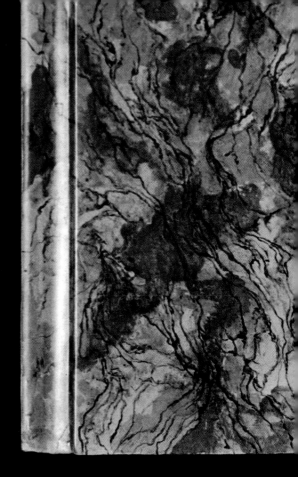

and mineral spirits to the consistency of water. A portion of the flat background color is also diluted to this consistency. The surface is brushed over first with flatting oil, then immediately with the thinned base hue. The

floating japan colors are introduced into this while the surface is wet. All tools are dipped in mineral spirits before they are loaded with paint.

Two to three floating colors are used. These, as they mingle with the base color and with each other, will combine to a number of other colors. Any of the methods of applying the floating colors may be used in combination. They are described below.

1. The thinned colors may be applied with the ¼-inch and ½-inch brushes, each dipped in a separate color; they are held at the tip of the handles and used as one brush. The several colors are laid on separately for contrast or they are blended together. The color must be patted on, not painted on, so that there is sufficient quantity to flow into the wet base coat.

2. A 12-inch square of cheesecloth is twisted into a rope and each section of it is loaded with a different color. The cloth is rolled over the wet surface in the same general direction a number of times; each time it is freshly loaded.

FAUX MARBRE: *Top left, serpentine; right, trompe-l'oeil.*
*Bottom left, fossiliferous; right, floating.*

3. Another 12-inch square of cheesecloth is rolled into a rope; each end is dipped into a different color. Held in the center, it is slapped against the surface.

4. The ends of the tassel made from cotton twine are divided into groups, and each group is loaded with one of the floating colors. Then the tassel is dragged and slapped on the wet ground.

5. The clipped brush with each group of bristles dipped in a different color is turned and twisted on the surface.

6. Several turkey feathers, each loaded with a different color, are used on the broad side to lay on color. The feathers are first dipped in mineral spirits, then are combed with a fine comb and dipped into the floating color.

7. A natural sponge is loaded with paint and rolled over the surface.

Interesting patterns form as the wet paints merge, provided that they have been applied in sufficient quantity. Time is allowed for the color to run and intermingle with the base paint or the adjacent hue. The several hues mingle, separate, grow great, dwindle and trickle off, just as the water in our metaphor at the beginning of this chapter. The preliminary experiments must be kept in mind, and especially the principle that all of the colors must flow in the same direction. Almost always interesting patterns will arrange themselves. If they do not, a large sash brush, or a natural sponge, deeply immersed in mineral spirits and then squeezed out on the marbleizing surface, will start an additional flow. However, the surface should not be flooded, because the effects of the happy accidents already obtained might be lost. Excessive moisture can be picked up with a piece of chamois, wet in water and wrung out, or with a ball of cotton dipped in mineral spirits, wrung out, and patted on a flat surface to pack together loose ends of its fiber. The chamois, acting as a blotter, removes the floating color and reveals the original surface. The cotton softens and blends the floating color. After use, either implement is patted on newspaper before it is reapplied to the surface.

The pattern produced so far is the result of accident and all patterns resembling the flow of marble must be recognized and retained. Areas that do not resemble marble are now blended and manipulated with the tools. The point of a feather dipped in mineral spirits is used to push wet paint into other areas where it can blend and float. The dry blender brush is whisked across color adjacent to a wet area to start a new flow. Variations of texture are created by pressing the sponge on wet paint; it is used dry, or wet with mineral spirits and squeezed dry. Diverse textures are achieved with crumpled tissue, newspaper, or cheesecloth. These texture areas are added discreetly: overuse of one implement makes a boring pattern—and nature is never boring. Any of these mottling tools absorbs paint and may be impressed upon a blank area. This method, called *frottage*, is often used by such contemporary painters as Max Ernst. If a repeat of the pattern formed by the tool is desired, the tool is blotted out on newspaper between each use. The water-wet chamois (acting as a blotting agent) reveals the background where desired. This type of *faux marbre* should be worked out freely, with no visibly labored passages, and thus requires intuitive decisions to direct the flow of color into color; there must be no violent or eccentric breaks. Hard edges of the floats are softened with the cotton or with the blending brush.

For additional interest, and for balance of color or value, islands are formed in the marble. These are irregular pools of different hue, and they simulate one of the effects of pressure on the impurities within natural limestone. An eyedropper releases a drop of one color in the middle of a pool of mineral spirits, then a drop of a second color; the mineral spirits marries the two hues and disperses them. A pool of color with the center dried out with a cotton bud receives a drop of mineral spirits, which pushes the color out and away. With a feather, the ends of the islands are extended; the centers are absorbed with a blotter, cotton bud, or the water-wet chamois.

At this point, other additional or corrective color is put down with the feather. A clean feather, dipped in mineral spirits, placed carefully on the edges of the paint, causes those edges to expand and float out into the surrounding area. As the paint begins to dry, unpleasant edges of mineral spirits sometimes appear; these residues are softened by rolling them with a cotton swab. While the surface of floating *faux marbre* is wet, the veining (to be discussed below) is painted in; the wet surface softens the veins. This type of floating marble is used for variegated, unicolored, and broccatello marble, or any marble with drifts of several colors.

## PROCEDURE FOR FLOATING THE COLORS ON A DRY GROUND

On a dry surface the floating colors must be as thin as water. A coat of flatting oil precedes the laying on of color. The tools and other devices are the same ones used for floating *faux marbre* on a wet surface. The badger blender is used to soften the color to transparency. This kind of floating renders impressions of onyx, white marbles, and marbles with transparent, sparsely placed drifts of muted color.

## FAUX MARBRE ON WOODWORK—PROCEDURE

Beams, dadoes, doors, window frames, baseboards, and other forms of woodwork have been painted in *faux marbre* in churches, palaces, and even provincial houses. Obviously, vertical surfaces like these must be rendered on a dry ground. Moreover, the floating background color must be laid on sparingly. Application is done with sponge, cheesecloth, or feather. The color is then softened with cotton dipped in mineral spirits and well wrung out. Such softening is essential, as the areas are part of the background of a room and must not be dominant. Colors related to each other are preferable. But if the *faux marbre* is used as a strong decorative element—for instance, on columns—the veining hues should include a dark value.

Around windows and doorways, provincial *faux marbre* often suggested a mitered corner. In rendering such a corner, an incised line is drawn at the joint to indicate where the floats should be cut off. Floats starting from opposite sides of the mitered line do not intermingle, but are placed asymmetrically and diversely.

In the chateaux and palaces of Europe, architectural *faux marbre* was used for areas where real marble was too heavy, too costly, or impossible to install—shutters, ceilings, concave niches. The rendering duplicates actual marble with almost unbelievable exactness. Here are a few memorable examples:

The palace at Versailles: in a vaulted ceiling over a grand staircase—where it would have been impossible to install real marble—the ceiling blocks are rendered in gray and white *faux marbre*.

The palace at Fontainebleau: under the silver-gilt decorated wall panels in one of the salons, apricot *faux marbre* is rendered on the dado; it also appears on the window shutters.

The Borghese Palace in Rome: on the second floor, one of the rooms is veneered with shaded blue and white vertical stripes of real marble; the curved niches are rendered in identical *faux marbre*.

## FAUX MARBRE—NEGATIVE METHOD

With the negative method, a pattern is revealed by the partial *removal* of a paint film from a surface previously protected and therefore reserved.

The negative method is best used for dark marbles such as the green serpentines, black and gold marble, and *brèche*; it is also one way of rendering marble that contains fossils and shell remains. This method calls for a surface which has been shellacked. It is then coated lightly with flatting oil. Over this, a coat of japan paint thinned with equal amounts of flatting oil and mineral spirits is applied. After a few moments, newspaper is laid over the wet ground. On this a pounce brush is rhythmically stroked. When the newspaper is removed, the surface will appear somewhat dappled and flowing in the areas where the brush was used. If a creased newspaper is used, the paint under the crease is absorbed, leaving a vein-like line. As the paint sets, further veins are added with a sharp, pointed stick or an eraser.

This method may also be used on small areas of floating *faux marbre*. Portions are rendered with torn pieces of newspaper placed here and there over the floating color. These are tamped with a stiff dry brush.

## BRÈCHE—PROCEDURE

Marbles combining angular fragments of limestone of various colors and pieces of older rock broken under pressure and re-cemented into solid rock, foreign matter and metallic oxides which have infiltrated it, are known as *brèche*. To simulate the angular forms of *brèche*, the ground is first coated with two or more colors of paint in a cream consistency; these are applied separately or mingled. A piece of newspaper crumpled into many spikes is then laid on the surface and allowed to absorb some of the paint. When it is removed, a network of irregular lines of the base hue shows through; some areas are mottled, some are still in deep color, and some are in lighter values (see drawing on next page).

With a #6 sable brush and mineral spirits, or with a pencil eraser, some of the areas bound by the fine lines are cleared out to reveal a block of the background color; this block must be so situated that it will contrast with neighboring ones. The removal of the paint is executed with delicacy so that the angularity of the boundaries is maintained. Perfect geometric forms—squares, rectangles, circles—should be avoided, for nature is always more or less irregular. The process just described may be used over an entire area or just in portions of an otherwise floated marble. A sharp pointed stick—for instance, an orangewood stick—is used to accent the outlines of the dark rock form. It removes the paint and reveals the surface below. A #3 brush loaded with the deepest color completes the boundaries of the lighter rock forms. Other blocks are darkened with one of the applied colors for further contrast.

Another method of forming such *brèche* conglomerates is to load a #6 sable brush (or the ¼-inch or ½-inch oxhair brush) fully with paint and let drops of it fall almost contiguously on the wet surface. As the paint expands, it assumes a pebble-like form with fine boundary lines ringing each drop. A large-pored natural sponge is coated with a paint brush loaded with another color. The sponge is then dabbed on the wet surface to create additional tiny fragments of rock in the background.

A further method of creating the forms of *brèche* is done with the #6 sable brush or the ½-inch oxhair one, but this time the paint load is light. The tip or the corner of the brush is lightly and irregularly drawn along for about 1″. In the process, the brush is pressed gradually to its fullest width, forming a triangular patch. It is then lifted perpendicularly at one end of the base of the triangle, and drawn off on its point for another inch before the action is repeated.

Lastly, it is possible to produce the effect of *brèche* by loading the edges of the coarse sponge with fairly heavy color and applying it over a surface that has been brushed with flatting oil. Blocks of various sizes are formed. Still others may be stamped on with an eraser cut in irregular shapes. Some of these forms are shaded with another color. In addition, various areas in the background are sprinkled with paint to form smaller pebbles.

## FOSSILIFEROUS MARBLE—PROCEDURE

Fossiliferous refers to marbles containing such matter as types of coral and other skeletal remains. These vestiges range in size from ½" to 4".

Over a dry ground, a thin glaze of color is painted. Into this some deeper color is dabbed with a soft sponge or a bunch of newspaper. The paint is pushed into ridges here and there with a soft rag, and these are dabbed with the paint-stained newspaper. With thin paint loaded on a stiff sponge, more color is laid on the surface; blending is done with a natural cosmetic sponge lightly loaded with color on its edges. Veining is added with a feather or brush, then the entire surface is lightly stippled with a small round stencil brush.

Fossil shapes are rendered either with a potato cut in the same way as a printing block or with a notched piece of cork; either of these when stamped upon the surface lifts the drying paint and reveals the undercolor. The potato must be wiped on newspaper between each imprint. This vegetable stamp may also be used as a color applicator, providing its printing surface has been dried out with talc. Additional markings of color in spirals and bent forms are touched in with a feather, and some few veining lines are accented with a #3 sable brush. When the surface has dried for several days, a thin tinted varnish glaze is brushed on, then removed here and there to reveal the color below and increase the variegation of hue.

## SERPENTINE MARBLE—PROCEDURE

Serpentine marble, so called because of its resemblance to the skin of the serpent, varies in quality but always has a green tonality and some trace of fossils. It is best rendered on a black ground that has been scumbled irregularly (pounced or mottled) with opaque white paint. When the ground is dry, a green glaze is brushed over all (see chapter on glazes), and square pieces of cork notched in two or three places serve to stamp on the fossils. This is an instance of the negative method, for the cork, placed firmly on the surface, lifts the paint and reveals the undercoat. The veins, rendered in shades of green paler than the glaze, are horizontal or vertical, and in some cases are fragmented into small segments as if they had undergone a violent concussion.

## LUMACHELLA—PROCEDURE

*Lumachella* is a marble distinguished by fossilized shell fragments forming small circles in close order. To achieve this effect, a glaze is scumbled over a dry ground and blended with a soft, clean, dry brush. After this, a natural cosmetic sponge or rag, moistened in a lighter value of glaze, is dabbed here and there upon the surface which is then lightly patted with a clean rag. A piece of rubber, linoleum, or cork, cut to resemble three-quarters of a circle, is pressed on the surface to make the shell shapes, which vary in diameter from 1″ to 2″. Further contrasting color is added with a brush or hard natural sponge; next, a spatter of color is distributed by knocking the spatter brush on a stick, and this is followed immediately by a spatter of mineral spirits, which spreads the paint spots, thereby ringing them with another color. The size of the spots is regulated by the size of the spatter. The #3 sable brush is used to edge some of the shells in deep color and to add thin veins to the light shells. The marbling should dry for several days, after which a glaze of harmonious color is brushed on and mottled with crumpled tissue paper.

## BROCCATELLO—PROCEDURE

*Broccatello* is a form of shell marble. Its name refers to the fact that, like brocade, it seems interwoven with metallic fiber. It is frequently rendered in tones of yellow. Gold leaf or Dutch metal should be laid haphazardly on the base. The technique then proceeds in the same manner as *lumachella*, all the way up to and including the drying period. After this, a thin glaze, possibly of yellow-orange, is added and immediately spattered with mineral spirits by rapping a brush on a stick, causing the base color to be revealed in small areas. Veins are added at this point, but it should be noted that in *broccatello* the veins do not cross the shell shapes.

# THE IMPORTANCE OF THE GRAND EFFECT

It must be clear by now that in rendering *faux marbre* any tool which serves to create texture or forms that even vaguely suggest nature should be used without inhibition; moreover, any of the tools and methods described may be combined to produce a fantasy of marble. *Faux marbre* conceived and executed with wit and rendered freely, rapidly, and with abandon is more successful by far than a fantasy having worked-over, studied areas and a pedantic concern for minutiae. The grand effect is the aim of the marbleizer.

# SCALE AND CONTRAST

The ultimate purpose of the *faux marbre* piece determines whether additional veining is necessary. On large surfaces of woodwork the color palette should be limited and closely related, somewhat neutral in hue and without dramatic contrasts. In the case of a dining table, the scheme should be simplified so that the surface serves as a background neither disturbing nor dominating the table appointments. However, on consoles, desks, chests, and incidental tables, the bold contrast and startling color of an imaginative and unreal palette are exciting, especially if the marbleizing is done with great verisimilitude. These pieces, of course, must be compatible in scale and contrast with other decorations in the room.

# VEINING—DESCRIPTION

No variety of marble is chemically pure. They all contain a greater or lesser amount of foreign material, sometimes chemically combined, sometimes present as separate minerals. It is these extra materials that give veins, markings, and flowering to colored marble. Shades of yellow, pink, and red are due to the presence of iron oxide, while shades of blue-gray to black are due to carbonaceous matter. Shades of green are caused by the intrusion of iron and copper sulfides, mica, and talc. When metamorphic changes were in progress, broken rocks with a vast number of fissures—large and small—became filled with crystallized rock and metallic ores carried by subterranean streams; intense heat and pressure determined the arrangement of these materials.

Deep veins in *faux marbre* should be soft in tone so that they will appear to lie well beneath the transparent surface. The craftsman keeps them in mind when floating the colors. Veins should be few and dispersed with regard to the decorative pattern, enhancing blank areas and emphasizing particularly harmonious effects within the float. The lines of veins vary in breadth and are angular rather than curved; they occasionally resemble the markings of the needle on a cardiogram. However, between periods of erratic movement, calm stretches occur. During the rendering of *faux marbre*, all repetitions should be guarded against. Nature is disciplined yet infinitely varied; no two pieces of marble are ever precisely similar, no two veins identical. Human beings, on the other hand, tend to stereotype irregularities, making them of equal height, equally spaced; they paint a scallop and go on scalloping *ad nauseam*, they zig and zag and repeat their zigzagging evenly. Once a direction has been established by a float, it should not be repeated in the veining. Veins should be rendered with spirit in a free and varied way.

### VEINING—PRELIMINARY PRACTICE

The following exercise with charcoal provides good practice in veining with paint, and it may be used later for rendering gray and white marble. On a surface which has been coated with flat white paint and tufbacked with 400 wet-or-dry paper and a soapy solution, veinings and some few floats are laid in with charcoal. Over this, a thin film of white is painted, and immediately the veinings and floats are blended with a soft dry brush. In a second exercise, oil pastels are used to lay in the floats and veins. If color overlaps color, the end of the crayon must be constantly wiped off with cotton. When the oil pastels are applied on a dry ground, they are blended with a rag, the palm of the hand, or a charcoal stump. This completed, a thin glaze of color is applied. On a wet ground, the soft veins are laid in with the oil pastels, followed by the finer veins; a pale color tint may be added to the background. The whole is softened with the badger blending brush.

These exercises provide quick and easy ways of rendering *faux marbre* effectively. All practice panels are useful for analysis of the intricacies of veining. Veining is free, with non-conformities and irregularities of edges and variations in width. Either a brush or a feather is used for rendering veins, which should be crisply dark on one side and softly light on the other.

### USE OF VEINING TOOLS

The veins may be rendered with brush or feather first dipped in mineral spirits and then in color. A preliminary veining may be laid in with mineral spirits; then the tool loaded with paint follows the path. If the veins are too strong in value, they may be rubbed over with dampened cotton when they are nearly dry.

When a brush is used for veining, its stem is held in the turned-up palm of the hand, as if it were an extension of the forefinger. The vein is swiftly laid on with the free movement of the outstretched arm. This is the

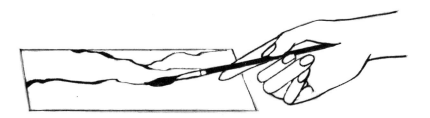

Italian method. My own method is to hold the brush as described and allow it to rotate in the palm as the arm moves across the surface. Another method uses a brush, loaded with paint, whose bristles have been separated with a steel comb.

A feather may be used in somewhat the same manner, its point pressing lightly and firmly to vary the width. For variety, some of the fronds of the feather are cut out along the edge; the feather is now dipped in water, then in mineral spirits; after combing, the fronds are loaded with color with a small brush. This feather is drawn along the surface to form fine veins running closely together. The veins branch off in different directions when the feather is sharply turned. This thread-like effect is also successful when used on a wet floating ground.

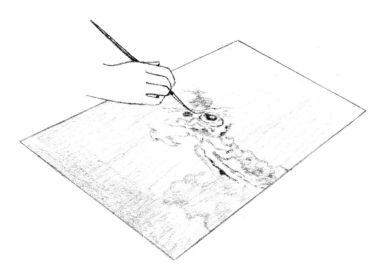

For the chevron, or feather, veining used by early American itinerant painters, the feather is used diagonally, brushed upward on its edge, and brushed downward with its full width. Such veining is lightly beaten with

a whisk brush to soften it. Another old method of veining consists of dipping a length of fine cotton string in the color, laying it irregularly on the surface, and beating portions of its length with a brush. Whatever the tool chosen for veining, it must be used loosely and freely. Veins, like plant life, branch and spring from a central stem and flow in the same general direction.

## ANTIQUING—PREPARATION

After the veining and glazing, the *faux marbre* surface undergoes a drying period of several days, then is brushed with a coating of thinned shellac or French varnish. In this case, the brush must be one with soft bristles to prevent the thin glazes below from running. The shellac coat must dry for an hour.

## ANTIQUING—PROCEDURE

*Faux marbre* may be antiqued in the standard way—by pouncing with thin japan spattering fluid, in a harmonious neutral tone deeper in value than the base hue, followed by blending with ooo steel wool. A more interesting effect is achieved with a lamb's-wool roller and the same thin spattering fluid, which has been further diluted with two volumes of mat varnish and turpentine mixed in equal proportions. After the roller is loaded, it is pressed out on the pan, drained, and rolled on newspaper until only a light dapple is left. The roller is guided by light pressure, and without pushing or dragging it moves in short diagonal strokes that proceed from the edges into the center of the surface. When the surface is covered, a second dry roller is used as a blotter. As one hand rolls it back and forth in short strokes on the wet solution, the other hand exerts strong pressure on it. This roller must be frequently wiped with a clean dry cloth to prevent re-deposits of the medium. Should dark, spotty areas occur, the clean roller is moistened lightly with mat varnish. A careful rolling over the heavy areas dissolves and spreads them. The molding edge of a marble surface can be antiqued with a 1-inch roller, or moistened cotton may be used to pat on the solution.

Antiquing increases the look of transparency, the appearance of stone, and the weathering of age. To further augment the effect of transparency and depth, the spattering fluid can be made of a value lighter than that of the marbleized surface.

*Faux marbre* requires a varnish finish of some depth to give credibility to the fantasy of polished stone. However, when woodwork and furniture proclaim by their very form the masquerade of fantasy, it is more sophisticated to finish them with protective mat varnish. After the surface has set for a week, the first varnish coat is carefully applied and allowed to dry. A second coat of varnish is applied and tufbacked with 600 wet-or-dry paper and a soapy solution. Other varnish coats are added until the surface is leveled, and the last one is rubbed down with a paste of rottenstone and lemon oil and a felt pad. By their very nature, of course, many types of antique *faux marbre* have uneven surfaces, for example, those used on a rustic or provincial piece of furniture. In such cases, the varnishing need not be carried to satin smoothness and may be finally coated with protective mat varnish.

## TROMPE L'OEIL FAUX MARBRE— PROCEDURE

*Trompe l'oeil faux marbre* differs from the *faux marbre* discussed previously in that it is executed with fine and minute detail, carrying the veining into a realm of jewel-like fantasy. It should be reserved for small and precious objects or for inlay.

The base for this type of *faux marbre* is prepared with four to five coats of paint tufbacked with 600 wet-or-dry paper and a soapy solution to satin smoothness. On this surface, a #6 sable brush is used to place the floating background in several colors. These are applied in small quantity, with a lightly loaded brush, to prevent rolling and dripping. The colors are controlled and blended with cotton that has been saturated with mineral spirits and then dried out. Some of the floats are soft and muted, others sharp and intense. Edges are softened with a cotton bud, or a #6 sable brush, dampened with mineral spirits. The colors cover about 60 per cent of the surface. Some areas may be rendered as *brèche* marble by blotting them with India paper (thin newspaper used for trans-Atlantic mailing) crumpled into countless tiny sharp edges or by using the pointed #6 sable brush in the way previously described for *brèche*. When the floating surface has dried overnight, it is reserved with a coat of thinned shellac. After this surfacing has dried, fine veins are applied with a #3 sable brush. Three colors are mixed for the veining—two hues analogous to the base color, and one sharply contrasting in hue and value. The two of least contrast are applied first, in thin, soft lines varying from hairline to $\frac{1}{16}''$, the width depending upon the light or heavy pressure of the brush as it is drawn across the surface. The veins more or less follow the general contour of the floating surface, occasionally diverging into the vacant areas; all flow, of course, in the same general direction. The veining is used as a harmonious element between floats and to break up and add interest to bland areas. After the first veining color has wrought intricate elaborations and embroideries, the second color emphasizes some part of these or begins new ones. The patterns to be avoided are those of repetition, regularity, parallelism, spider webs, train tracks running from a central depot, street maps, and regiments on parade. The third veining color—selected for sharp contrast —is used with more density, achieving a strong, dramatic effect. Its delicate variation contributes both accent and balance to the composition, and heightens its decorative quality. This type of veining is one of the most pleasurable adventures of *faux marbre*. It is an esoteric refinement of doodling. Veining must be planned to give the effect of all-over design, but one rhythmically punctuated by dominant elements within. It must be rendered with such exquisite detail that it induces the beholder to examine it closely.

## TROMPE L'OEIL FAUX MARBRE—ANTIQUING

Three ways are described here for the antiquing of *trompe l'oeil faux marbre*.

1. The surface is spattered and pounced with one of the antique anilines, made very thin with alcohol, in the color most related to the hue of the marble.

2. A thin solution of casein in a harmonizing color is spattered on or pounced on, and then patted with cheesecloth.

3. Having been protected with thinned shellac, the surface is pounced with a thin japan spattering fluid, or it is first spattered and then pounced with this fluid.

*Faux marbre* is one of the most rewarding of the fantasy finishes. It can be used on likely and unlikely surfaces and provides a gay and lively pleasantry. A demanding technique? Yes. But as fear diminishes and freedom grows, as the realization that nothing is ever lost, and that all is mutable, is reached, bravura leads to increasingly dazzling creations.

## FAUX MARBRE

*Materials*
Flatting oil
Shellac
Alcohol solvent
French varnish
Turpentine
Charcoal sticks
Oil pastels
Japan colors
Flat white paint
Protective mat varnish
Clear gloss varnish
Mat varnish with high wax
  content
Rottenstone
Lemon oil
Mineral spirits

*Tools*
Shellac brush
400 wet-or-dry paper
600 wet-or-dry paper
Stiff-bristle brush
Oxhair brushes (¼″, ½″, 1½″)
Turkey feathers
Camel hair whisk
Natural sponges (cosmetic and
  large-pored)
Chamois
Wooden block
2″ spatter brush
Badger blender
Eyedropper
Pounce brush

#3 and #6 sable brushes
Metal comb
000 steel wool
Two lamb's-wool rollers and pan
Orangewood sticks
Stipple brush (stencil brush)
Erasers (for veining, erasing,
  stamping)
Large sash brush

*Miscellaneous*
Felt pad
Non-detergent soap flakes
Synthetic sponge
Cotton twine
Cheesecloth
Absorbent cotton
Cotton buds
India paper
Baking tin
Sheets of paper (for tests)
Scissors or clippers
Newspaper
Tissue paper
Sample boards
Blotter
Rags
Corks
Potatoes
Talc
Rubber or linoleum (for small
  stamps)

# FAUX
# TORTOISE SHELL

## NATURAL SHELL: DECORATIVE USE IN
## FAR EAST

Tortoise shell was used as ornamental veneer in the Orient. With its soft tawny mottling, its translucency, and its pliability, it is a versatile decorative material. As early as the eighth century, tortoise-shell overlay was used on different backgrounds—white, yellow, green, red or golden—which imbued the shell with greater textural depth, emphasizing or altering its color according to the density of the natural tortoise markings.

The dorsal shell of the hawksbill tortoise, *caretta imbricata*, was most sought after because of its black, yellow, and flame markings. This shell consists of layers of horny, translucent, and mottled plates. The plates are peeled, partially liquefied by heat, molded and compressed, and then solidified firmly. When used as inlay, this substance was embedded with a hot iron between decorative channel walls of ebony, ivory, or ormolu.

FAUX MARBRE: *Top left, black-and-gold, negative; right, brèche.*
*Bottom left, feather; right, trompe-l'oeil.*

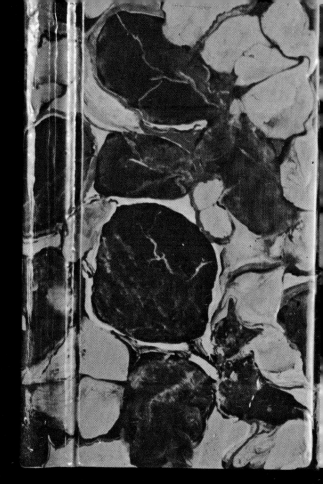
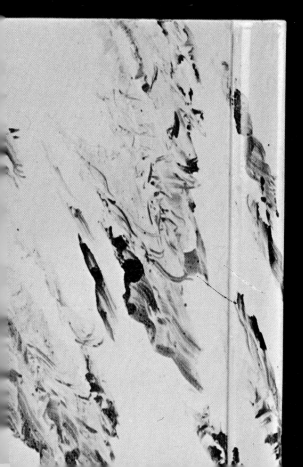
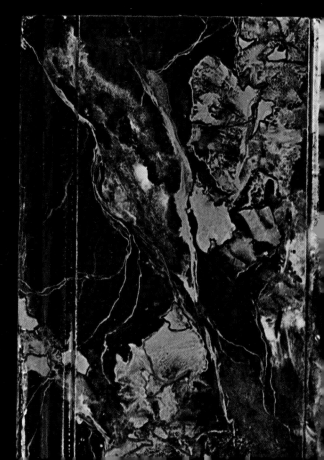

## NATURAL SHELL: DECORATIVE USE IN WESTERN WORLD

One can assume that examples of Oriental tortoise shell inlay reached western Europe through the Dutch East India Trading Company. In the eighteenth century André Charles Boulle, *ébéniste* (cabinetmaker) to Louis XIV, rediscovered the charm of tortoise as inlay or veneer. He used the shell as a decorative surface on commodes, table desks, secretaries, and clock cases, elaborately combined with silver, pewter, or ormolu.

Boulle was inspired by the technique of Florentine craftsmen to effect a marquetry of brass and tortoise shell. As F. J. B. Watson, the British antiquities historian, explains:

> To prepare this marquetry a sheet of brass and a
> sheet of shell are glued together; the decorative
> design is then laid down on the top and cut out
> in the usual manner by means of a marquetry saw.
> When separated, the layers of veneer can be com-
> bined in two different ways: in the one a
> shell ground is inlaid with the design in brass
> (*première partie* or first part), in the other
> the design appears in shell against a background
> of brass (*contre-partie* or counter part).

A museum is fortunate indeed if it owns both forms of a single design. Admiration for Boulle's use of the shell over a painted ground led to two of the painted fantasies which bear his name: red Boulle and green Boulle.

## SIMULATED SHELL

In the seventeenth and eighteenth centuries there were Venetian, French, English, and American variants of what was then described as tortoise lacquer. The vogue for all things Oriental which swept the Western world had created a craze for lacquered furniture, and this in turn had led to the imitation of lustrous tortoise in that much-admired finish. Cabinets, commodes, and other furnishings, small decorative objects such as mirror and

TORTOISE SHELL: *Top left, Italian; right, green Boulle fantasy.*
*Bottom left, red Boulle fantasy; right, English.*

picture frames, and molding trim on painted pieces, all were rendered in this fashion. (One fine example is an American tallboy in Queen Anne style at the Winterthur Museum.) These pieces were usually further embellished with gold, often raised, in a *chinoiserie* design.

In France and England, *boiserie*, ceilings, cornices, and woodwork were painted in the tortoise fantasy well into the nineteenth century, as is confirmed by contemporary manuals and periodicals that were intended for the house painter. In America a naive and provincial tortoise was rendered on chairs and wardrobes by itinerant painters.

Today there is a resurgence of interest in painted tortoise as a decorative finish—it is being reproduced even on leather, plastic, and paper. But of course the mechanics of reproduction are incapable of the spontaneity and charm of freely executed painting.

## SUITABLE SURFACES; PROPER DIMENSIONS

There are many versions of painted tortoise, ranging from the *faux* rendering in naturalistic style over a white or yellow ground to the Boulle fantasies, and even to the golden conceits inspired by the Orient. Tortoise forms and the tortoise palette stimulate still other decorative finishes which bear little resemblance to their progenitor but retain some of its charm. Painted tortoise is at its best on flat or rounded surfaces to which the shell itself might reasonably have been applied. Broken surfaces and carved elements obviously could never have been tortoise. Furthermore, on uneven surfaces the transparency is lost and the fantasy fails. Carved elements and small moldings must therefore be finished to resemble metal, ivory, or ebony. Since large pieces of tortoise shell would not be true to nature, the fantasy pieces are not more than 6″ in largest dimension, which is consistent with actual tortoise plate. This size limits their use to small areas, where they are combined decoratively in rectangles, squares, and strips, or in baroque designs such as those of Boulle. The sections are controlled by fine joining lines as well as with mounts of ivory, ebony, or metal.

## CARE OF NATURAL SPECIMENS

In the pursuit of *faux* tortoise, a sample of real tortoise is a tremendous help as an inspiration and a control. If the real shell is mounted on a small box or other object, it is essential to know how to care for it since central heating is apt to produce lifting and cracking. The shell can be kept moist with senna powder mixed to a paste with olive oil; this is rubbed on with the palm of the hand about once a week.

## NATURAL-COLOR FAUX TORTOISE—PREPARATION

The ground hue for tortoise is selected from the tones ranging from ivory to a pale yellow, and is mixed by adjusting the proportions of the following formula:

8 volumes flat white paint
½ volume French yellow ochre japan color
1 volume chrome yellow light japan color

Three to four coats are applied to the surface; each coat following the second one is tufbacked with 400 wet-or-dry paper and a soapy solution. The surface is then bound with thinned white shellac and lightly rubbed down with ooo steel wool. On this surface, the pieces of tortoise shell are marked out with a 2H pencil. A provincial piece might be painted with sections of dissimilar shape; such variety sometimes displays the painted fantasy in a diverting way. A more elegant piece, on the other hand, is treated as fine veneer, the segments of tortoise laid in matching, symmetrical fashion. Before a section is painted, it is bordered with rubber cement to protect the adjacent areas.

## NATURAL-COLOR FAUX TORTOISE—PROCEDURE

Natural tortoise shell is made up of a series of free forms, radial in direction and progressing from light to dark in value. A form is largest at its lightest point, diminishing in size as the value deepens.

### THE RADIAL PATTERN

The pattern of tortoise is simulated with a series of strokes of varying width and length: brush splashes which radiate from a central point. These markings appear to consist of many transparent tones ranging gradually from a delicate tawny hue in the larger areas to a deep brown-black in the smaller ones. The beauty of real tortoise shell lies in the semi-transparency of its layers, which creates a rich depth of changing tonalities. The illusion of this is achieved by painting in the large light transparent markings first, proceeding to deeper but still transparent yet diminishing markings, and ending with those that are small and almost opaque.

When natural shell is cut for inlay the point from which the markings radiate is removed because of its coarseness. Therefore, when planning a painted fantasy, an imaginary point of radiation—about 6″ beyond (above, below, or to either side of) the particular section to be painted—must be visualized. Each stroke appears to originate from this point and radiate from it like one of the spines of an open fan. The size of each section regulates the arc of the radial strokes. Their fanning direction is determined by the position of that imaginary point, which is preferably off-center.

### THE FIRST, TRANSPARENT STROKES
For the first transparent radial markings, an asphaltum wash is used thinly in each section.

|  |  |
|---|---|
| ASPHALTUM I | 1 volume asphaltum |
|  | 1 volume japan drier |
|  | 1 volume undiluted spar varnish (warm) |
|  | 2 volumes thinner (mineral spirit) |

The wash can be applied in one of several ways. A lightly loaded 1-inch oxhair brush may be used on its broad side as a pencil is used to shade a drawing. The ends of the strokes are whisked and drawn out unevenly with a small piece of absorbent cotton. In fact, the wash may even be applied with a cotton-fabric bob, or a natural cosmetic sponge, well wiped out on paper toweling. About 60% of the background is covered with these first radial strokes. When the asphaltum has dried, it is coated with thinned orange or white shellac, the choice depending on the tone of yellow desired. This prevents the asphaltum from dissolving when it comes in contact with any paint mixed with mineral spirits or turpentine.

### THE SUCCESSION OF COLORS
As the essential characteristic of tortoise shell is its shadowy transparency, oil color is the best medium for the fantasy. The palette should consist of:

French yellow ochre oil paint
Raw sienna oil paint
Raw umber oil paint
Burnt umber oil paint

Diluted clear varnish (40% turpentine) is used as the mixing agent in order to emphasize the transparency of tone. One drop of japan drier added to the varnish expedites the drying of the paint. Tortoise shell ranges in hue from closely related soft and tawny tones to flame color to deep browns. In *faux* finish, the colors may be closely related or in strong contrast; moreover, there is a wide choice in the proportions of the dominant tone of this palette. On an extensive surface—a table or chest top—it is preferable to narrow the color range, as strong contrast on such an area is disturbing; dramatic contrasts should be reserved for smaller objects. Some will prefer to work from light hues to dark, others vice versa. This is a matter of personal preference. However, in teaching, the progression from light to dark has proved to be more practical.

Before the oil color is applied, each section is wiped with cotton dipped in flatting oil. This softens the paint and increases the effect of transparency. The first colors laid on are French yellow ochre and raw sienna alone or combined in varying hues. These amorphous strokes are applied, with a #11 round sabline brush (a mixture of oxhair and sable), over about 50 per cent of the surface, some of them upon the background, some upon the asphaltum strokes. They range from thin to thick, long to short, have irregular edges, and occur in groups of different dimensions. Rigid parallel forms must be avoided as they are not characteristic of either nature or traditional painted fantasy. After each group is brushed on, the ends of each stroke are lightly whisked with a small ball of cotton; not only does

the paint gain a more transparent quality, but also the frayed ends become more like those in actual shell. With skillful use of the cotton, additional irregularity of the strokes can be contrived. After the drying interval, a coat of thinned shellac is applied and another series of the radial strokes in deeper colors is laid on. As many combinations of the palette as are desired may be applied provided there is an intervening coat of thinned shellac. When the stroking is concluded and dry, the entire section is lightly washed with some tone of the oil color that deepens or adds warmth to the general effect.

## ACCENTS

Now 1 volume burnt umber japan color is combined with ¼ volume lampblack japan color to a brown-black: this color is the definitive accent that creates the tortoise effect. With a #6 sable brush, the color is pressed, rather than painted, in a series of small irregular lozenges and dots. These are placed singly and in clusters at a slight angle to the existing radials. The black-brown forms accent the background and the radials with dramatic insistence.

When the oil paint is used from light to dark, the first asphaltum application may be omitted. In such case, asphaltum is reserved for a final loose spattering to harmonize the work. As the spatter begins to dry, it is blotted gently with a white blotter.

## CONCLUDING STEPS

When the tortoise effects have been completed, the surface is again coated with thinned shellac. If the sections of shell simulate ones that are joined, the fine lines that symbolize the joinings are indicated with a #3 sable brush and raw umber japan color. Then inlay bands simulating ivory or ebony may be added in widths of from ⅟₃₂″ to ⅟₁₆″. Ormolu, silver, or pewter mounts may be applied in an over-all continuous design. For ivory a faintly yellowed flat white paint is used; for ebony, lampblack japan color with drier; for ormolu, silver, or pewter, one of the metal leafs. The leaf, of course, must be toned with an antique patina. Finally, the usual many coats of clear gloss varnish are applied and tufbacked with 600 wet-or-dry paper and a soapy solution. The last coat is rubbed down with rottenstone and lemon oil for a superior finish.

## LIGHTLY DAPPLED NATURAL TORTOISE

On one occasion, a decorator wished to have armchairs with rounded surfaces rendered in tortoise. Since the markings of natural shell were too strong and spotty for this purpose, they could not be used. Instead, the following variation was developed. The chairs were painted with five coats of tortoise base paint and tufbacked with 400 wet-or-dry paper and a soapy solution. A coat of thinned white shellac was then applied. When dry, each member was rubbed over with flatting oil before the application of color. The palette consisted of oil paint in French yellow ochre and raw sienna. Small cotton balls were first dipped in flatting oil and then loaded with the oil paint and patted on the surface; these, with different pressures and some overlapping, achieved a number of tones. Where necessary, they were blended with another cotton ball dipped only in flatting oil. The effect was a light dappling in tawny tones which only faintly resembled tortoise. When the surface was highly varnished and rubbed down, the result was elegant and effective. This technique is excellent for moldings on a piece otherwise painted in color.

## TOLE-INSPIRED TORTOISE

Another delightful fantasy was inspired by tortoise painted on eighteenth-century tole. The surface was first prepared in the usual way. In this case, yellow yellow-green was used as the background; after tufbacking, it was coated with thinned white shellac. One-inch bands, alternating with $1\frac{1}{2}$-inch bands, were ruled on the surface. The $1\frac{1}{2}$-inch bands were masked off, and the remaining 1-inch bands were coated with Asphaltum I and pressed with crumpled newspaper. When these were dry, the rubber cement was removed, and $\frac{1}{16}$-inch lines of India ink were painted down each side of the asphaltum bands. The whole was coated with thinned white shellac and then varnished.

The student of these fantasies will discover, after he has learned their techniques, that they lead on to original variations on the theme.

## NATURAL-COLOR FAUX TORTOISE

*Materials*
Flat white paint
French yellow ochre japan color
Chrome yellow light japan color
Raw umber japan color
Burnt umber japan color
Lampblack japan color
White shellac
Orange shellac
Alcohol solvent
Asphaltum
Japan drier
Spar varnish
Mineral spirits
French yellow ochre oil paint
Raw sienna oil paint
Raw umber oil paint
Burnt umber oil paint
Clear gloss varnish
Flatting oil
Turpentine
Rottenstone

Lemon oil
India ink

*Tools*
2H pencil
1″ oxhair brush
Shellac brush
Varnish brush
Natural cosmetic sponge
Round sabline brush, size 11
#3 and #6 sable brushes
400 wet-or-dry paper
600 wet-or-dry paper
000 steel wool

*Miscellaneous*
Absorbent cotton
Ruler
White blotter
Rubber cement
Fine cotton fabric
Newspaper

## BOULLE TORTOISE

Red and green Boulle made use of the transparency of tortoise shell; over brilliant color, it created an effect unrelated to the natural tone. Antique pieces of Boulle which have split and dried reveal that the brilliant color was on a thin sheet of paper glued to the wood surface over which the tortoise was laid. The color of the paper was either red red-purple or blue blue-green. Over the red, the golden and brown tones of the tortoise became a warm rich red. Over the green, the tones became a yellow-green. In both cases, the deeper brown tones were dramatized by the color surrounding them. Each of these combinations lends itself to exaggeration in the painted fantasy. The red red-purple and the blue blue-green are glimpsed as though through the palest part of the shell. The deeper tones become the golden red and green. The amber hues are somewhat lost but are replaced by the warm tones of the reds and greens in contrast with the black-brown.

# RED BOULLE—PROCEDURE

## *THE BASE*

To create the fantasy of red Boulle, the surface is prepared with a warm red made to this formula:

1 volume orange-red japan color
$\frac{1}{10}$ volume japan drier
$\frac{1}{2}$ volume turpentine (as needed for thinning)

Four or more coats of the mixture are necessary; the second coating and each one thereafter is tufbacked with 400 wet-or-dry paper and a soapy solution. When this has been done, the surface is coated with thinned orange shellac.

## *FIRST SERIES OF STROKES*

The asphaltum mixture already described (Asphaltum I) for natural tortoise is used and applied in the same manner. Fifty per cent of the background is covered with radial strokes. In this rendering, they are the largest and lightest radials, and they initiate the illusion of transparency. When they have dried, a bonding coat of thinned orange shellac is applied.

## *SECOND SERIES OF STROKES*

A heavier asphaltum is prepared for the second series of strokes.

ASPHALTUM II　　2 volumes asphaltum
1 volume undiluted spar varnish (warm)
$\frac{1}{2}$ volume thinner
$\frac{1}{4}$ volume japan drier

This series, laid partly on the first set of strokes and partly on the remaining red ground, covers about 65% of the surface. It dries overnight.

## *ACCENTS*

The black-brown accents (which vary from $\frac{1}{2}''$ to $1\frac{1}{2}''$ in length) are now painted on in the way described for natural tortoise: singly and in twos and threes, some of the clusters touching. These accents are placed on the existing strokings, on the background, and occasionally on parts of both. They continue to follow the fan pattern, but at a slightly different diagonal. The over-all decorative pattern must be considered and these strokes added for stylistic emphasis. After overnight drying, a thinned coat of orange shellac is applied with the oxhair brush as the stiff shellac bristle would disturb the asphaltum.

### GLAZE

Now a glaze is made to this formula:

> 1 volume thalo red rose oil paint
> 1/8 volume Indian red oil paint
> 2 volumes undiluted clear gloss varnish
> 4 volumes turpentine
> 1/4 volume japan drier

The oil paints are mixed with the turpentine before the other ingredients are added. With an oxhair brush of suitable size or with a finger of absorbent cotton, the glaze is applied in radial splashes. It must overlap—but with a slight variation in direction—about 50 per cent of the established pattern. Only 15% of the original ground color remains exposed. When the glaze has dried for a week, the surface is coated with thinned orange shellac. Leveling coats of thinned clear gloss varnish tinted with cadmium red oil paint are added, and are rubbed down with 600 wet-or-dry paper and a soapy solution.

### CHARACTERISTIC BOULLE DECORATION

The decoration added to Boulle tortoise simulates ormolu, pewter, or silver inlay, and may be rendered in common or precious leaf and antiqued with the suitable aniline. This decoration should be baroque in design, or it might be a diaper pattern. To emphasize the inlay, the metallic pattern is highlighted with French yellow ochre japan color and underlined with burnt umber japan color. Finally, the entire piece is spattered with a thin solution of antique aniline, or is antiqued with raw umber japan spattering fluid, before the concluding coats of clear gloss varnish.

# RED BOULLE VARIATIONS

### ENGLISH TYPE

There are a number of variations of red tortoise shell that probably derived from the much-admired red Boulle. In England, a lacquer tortoise was rendered on Japanware and was dried over a long period in an oven, as was English black lacquer. A facsimile of this type of tortoise has been achieved in the studio. A ground of red red-orange japan color is prepared in the usual manner. After this surface has been coated with thinned white shellac and has dried for one hour, a coat of quick-drying varnish is applied. Into this are immediately floated: a) 1 volume Indian red oil paint thinned with 4 volumes turpentine; b) Asphaltum II; c) the red red-orange japan color of the base coat, which has been thinned to milky consistency. These floats are applied in the radial pattern. This type of *faux* tortoise resembles that used on ceilings, wood paneling, and woodwork by English painters during the late nineteenth century.

## FRENCH TYPE

In France, the ground color was rendered in red red-orange japan color. The tortoise splashes on this ground were in red ochre, black, and red lake oil paint, alone and combined, and often additionally spattered with the red ochre oil paint. Distemper (a medium described in the chapter on *Faux Bois*) was sometimes used for the pattern. Over this an appliqué design in either Dutch metal or black japan color was rendered.

## RINGED VERSIONS

In the studio, several ringed variations have been inspired by Boulle tortoise. *In the first version* the surface is painted with red red-orange japan color combined with 10% japan drier and thinned with turpentine and prepared as for any tortoise base. This surface is protected with a coat of thinned orange shellac. After drying, it is rubbed over with flatting oil and brushed with a coat of the following asphaltum mixture:

ASPHALTUM III  3 volumes asphaltum  
        2 volumes undiluted spar varnish (warm)  
        1 volume thinner  
        ½ volume japan drier

When the asphaltum is surface dry, three bobs of fine cotton (ranging from dime size to the size of the tip of a cotton swab) are pressed on the surface to create a variety of rings, some isolated and some overlapping. Differing values are achieved with the asphaltum over the red according to the amount of pressure exerted. Concentric circles are formed by twisting the bob, first to the right and then to the left, without lifting it from the surface. If the asphaltum does not move, the bob, barely moistened in flatting oil and blotted out on newspaper, is touched to the surface. A coat of thinned orange shellac is applied with an oxhair brush. Lastly, concentric circles and harmonizing dots of red red-purple japan color, red-orange japan color, burnt sienna japan color, and burnt umber japan color are added with a #3 sable brush.

*A second ringed version* was evolved to recreate the finish on a beautiful eighteenth-century French workbasket. In this instance, the red red-orange surface is coated with thinned orange shellac. Over this is laid a thin coat of Asphaltum I, deepened in some areas by a second coat. Cotton wrung out in flatting oil is used to remove small circles of the asphaltum. If these circles close up too much, the flatting oil was applied too soon. Because of the heavier asphaltum areas, a three-toned effect is achieved. After the surface has set for an hour, smaller circles are made with tiny cotton-tip and toothpick bobs covered with cotton fabric. Asphaltum III is used to add centers to the circles. Additional circles and centers are painted in with a #3 sable brush and red red-orange japan color. When dry, a coating of thinned orange or white shellac is applied and the whole is finished with the usual varnish coats tinted with Indian red oil paint.

*The third ringed version* is even farther afield from the original tortoise but can be produced over the same red red-orange base coat. This is covered with thinned orange shellac. A light coat of flatting oil is applied, followed by a thin, even coat of Asphaltum III. The surface is then spattered with flatting oil, which causes the asphaltum to withdraw and reveal small rounds of the base hue. The time interval before spattering depends on the humidity of the day. If, after spattering, the revealed rounds of base color close up, the spattering was done too soon. The asphaltum coat must be very thinly applied or the rings will have gummy edges. If such should occur, they may be lessened with a cotton fabric bob rolled over them. When nearly dry, the surface is spattered with the glaze used for Boulle tortoise. Such a finish requires many coats of clear gloss varnish to level the surface. If the varnish is tinted with cadmium red oil paint, the translucency and shell-like appearance of the surface are increased.

## EARLY AMERICAN TYPE

A tortoise fantasy inherited from early American craftsmen is rendered on a red-orange japan color base, or on one prepared with a mixture of 2 volumes flat white paint and ¼ volume Indian red oil paint. Over this, the following coating is applied with an oxhair brush:

> 1 volume asphaltum
> 2 volumes quick-drying varnish
> ¼ volume turpentine

Onto the wet surface are flowed alizarin crimson oil paint and burnt umber oil paint, each mixed with a solution that is 1 part turpentine and 2 parts quick-drying varnish (warmed). The two colors are not brushed over, but instead are allowed to flow together. Then a stiff-bristle brush dipped in turpentine lifts portions of the wet paint in radial splashes, thus revealing some of the pink or red ground. This variation responds well to many applications of cadmium red tinted gloss varnish.

## ALUMINUM-SPLASHED VERSION

A dramatic version vaguely related to red Boulle is produced on a black surface which has been properly tufbacked, shellacked, and then laid with large radial splashes of aluminum leaf. With an oxhair brush, the following glaze is applied over all:

¼ volume alizarin crimson oil paint
½ volume quick-drying varnish
¼ volume turpentine

After the glaze has dried overnight, a coat of thinned French varnish is applied. An asphaltum glaze (1 volume asphaltum, 2 volumes quick-drying varnish) is laid on in radial splashes with the tip of a 2-inch oxhair brush. The edges of these splashes are softened with a brush loaded with a mixture of 2 volumes quick-drying varnish and ¼ volume mineral spirits. The resulting effect is brilliant and lustrous, and is most striking when painted with bravura. After being shellacked, this version, too, is concluded with the customary varnish coats.

### O'NEIL STUDIO VERSION
A studio version stemming from the methods just discussed uses 1 volume Venetian red oil paint combined with 2 volumes flat white paint for the base coat. When this is dry, a coat of Asphaltum I is brushed on. While it is still wet, radial splashes are laid on with alizarin crimson oil paint thinned with turpentine.

### THE LAST STEPS FOR ALL TYPES
It should be noted that any of these tortoise finishes is coated with thinned clear gloss varnish, tufbacked with 600 wet-or-dry paper and a soapy solution, and finally polished with a paste of rottenstone and lemon oil to approximate the lustre of the shell.

## RED BOULLE

*Materials*

Red red-orange japan color
Red-orange japan color
Japan drier
Turpentine

Orange shellac
White shellac
Alcohol solvent
Asphaltum
Spar varnish

French varnish
Thalo red rose oil paint
Indian red oil paint
Clear varnish
French yellow ochre japan color
Burnt umber japan color
Flat white paint
Cadmium vermilion oil paint
Black oil paint
Mineral spirits
Flatting oil
Burnt sienna japan color
Red red-purple japan color
Cadmium red oil paint
Rottenstone
Lemon oil
Venetian red oil paint
Quick-drying varnish
Lampblack japan color
Alizarin crimson oil paint
Burnt umber oil paint

Red ochre oil paint
Common or precious leaf

*Tools*
Varnish brush
Oxhair brush
#3 sable brush
#6 sable brush
Spatter brush
Stiff-bristle brush (for turpentine)
2″ oxhair brush
400 and 600 wet-or-dry paper

*Miscellaneous*
Absorbent cotton
Wooden block
Cotton bobs
Cheesecloth
Newspaper
Toothpicks

## GREEN BOULLE—PROCEDURE

The green Boulle fantasy follows all the methods of application described under red Boulle, and varies only in color.

The base hue is yellow-green and is made to the following formula:

1 volume green green-yellow japan color
2 volumes chrome yellow light light japan color
1/16 volume red red-purple japan color
¼ volume flat white paint
1/10 combined volume quantity japan drier
turpentine (as needed for thinning)

The glaze is blue blue-green, and is made by combining:

1 volume viridian green oil paint
2 volumes undiluted clear gloss varnish
4 volumes turpentine
5% japan drier

Antiquing of green Boulle is done with Antique Aniline Warm (see chapter on antique patina for leaf); it is spattered on in large drops.

## VARIATIONS

### RINGED GREEN BOULLE
In the studio version of ringed green Boulle, additional circlets are rendered in emerald japan color, green green-yellow japan color, and burnt umber japan color. Otherwise, the procedure for ringed red Boulle is followed.

### ITALIAN GREEN BOULLE
A beautiful Italian antique green Boulle box that was brought to the studio had been rendered by a technique similar to the one just described. However, the base hue was more yellow. To reproduce this finish, the following formula and procedure are used:

> 6 volumes French yellow ochre japan color
> 4 volumes flat white paint
> ¼ volume yellow-green green japan color

After the surface is prepared with this ground color, it is coated with thinned white shellac. A coating of Asphaltum I is added and allowed to dry for about one hour. Cotton moistened with flatting oil is then used to contrive touching circles of various sizes. In this case, the remaining asphaltum is somewhat transparent and the hue is lighter, in less contrast with the base color. Finally, ovals of viridian green glaze are centered in some of the forms. This finish may also be rendered by substituting walnut aniline for the Asphaltum I, and by using alcohol to form the circles of various sizes.

## GREEN BOULLE (see also list for RED BOULLE)

*Materials*

Green green-yellow japan color
Chrome yellow light light japan color
Red red-purple japan color

Emerald japan color
French yellow ochre japan color
Flat white paint
Japan drier

Turpentine
Viridian green oil paint
Clear gloss varnish
Burnt umber japan color
Asphaltum
Flatting oil
Walnut aniline
Alcohol

*Tools*
Oxhair brush
Spatter brush
Varnish brush
#6 sable brush

*Miscellaneous*
Absorbent cotton

# TORTOISE CONCEIT

In Tortoise Conceit, a golden surface glimmers around and through a galaxy of semi-transparent circles. This fantasy is called a conceit because the markings so greatly diverge from natural ones. It derives, however, from the Oriental practice of placing real tortoise shell over a golden ground. The circles vary in size and range in tone from amber to deep brown, mingling and overlapping in every conceivable arrangement. The result is a luminous effect, one even more fantastic than when shell itself is laid over gold.

The surface to be rendered is first covered with Dutch metal leaf. The circles are put in with oil paint or with aniline solutions, either of which is applied in this order: first the lighter or amber colors, then the deeper tawny tones, and finally the dark browns.

### OIL PALETTE PROCEDURE

The golden surface is first coated with thinned orange shellac. The oil palette for the circles is identical to that used for natural tortoise markings and is applied in similar stages, beginning with yellow ochre oil paint and raw sienna oil paint. For a slightly exotic note, a little terre-verte is used as one of the hues. The oil paint is mixed with a combination of 60% clear gloss varnish and 40% turpentine. In the Pitti Palace in Florence are columns which have been rendered in this fashion.

The following tricks—which are best done with an eyedropper—may be used to render the circles of color.

TORTOISE SHELL: *Top left, natural; right, conceit with oil.*
*Bottom left, lace; right, conceit with aniline.*

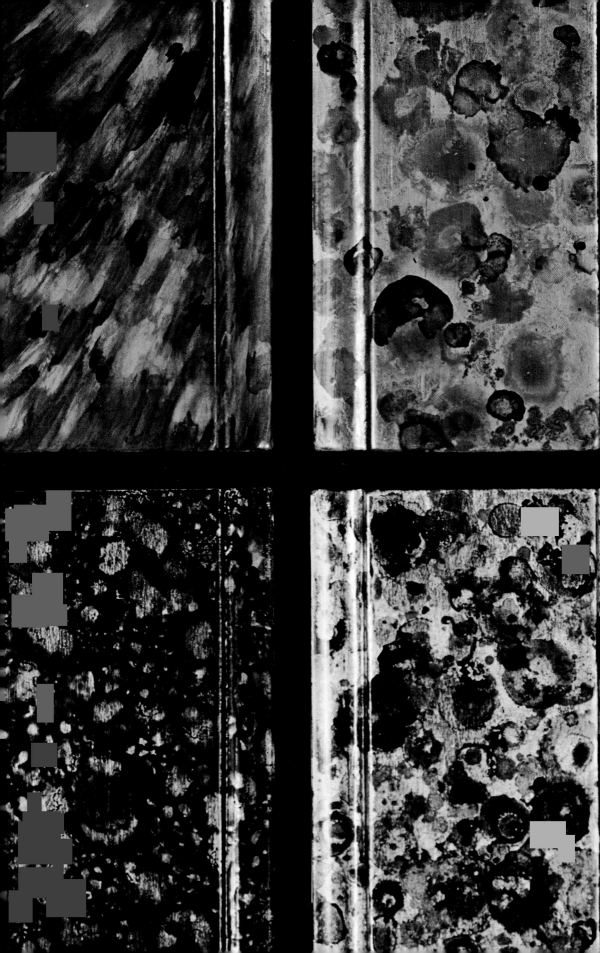

A small circle of flatting oil is inserted with a dot of color, the edges of which expand into the oil. As this dries, another color may be added to the center.

A drop of flatting oil added to the center of a drop of oil paint makes the circle expand; the gold center is left partially revealed and is subsequently dried out with a cotton bud.

A drop of water placed on the surface has a dot of oil paint added to it; the result is a ring of color. The water takes quite a while to evaporate.

Alcohol is dropped into a drop of oil paint in order to fray its edges.

The first application of yellow ochre oil paint and raw sienna oil paint, applied singly or in mixture, must dry. It is then sealed with a coat of thinned orange shellac before the deeper mixtures are added. The orange-brown warmth of tortoise is heightened by successive transparencies of brown, made more translucent by increasing the proportion of varnish. When 80% of the surface has been covered, some dark spottings are added, either as overlaps or as the centers of existing circles. A further interesting effect is obtained with a drop of Asphaltum II having a smaller drop of yellow ochre oil paint tipped to its center. When all the applications have dried, the entire surface is spattered with Antique Aniline Warm before the final varnishing coats.

### ANILINE SOLUTION PROCEDURE

To execute Tortoise Conceit with aniline solutions, the following palette is used:

yellow maple aniline powder } each mixed with white shellac
light maple aniline powder

dark golden oak aniline powder
walnut aniline powder } each mixed with orange shellac
light golden oak aniline powder

The powders, as usual, are dissolved in alcohol, and then combined with an equal amount of shellac, which is undiluted 4- or 5-pound cut. There are

LAPIS LAZULI: *Top left, French; right, Italian with gold skewings. Bottom left, provincial; right, jewel.*

a number of ways to apply the aniline circles; in any of them a coagulation of shellac gum must be avoided at all costs.

A drop of flatting oil dropped into aniline reveals a golden center.

A drop of aniline released within a drop of water produces a dark ring with a light center.

Aniline may be floated into a ring of alcohol with a #6 sable brush.

Alcohol added to an aniline droplet spreads the color.

Drying time must be allowed between applications or gummy edges are bound to appear; if, despite all precautions, some are apparent, they can be blotted with a fine cotton fabric bob rolled lightly on its edge. When 80% of the surface has been covered and dried, it is lightly rubbed with ooo steel wool. Japan paint mixed to black-brown may be used for accents—superimposed small dots, small circles, and the centers of the aniline circles. Any uncovered areas of the Dutch metal may be tarnished with sodium sulfite, which adds an exotic, faintly green tinge. When all is complete, the usual coats of thinned clear gloss varnish are applied.

## LACE TORTOISE

An interesting box that was brought to the studio proved upon examination to be another expression of this fantasy—lace tortoise. A Dutch metal ground which had been shellacked was used as the base. To recreate this finish, Asphaltum III is brushed over the prepared surface. Cotton, dipped in flatting oil and wrung out thoroughly, is used to diffuse the asphaltum and reveal the gold. The more often the cotton is touched to the surface, the more the asphaltum retracts and the areas of gold enlarge. When dry, the surface is coated with thinned orange shellac. Following this, the varnish coats are applied.

## BLACK AND WHITE CONCEIT

A contemporary variation of *faux* tortoise is rendered on Dutch metal or aluminum leaf. The leafed surface is first coated with thinned orange or white shellac. Then the following mediums are prepared:

BLACK GLAZE    ½ volume lampblack oil paint
½ volume quick-drying varnish
½ volume turpentine

WHITE SCUMBLE    ½ volume flat white paint
                ½ volume quick-drying varnish
                ½ volume turpentine

The black glaze is patted on with a ball of cotton, as is the white scumble, leaving the metallic base visible here and there. While wet, the surface is spattered additionally with the white mixture. When completely dry, it is shellacked. A thin glaze of Asphaltum I is added. This is spattered first with turpentine, then again with the white glaze. Cotton, wet with turpentine and wrung out, is used to soften the spattering here and there. After the drying interval, a coat of thinned white shellac is added. Then come the usual coats of clear gloss varnish.

Throughout the ages the shell of the tortoise, with its spectrum of color—pale yellow, gold, amber, topaz, carnelian, flame, and brown—and its warmth, vitality, and exoticism, has appealed to the imagination of creative craftsmen.

# TORTOISE CONCEIT

*Materials*
  Dutch metal and aluminum leaf
  Orange shellac (4- or 5-lb. cut)
  White shellac (4- or 5-lb. cut)
  French yellow ochre oil paint
  Raw sienna oil paint
  Terre-verte oil paint
  Turpentine
  Flatting oil
  Clear gloss varnish
  Asphaltum
  Alcohol
  Aniline powders (alcohol soluble)
    light maple
    yellow ochre
    raw umber
    dark brown
    yellow maple
    dark golden oak
    walnut aniline
    light golden oak

  Lampblack japan color
  Burnt umber japan color
  Sodium sulfite
  French varnish
  Quick-drying varnish
  Raw umber oil paint
  Burnt umber oil paint
  Flat white paint

*Tools*
  Eyedroppers
  Shellac brush
  Varnish brush
  #6 sable brush
  ooo steel wool
  Spatter brush

*Miscellaneous*
  Absorbent cotton
  Cotton buds
  Fine cotton fabric

# LAPIS LAZULI

## DESCRIPTION

*Lapis* is the Latin word for stone; *lazuli,* the Arabic word for heaven. They were combined by the Romans to designate a semiprecious substance of rich deep blue flecked with tiny yellow pyrites called "fool's gold." Lapis lazuli is composed of lazurite and numerous other minerals and occurs in masses in metamorphic limestone. Its beauty lies in the glint of gold, deep within the blue, which is a mass of tiny particles in subtly varying tones. In the fifteenth century, Italian painters ground this stone to produce the sky-blue pigment used in precious altarpieces for the Virgin's mantle and the robes of saints and angels. Today lapis is far too valuable to be used as a pigment, and its color is reproduced synthetically in commercial ultramarine.

The deepest darkest lapis lazuli of gem quality was found in Persia, China, and Siberia. The stone is now even more scarce than in earlier times, and the present supply from Afghanistan, Chile, and the United States is a softer blue mingled with gray drifts of matrix.

Lapis lazuli was valued by the ancient Egyptians and the Romans, who used it for superb intarsia work. In a later age, Europeans reserved it for jewelry and inlaid veneer. As the stone became increasingly rare and costly, eighteenth-century Italian craftsmen painted a somewhat exaggerated fantasy of it on chairs, chests, consoles, and as architectural ornaments; they also used it in false inlay, along with fantasies of other semiprecious minerals. The sophistication of the painted facsimile was relative to the place of conception and the technical skill with which it was executed. In the provinces, the paint technique was soft and free, the color naive—ultramarine mixed with Prussian blue, plus raw sienna to represent the yellow pyrites. On objects made for the sophisticated court, leaf was frequently used as the background, or gilt particles were added to the color ground.

A successful painted rendering exaggerates the characteristics of the stone. The color varies widely, yet subtly, in tonality and hue, magnifying the differences of nature to intrigue the beholder. The fragmentation of color is obvious. The particles representing the pyrites are discreetly and sparingly placed. Obviously, the provincial interpretation is bold and free, far removed from actuality.

## PROVINCIAL LAPIS—PREPARATION

### COLORS

The base paint for the surface is made by combining:

> 2 volumes flat white paint
> ½ volume French yellow ochre japan color
> ½ volume raw umber japan color
> ½ volume chrome yellow light light japan
>     color

Four to five coats of this paint are applied in the usual manner. These are tufbacked with 400 wet-or-dry paper and a soapy solution to obtain a smooth body. Oil colors, because of their transparency, are best suited to make up the palette for the particles in the matrix. The following four are used:

> Indian red oil paint
> Prussian blue oil paint
> Raw sienna oil paint
> Ultramarine blue oil paint

Each of these colors—with the exception of the ultramarine—is mixed with turpentine to the consistency of milk (the turpentine is added little by little or the oil color will not dissolve sufficiently). Then a few drops of japan drier are added to the mixture. The ultramarine is prepared by combining:

½ volume ultramarine blue oil paint
2 volumes quick-drying varnish
1 volume turpentine
1 drop japan drier

### APPLICATORS

Four small cotton balls are prepared. They are dipped into a mixture that is half flatting oil and half turpentine, then are wrung out and pounded on a flat surface to blunt the wisps. One of the cotton balls applies a preliminary coating; the other three are the tools for applying the raw sienna, the Prussian blue, and the ultramarine blue. The Indian red is put in with a #6 sable brush.

## PROVINCIAL LAPIS—PROCEDURE

### APPLICATION OF COLORS

First, a thin coat of the flatting oil and turpentine mixture is applied to the surface with a cotton ball.

Immediately, with a #6 sable brush, a few dots of the Indian red are laid on to simulate the fragments of iron.

Then raw sienna is dabbed with a cotton ball over 30 per cent of the surface.

Prussian blue is patted over part of the raw sienna, eliminating it in some areas and bringing out a greenish blue in others; then more of it is added elsewhere until its coverage totals about 60 per cent of the surface.

Ultramarine blue is now patted over the Indian red, over some of the isolated Prussian blue, and on the background color, obtaining a coverage of about 95 per cent of the surface.

Some minute areas of the background are left uncovered, while other areas are only transparently filmed in order to achieve a variety of blues. Since the color should appear in irregular drifts—thin in some places, more opaque in others—the cotton balls are manipulated in such a way that rounded or cloud-like forms are avoided. Moreover, the work must be done quickly. The drifts of ultramarine and Prussian blue may be emphasized to mimic the drifts in real lapis. They should be of differing deep blues and lighter greenish blues, interspersed minutely with raw sienna, bits of iron red, and occasional outcroppings of the background color. The effect is one of overlapping transparencies.

## FRAGMENTATION OF PAINT

Just before the paint film dries to mat, turpentine is finely sprayed on it with a spatter brush—a procedure done *with restraint* so that the surface is not flooded. This spattering causes the paint film to separate into fine particles. As a result, the base hue and the colors first applied are in part revealed, suggesting the tiny grains of varying hue characteristic of real lapis lazuli. If the surface remains opaque, a careful light blotting will accentuate the fine particles. If the rendering lacks unity, it may be additionally spattered with (1) a very thin solution of the Prussian blue oil paint, or (2) the ultramarine oil paint lightened with an equal volume of flat white paint, or (3) a thin solution of turquoise japan color made to the following formula:

> 2 volumes flat white paint
> 1/8 volume blue blue-green japan color
> 2 volumes emerald green japan color

## VARNISH COATS

At least a full week must be allowed for drying time, longer if the humidity is high. It is possible to hasten the drying by dusting the object with either ultramarine blue or Prussian blue dry powder; this is brushed off several days after the application. When the surface is completely dry, thinned gloss varnish coats—which may be tinted with ultramarine blue oil—are added. They continue, with the usual intervening tufbacking, until the surface is level. Since provincial lapis is meant to look naive and obviously unreal, the final coat is a mat varnish.

## ANILINE SPATTERS

In a more sophisticated rendition, a spattering of aniline precedes the varnishing. The spatter is made by combining 1 volume ultramarine blue, or blue-green, aniline powder dissolved in alcohol (see standard formula, in the section on tinting leaf) with 1 volume undiluted white shellac.

# FRENCH AND ITALIAN VERSIONS OF PROVINCIAL LAPIS

A refined form of lapis lazuli was painted in the eighteenth century in both France and Italy. It can be duplicated with a technique related to that used for floating *faux marbre*. Very thin ultramarine blue casein is floated over a flat-white paint ground (probably gesso in former days). Heavier floats of ultramarine blue casein and Prussian blue casein are mingled. Small areas of the white and larger transparent blue areas are reserved. To this are added small floats of soft gray made to this formula:

> 4 volumes white casein
> ½ volume black casein
> 2 volumes raw umber casein
> ⅓ volume pale yellow casein

When the surface is dry, fine golden veins of either metallic powder or French yellow ochre casein are applied with a #3 sable brush. This type of lapis is coated with a flat varnish of high wax content. It is then antiqued with raw umber japan antiquing fluid, or raw umber powder and wax, either of which is applied by pouncing.

A variation of the lapis lazuli fantasy may be observed on the doors of an apartment in the Pitti Palace in Florence. Here the ultramarine blue was lightened with an equal amount of white, drifted with white, and scumbled with deep blue. Then the surface was veined and spattered with gold. Today japan paint and flatting oil and turpentine would be the simplest means for approximating this variant.

### GOLD ACCENTS

When a sophisticated fantasy is required, it may be accented with golden particles in either of the following ways.

1. After two coats of varnish have been applied and rubbed down, small amounts of quick size thinned with turpentine are floated on the surface. Into each float, a grain of rich gold bronzing powder is tapped. The particle expands into a fine hair-like vein.

2. After the first two coats of varnish, the article is surfaced with quick size. With the flitter tube described in the chapter on burnishing, tiny flakes of gold are deposited wherever desired, and are flattened with the finger.

In France, there are examples of *faux* lapis that were first surfaced in cobalt blue oil color lightened with one-third white; this was spattered with white, then was lightly pounced to form irregular particles. Raw umber lightened to a middle value with white was used as a veining medium. Today this variation would be rendered with japan color and flat white paint. Here, as in the Pitti Palace version above, varnish coats may be applied between scumbles and drifts to reserve what has been achieved before further drifts or scumbles are added.

## GEM LAPIS—PREPARATION

The following methods of simulating lapis achieve a more jewel-like effect than the ones described for provincial lapis, and the results more nearly resemble the stone.

The surface is leafed with Dutch metal and coated with thinned orange shellac. This metallic surface substitutes for the raw sienna simulating pyrites used in provincial lapis. The ultramarine blue oil paint, the Prussian blue oil paint, and the Indian red oil paint are mixed as previously described. Oxhair brushes, plus a quantity of facial tissue, are the essential tools.

## GEM LAPIS—PROCEDURE

### COLOR FLOATS

It is necessary to work quickly for the best results. With a 1-inch oxhair brush, floating forms of ultramarine blue oil paint are applied opaquely over 70 per cent of the surface. With a #6 sable brush, a few small dots of Indian red oil paint are floated into the ultramarine blue. A facial tissue

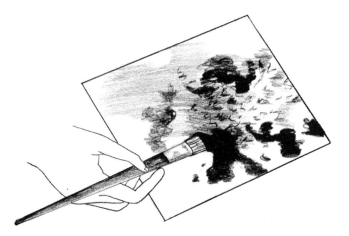

crumpled in sharp points is pressed lightly on a section of the paint to expose definite lines of the golden background. The pressure must be light to keep the strong contrast between the gold and the deep blue, and the area must not be re-blotted or the color will blur. The same tissue with the blue paint it absorbed on its points is pressed on the peripheral edges of the ultramarine blue patch so that the imprint mingles with the remaining gold ground. The blotting process is now repeated—each time with a clean crumpled tissue—on one section of color after another.

Next, the Prussian blue oil paint is patted on the remaining 30 per cent of the surface, and thinned ultramarine blue oil paint is floated into it here and there. Certain areas are deepened, and the floating effect is accentuated with a #6 sable brush. These sections in turn are blotted with clean crumpled tissue. Specks of gold appear minutely here and there over the entire surface, resembling the gold in genuine lapis.

### FRAGMENTATION OF PAINT

When the paint surface is almost mat dry, it is spattered finely with turpentine to separate the paint into tiny particles. If the values are too closely related, they may be lightened with a spatter of the turquoise japan color or the ultramarine blue mixture described in the provincial method. This rendering must dry for over a week. Should the final result fail to please because of a lack of harmony, aniline spatters may be added, or the whole surface may be glazed with a thin solution of the ultramarine blue oil paint, followed by a spatter of thinned Prussian blue oil paint. A viridian green oil glaze may be introduced as an interesting substitute for the conventional ultramarine blue hue.

## *SIMULATION OF VENEER*

As this procedure results in a fantasy of lapis which more nearly resembles the jewel stone, the area covered is now divided into sections that simulate the joinings of thin slabs of lapis used as veneer. With a stylus that has been dipped in turpentine, fine lines are drawn against a straight edge to mark the joinings. These lines will obviously expose the gold, but so finely that they produce the illusion of carefully fitted segments. Sufficient thinned clear gloss varnish coats are applied to level the surface, which is finally rubbed with a paste of rottenstone and lemon oil so that it resembles polished lapis lazuli.

# LAPIS VARIATIONS

There are other unusual methods of creating *faux* lapis. One of them requires a white base that has been tufbacked and then coated with thinned white shellac; this is spattered with quick size thinned with turpentine. When the surface becomes tacky, common color powders or fresco colors are sprinkled on or are applied with a cheesecloth bob. These powders range through the blues, blue-purples, and blue-greens (for example, turquoise, ultramarine, and Prussian). After the first color has been applied, the surface must dry overnight; it is then sprayed with acrylic fixative. The sizing and powdering with one shade of blue after another is repeated until a pleasing effect is achieved. The final spattering with size is dusted with gold particles. After an application of the acrylic fixative, the surface is finished with the usual varnish coats.

A variation of this is rendered on an aluminum or silver ground which has been coated with thinned white shellac. In this case, the metal glints are brought out, after the dusting with powder, by sharp pouncing with a stencil brush.

This fantasy when rendered in the provincial manner combined with *faux bois* was one of northern Italy's most delightful creations. In the more realistic, jewel-like rendering, it is particularly effective when used with other *faux* inlay materials or in combination with marble and malachite.

## LAPIS LAZULI

*Materials*
Mat varnish (with high wax
  content)
Flatting oil
Clear gloss varnish
Quick-drying varnish
Turpentine
Japan drier
White shellac
Orange shellac
Alcohol solvent
Common dry powders
Fresco dry powders
Quick size
Rich gold bronzing powder
Gold leaf
Dutch metal
Aluminum leaf
Flat white paint
Raw umber japan color
French yellow ochre japan color
Lampblack japan color
Ultramarine blue japan color
Cobalt blue japan color
Prussian blue oil paint
Raw sienna oil paint
Indian red oil paint
Ultramarine blue oil paint
Rottenstone

Lemon oil
Acrylic fixative
Casein paints
Chrome yellow light light japan
  color
Blue blue-green japan color
Emerald green japan color
Viridian green oil paint
Aniline powders

*Tools*
1″ oxhair brush
#3 and #6 pointed sable brushes
Varnish brush
Shellac brush
Spatter brush
Pounce brush
400 wet-or-dry paper
Stencil brush

*Miscellaneous*
Absorbent cotton
Facial tissue
Wax
Flitter tube
Stylus
Straight-edge ruler
Cheesecloth

# FAUX BOIS

## PAST USES OF FAUX BOIS

The fantasy of painted wood goes back for thousands of years, inspired, it seems, by an interest in rare and exotic species. In the Bronze Age, the Mycenaeans decorated pottery with an imaginative impression of wood. Egypt, a country poor in wood, produced a more realistic version. There, during the Third and Fourth Dynasties, unusual varieties were simulated with all their knots and waviness. The Orientals with marvelous artistry stylized their fantasy, using symbols for the knots and graining.

Coming up to the Modern Age, we find the French designating their version of this fantasy as *faux bois,* which means "false wood." The phrase distinguished the technique of the artist from the coarse wood grainings of the house painter.

In Europe and America *faux bois* was used, as was marbleizing, on architectural elements, in which case the fantasy sometimes formed the background for *trompe l'oeil* decorations. Doors and wainscoting in the palace at Fontainebleau are painted as cypress—with a pale gray ground, paler gray peck marks (signs of a type of rot), and a raw sienna graining. In the Villa Borghese in Rome there is a *faux bois* door, complete with hardware, which opens on a *trompe l'oeil* vista and balances an actual door.

This fantasy was also used to embellish furniture. For instance, in northern Italy beautiful desks and *poudreuses* had elaborate inlays of *faux bois*; this was executed with almost jewel-like perfection in colors unknown to nature but with the characteristic knots and grains freely and wittily retained.

In country houses, *faux bois* was used in a naive form; the style is loose and has little relation to any natural wood. Pieces of this type were painted in this way in northern Italy during the eighteenth century; they have an air of uninhibited innocence. The inspired Venetians combined other *faux* finishes—lapis, malachite, and marble—with *faux bois*. In Germany, Austria, Norway, and Sweden, the interpretation was heavier; however, it was not without a certain individual appeal.

European examples from the eighteenth century are now regarded as treasures. Some were executed as painstakingly as miniatures, elaborately imitating marquetry. Then, in the early nineteenth century in France, shop fronts appeared that were painted entirely in *faux bois*, while interior paneling and woodwork were embellished with gold and ebony-painted inlay.

House painters, of course, were among the artisans who came to America, and many brought with them the graining methods practiced in the larger cities of Great Britain and continental Europe. In the 1800s when rosewood supplanted mahogany as the fashionable wood for American furniture, artisans learned to imitate it with paint, as rosewood itself was rather scarce. Later on, "fancy" chairs in the style of Hepplewhite were grained. The provincial furniture of America includes naive interpretations of *faux bois* which wander so far afield that they are sometimes mistaken for *faux marbre*. As the century entered the Victorian era, the painted fantasy deteriorated to wood graining, a travesty of both the real and the fantasy; this coarse decoration continued into the early 1900s.

# NATURAL WOOD: GENERAL CHARACTERISTICS

The various species of wood have peculiar qualities, each one differing in grain, pore, and color. Moreover, the hue of a well-polished piece of wood changes in appearance according to the light falling upon it. The chatoyancy (changing luster) varies with the angle of the light and the density of the wood grain; the tonal quality is modulated while the pattern of the grain remains unaltered. The diversity of woods is characterized by the differences in the grain.

# FAUX BOIS—GENERAL CHARACTERISTICS

The technique of *faux bois* should be undertaken with a conscious understanding of the finely marked and varied grains of wood and the eccentricity of the knots, though it is not necessary to have in mind a specific variety of natural wood, particularly insofar as color is concerned. In a highly imaginative rendition of *faux bois*, natural color and specific form may both be defied, as long as the essential presence of knots, followed by the rhythm of surrounding grain, is maintained.

A decorative exaggeration is essential to the rendering of the provincial fantasy. The execution is free and bold, yet with full regard for the composition. The design is one of approximate symmetry, an imitation of matched veneers that vary slightly with each cut. As one studies the grain of wood, one becomes aware of the endless variation of line: thin, thick, curving or jagged, never exactly the same. Primarily, in painting, the knots are disposed to make the panel pleasing. The flow of the grain in real wood emanates from the knot, first clinging to the form of the knot and gradually straightening, then slowly curving again as it prepares to surround another knot. The grains are heavy and strong near the knot, becoming finer as their distance from it increases. There is always a subtle non-conformity of form and line. As has been stated before, nature is ever creative, never reiterative. The painted fantasy must be no less fanciful.

# PREPARATION OF BRUSHES

The brushes used for *faux bois* are of utmost importance. The exactitude with which each one is prepared determines its excellence as a tool.

*For the wood knot,* two *round* stiff brushes (glue brushes) of different size are prepared in the following manner: the bristles are tied about 1″ from the ferrule and cut off with a razor and hammer at that point (this is the only way they can be cut evenly); they are shortened to give them

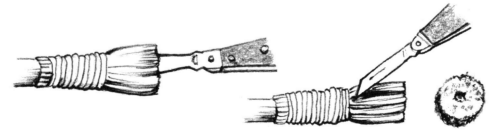

more elasticity. The brush is now cored: a sharp knife pressed from the free end of the bristles as deeply as possible into the middle of the brush is turned around to cut out one-third of the bristles from the center of the brush. Tweezers aid the removal of these central bristles. The brush is then laid on a board and clumps of the outer bristles are cut out near the ferrule, care being taken that the cutting does not penetrate as far as the middle of the brush. These clumps are cut out so that the remaining hairs can change place and undulate when the little rings of the knots are sketched. As the brush is rotated horizontally on a flat surface, the remaining clumps of bristle are cut off at the end in a slanting direction so they will not be united and the hairs can be placed as desired. Now the brush is held vertically and pressed down on a board; as it is turned, the ends of the hairs are further abraded in a slanting direction. Finally, the brush ends are turned and twisted on a piece of wet carborundum to round them.

*For the wood grain,* several *flat* stiff-bristle brushes (similar to a shellac brush) of different widths are used. These, too, are chopped off to 1-inch length with a razor and hammer. The bristles of the brush (held vertically) are divided horizontally in the center with a cardboard or a steel comb. On one side of the divider, with a sharp, pointed knife or manicure scissors,

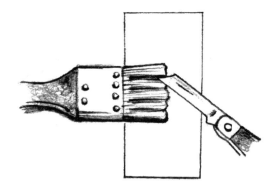

four or five clumps of bristle are cut out near the ferrule. On the other side of the brush, additional clumps of bristle are removed; these must alternate with those already removed; in addition, there must be a slight space on either side of the clumps. The ends of these bristles are serrated in a slanting irregular way, and then the longest hairs only are ground on the wet carborundum. The round and flat brushes just described, a metal

FAUX BOIS: *Top left, Oriental with gold; right, provincial.*
*Bottom left, Oriental; right, crotch faux bois.*

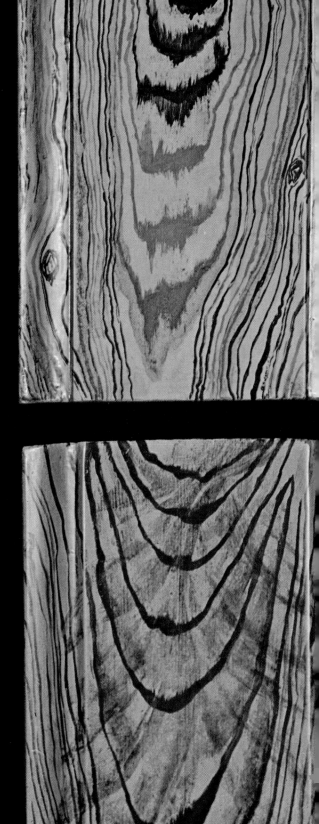
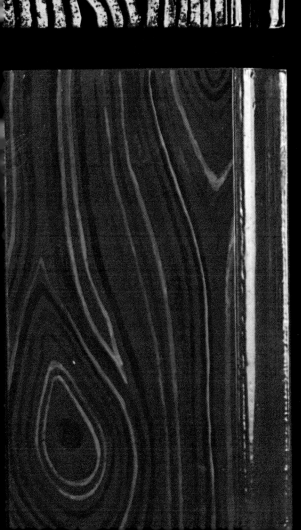

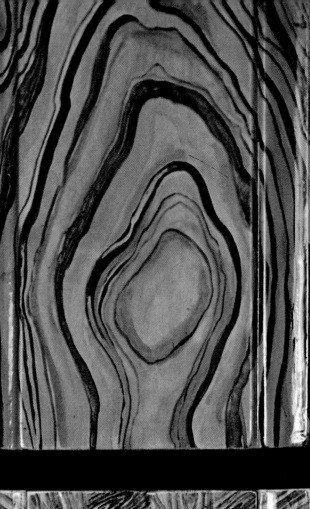

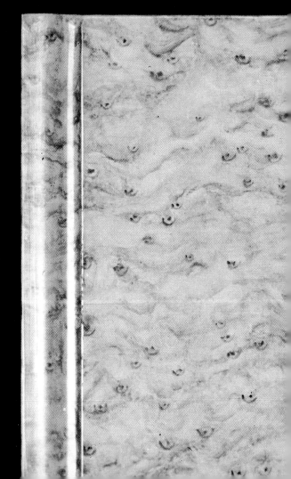

comb and a badger blender, a natural cosmetic sponge and a glazing brush, a short whisk brush, several pointed sable brushes (#3 and #6) and a pipe-over grainer (commercial brush) are the required tools for painting *faux bois.*

## PRELIMINARY STUDIES

Careful study of wood grain and practice with the tools must precede any attempt to render *faux bois* in paint. Samples of veneer may be obtained from lumber yards. For observation purposes, these should be oiled or varnished to intensify the grain. The prepared tools should be tried out with India ink on heavy brown paper to see what effect they produce and to determine whether the cutting needs rectifying. A sketch of the particular grain to be simulated should be made first before undertaking it with paint. With the design firmly in mind, the craftsman will not be hindered by the use of paint for the actual rendering.

We now come to a discussion of the various shapes of wood grain and the techniques of rendering them; these should be practiced on brown paper with the India ink.

### KNOTS—TECHNIQUE

The knots are put in with the round stiff brush. It is filled with the medium, rubbed out on paper until half dry, and gently pushed against the steel comb in a slanting direction to spread the hairs. The points of the bristles are rounded by rolling them on the palette. The lightly loaded brush is then placed on the surface to be painted and is rotated with a slight pressure, thereby producing a knot with an open center.

FAUX BOIS: *Top left, stylized; right, North Italian.*
*Bottom left, marquetry; right, pecky faux bois.*

### RINGS—TECHNIQUE

The rings surrounding a knot are added next; the upper section of each is drawn with one stroke, and the lower section with a second stroke. The points of joining are whisked with a badger whisk to make them imperceptible. The grains in the vicinity of the knot formation are at first relatively broad and widely spaced but they thin out and draw together as they depart from it.

The above procedure is now explained in detail. After the brush is loaded, it is knocked against the steel comb to separate the bristles—thus insuring a variety of graining lines. The brush is held at the ferrule between thumb and fingers. The ascending stroke begins with the brush held in a slanting horizontal position with the palm turned toward the surface. At the top of the curve, the brush assumes a more perpendicular position but

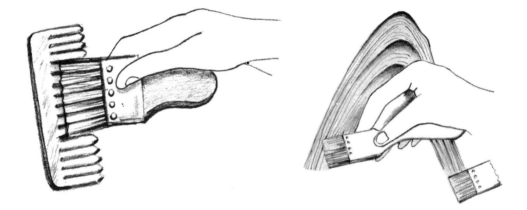

again falls into the slanting horizontal direction as it descends. The segments of the growth rings along the side fall densely together and those at the top become more widely separated as they extend upward, for a tree increases in height more than in width. As the brush runs along the knot, it rotates to narrow the grain.

### VARIED USE OF GRAINING BRUSHES

For the straight veins on either side of those that surround the knot, a graining brush or a pipe-over grainer is used. The bristles are separated by the comb, then the brush is placed flat on the panel. The grain remains uninterrupted, and one follows another. As a tree increases in height, the widely extending veins become more compact on the sides, and this fineness of grain is produced by moving the brush now upward, now downward.

The grain flowing from the cut brushes varies in these respects: if the brush is used on its corner only, a thin veining results; if the brush is held more horizontally and has been knocked out against the comb, the graining is wider; if the brush is held upright, the veins become thin, and thicker and broader as the brush slants.

## *VEINY CROTCH WOOD—TECHNIQUE*

Crotch wood, so called because it occurs at the parting of two heavy branches, is most beautiful when veiny. Fine marquetry furniture often uses this part of the wood as veneer. The curvy graining lines which characterize crotch wood are stroked in with the flat brush, which is kept in a perpendicular position. The strokes move from the bottom perpendicularly and as pressure is exerted on the left side of the brush, they gradually slant and widen as the brush descends. The strokes are kept close together as they descend on the right of the curve, and widen as they reach the bottom

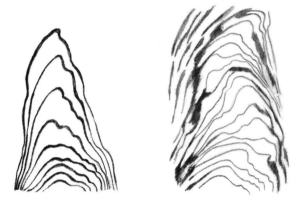

of the form. With a thinly loaded natural cosmetic sponge, light, interrupted strokes are wiped diagonally across the two curves to the left and to the right. These strokes must not reach the middle of the vein. The paint deposited by the sponge is then partially removed from the lower side with a solvent applied with sponge or brush. Stroking and hacking with the whisk brush then serrates this lower edge of the sponge stroke. To form a feathery

effect from the center outward of the graining form, the corner of the whisk brush dipped in a deeper color is used. These are softened with the badger blender when paint rather than ink is used.

### SOFT CLOUDY GRAINS—TECHNIQUE

Cloudy portions of *faux bois* are obtained with a fine natural cosmetic sponge. As they are difficult to render in ink, the sponge is filled with a glaze consisting of ½ volume oil paint diluted with 4 volumes turpentine and 3% of the combined quantity japan drier and is rubbed over the surface so that a half tint is left behind. A piece of chamois wet with water and wrung out is formed into a roll and rolled down the surface, thereby removing the color in irregular patches. Then, with the sponge filled but not drenched with the same glaze, horizontal undulating lines are sketched in

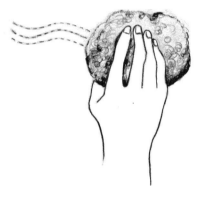

from top to bottom of the surface. From the bottom, the sponge is stroked upward in the direction of the high curve of the undulation. It is pressed softly at first and then harder; irregular cloudy portions, small and large, are thus formed. The effect is of light above the dark clouds formed by the stroke of the sponge. The badger blender, manipulated with an undulating motion in a slanting direction, then erases the strokes of the sponge so that only the clouds remain. If very fine curly lines are a part of the wood specimen, a flat bristle brush, which has been dipped in color and pressed against the steel comb, is drawn through the work in wavy curling lines inclining downward. Immediately a feather with the fronds separated is moved over the surface in the same direction, turning at times sharply and then proceeding downward. This splits the grain into a variety of forms. When the operation is complete, the surface is beaten with a badger blender. The tiny knots in the midst of the clouds require a small short-haired pointed sable brush; this is divided in the middle of the bristle with a piece of cotton

thread tied to the handle. It is dipped in paint and the knots are laid on in the light part of the clouds while the surface is still wet. These tiny pecky knots of color are placed in the undulations. Two knots may be placed immediately next to each other, and a half-circle painted beneath them.

## DISTEMPER AS A GRAINING MEDIUM

The surface for wood graining must be prepared to a satin smoothness, as all fine wood has a surface without blemish. When this has been accomplished, various mediums discussed in this chapter may be applied. The first of these is distemper. In the nineteenth century, beer was commonly used by decorative painters for tempering—that is, mixing—the graining medium. The weak, glutinous nature of beer makes it peculiarly fit for spreading and binding the pigment to the surface. Distemper has the advantage of quick drying. Its disadvantage lies in the fact that it is not so durable as oil paint.

## DISTEMPER—PREPARATION

The surface to be grained is first given four or five coats of japan paint in the lightest value of the wood. Each coat dries overnight and the whole is tufbacked with 600 wet-or-dry paper and a soapy solution. The surface requires this washing before the application of the distemper, as any grease will prevent the medium from lying smooth. As a further precaution, onion or garlic juice is rubbed over the base paint.

A distemper paste is made to this recipe: dry pigment powder of the desired color and hot soapy water are combined to a paste. Flat beer or ale is added as a diluent (½ beer and ½ water) and then the mixture is strained.

# DISTEMPER—PROCEDURE (NEGATIVE METHOD)

### GRAIN

As in other fantasy finishes, either a negative or a positive method is used for graining with distemper. To render *faux bois* in the negative manner, revealing the color underneath, the surface is first dampened with water or a soapy lather in order to prevent the medium from crawling. Then the distemper paste is laid on with a natural cosmetic sponge or a brush. A series of rubber combs is now run over the distemper. In part they remove the color, in part they push it aside, leaving a track to indicate the grain of the wood. During this patterning, they are held perpendicular to the surface; after each use, they are wiped clean. The first combing is done with a large, widely spaced rubber comb. A metal comb with a piece of a child's balloon stretched over its prongs also works admirably. A comb with closer-spaced teeth follows with an uneven pressure and a slightly tremulous motion. Pressure must vary to produce broad or fine lines. Combing proceeds in a series from the broadest combing near the knot to the finest on the periphery.

### KNOTS

Knots are rendered with a damp chamois or a chamois tip on an orange-wood stick. The chamois, placed around one's first and second fingers, is laid firmly on the work and turned without lifting to give a curl to the knot. The grain flows up and around the knot. Each combing is followed by one which overlaps a little and varies in direction so as to produce a gradual change in form. The broadest graining lies near the knot and becomes gradually finer. After the pattern has been established, the position of the comb is varied, slanting it one way or another for coarse or fine strokes, just as with a brush.

### OAK FIBERS

In the case of oak, after the grain has been made, a very fine and sharp metal comb is run over the whole piece. Held perpendicular to the surface, it is pushed back and forth to create the fibers of the grain. The surface is then beaten with a slightly dampened badger blender, the points of the brush going against the grain. Should the surface become too dry, it may be wet anew with a damp badger brush.

### SURFACE HIGHLIGHTS

With a 1-inch strip of cloth or chamois, laid over the index finger and held with the thumb and middle finger, the glittering highlights are put in. These highlights are light diagonals which indicate the changing light on the surface of the wood. A dry natural cosmetic sponge may also be used.

When completed, the lines of the grain are brushed horizontally with a badger blender to soften their edges; or the blender may be pounced lightly over the lines to break them up. If a panel is implied, a comb is drawn against a stiff, folded paper to indicate the straight edge of the joining; for a dramatic effect, the grain on one side of the joint goes in a direction slightly askew to that of the grain on the other side. Dark, defining touches around the knot and among the grains are added with a deeper japan paint. Quickness and spirit in the execution of this work are necessary for a lively rendering.

A panel may also be executed with three color values, each of which is applied with an oxhair brush and immediately combed, the grain being directed around the knots. The darkest of these colors is applied first. The two other values are used to fill in between the darks.

### WOOD PORES

When the surface has dried and been coated with thinned shellac of the appropriate color, the entire surface is lightly speckled with japan spattering fluid of the deepest hue. The steel comb is held over the surface and a lightly loaded spattering brush is run through the teeth. This projects a fine spray, which is immediately whisked in the direction of the graining. The fine particles now resemble the pores of the wood.

### SURFACE GLAZE

Finally, when fully dry, and after it has been sprayed with acrylic fixative, the surface is filmed with an oil glaze, of any desired color, made to this recipe:

> ½ volume oil paint
> 2 volumes undiluted clear gloss varnish
> 5 to 6 volumes thinner
> 3% combined volume quantity japan drier

When painting wood, it is assumed that the light falls directly upon the surface. Wherever the grain turns, there is a change of light. Light areas are generally in a slanting direction above the point of turning. The glaze at these points may be removed with sponge, chamois, or well-dried brush. In another method, a thin glaze is applied with a wide whisk brush, which is moved diagonally from top to bottom to regulate the dark or light tints by greater or lesser pressure on the brush. When this surface has dried, it is given sufficient thinned clear gloss varnish coats and the usual tufbacking to level the surface.

## DISTEMPER—PROCEDURE (POSITIVE METHOD)

Three distemper mixtures are prepared: a light, a medium, and a dark color.

After the surface has been dampened with soapy water or rubbed with onion juice, one of the flat stiff-bristle cut-out brushes is loaded with the lightest color and the bristles are spread against the metal comb. This first color is applied throughout the surface. The edges are blended and softened with a natural cosmetic sponge and soapy water. The medium color is loaded on the tips of the pipe-over grainer and applied in veins. These strokes are whisked with the badger blender. Knots are laid in with the medium color and a #6 sable brush. The deepest color is used for accents, which are applied with a #3 sable brush. Highlights are added with a water-wet chamois. All surfaces rendered in distemper must be sprayed with acrylic fixative before varnishing.

## OIL GLAZE AS A GRAINING MEDIUM— PREPARATION (NEGATIVE METHOD)

As previously mentioned, the surface for *faux bois* must be very fine and smooth. It is prepared with four to five coats of flat paint of the desired color, which is tufbacked with 600 wet-or-dry paper and a soapy solution. Flat paint is preferable to enamel or semi-gloss because when sanded it produces a finer surface; however, it calls for a coating of thinned shellac, which enamel and semi-gloss do not require.

## OIL GLAZE—PROCEDURE
## (NEGATIVE METHOD)

A glaze is made to the following formula:

> ½ volume japan color
> 2 volumes undiluted clear gloss varnish
> 3 volumes thinner
> 2 volumes flatting oil
> 3% japan drier

This is flowed on the painted surface with a bristle brush. Some variation in the coating will not matter as the subsequent graining will veil its inequality—in fact, the effect will be better than that achieved on an evenly glazed surface. The *faux bois* graining is produced by removing the drying glaze in striations in a rhythmic pattern with a rubber comb. The comb moves unsteadily with wiggles and jerks. Occasional halts and backtrackings are necessary to produce the irregularities that are naturally formed around knots. Nevertheless, the tool must maintain firm contact with the surface. A stiff-bristle brush may also be used; before each stroke, the bristles are wiped clean, reloaded, and dragged across the metal comb. If the glaze dries too rapidly for easy striation, the brush is lightly moistened with flatting oil and thinner. To lighten the striations, a muslin or cheesecloth rag can be dragged over certain areas. A sponge used in a rhythmic diagonal movement highlights the wood. A water-wet chamois or chamois tip is also used to highlight and lay in the knots. Japan paint on a #3 or #6 sable brush defines the knots and accents the veins. Finally, the surfaces are whisked with a badger blender to soften all edges. The piece is then set aside to dry for a week, after which it receives the thinned clear gloss varnish coats necessary to achieve perfect smoothness. These varnish coats, if tinted, eliminate the necessity of applying a thin oil glaze to the entire surface, as in methods using distemper.

## OIL GLAZE MEDIUM FOR STYLIZED
## FAUX BOIS—
## PREPARATION (POSITIVE METHOD)

The Italian method in the eighteenth century used paint in the positive method; stylistically, therefore, it is the most decorative. A very fine preparation is essential. The base coats of the lightest value are smoothed and polished, particularly when *faux bois* is to be rendered with glazes, as the least defect will mar the finished work. The base coats are tufbacked with 600 wet-or-dry paper and a soapy solution, and when dry are protected with a thinned coat of white shellac.

## PROCEDURE

The color for stylized *faux bois* may be divergent from natural tones. The graining is rendered in one or two contrasting colors of middle value, the accents in a deeper value. A wash deeper than the base, lighter than the grain, is added here and there further to enhance the whole.

After careful consideration has been given to the general design to be rendered in *faux bois*, it is lightly indicated with chalk on the surface. Oil glazes for the grain are made to the following formula:

$\frac{1}{2}$ volume oil paint
3 volumes turpentine
3% japan drier

A stiff graining brush is loaded and knocked several times against a steel comb. A trial is made to determine whether the grain is too broad or too slight. If too broad, some liquid is pressed from the brush on a cloth; if too slight, the brush is re-loaded. In addition, one corner of the brush may be loaded, by means of another brush, with a deeper value of glaze so that two values will be applied simultaneously. Thus the principal vein as well as the thin spreading veins are laid in with one stroke.

Now all the techniques of graining practiced before are brought into play. The variety of wood to be painted is well studied. The work proceeds through the laying of the knots, to the painting in of the veins around the

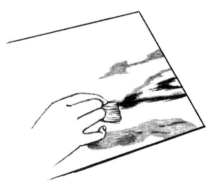

knots, to the stroking in of the straight veins, then on to the heart veins surrounding another knot. The surrounding veins are whisked at either end both away from and toward the knot. This fills in the open areas around the knot and assists the transition to the surrounding straight grain. The

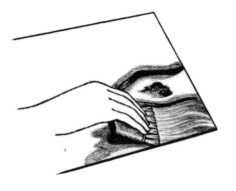

outer edges of the graining lines may be softened, if desired, by whisking, or by rolling a cotton swab along them. When the entire surface has been grained, the highlighting is done with the chamois or the natural cosmetic sponge. To dramatize the pattern, the accents on knots and emphasis on graining are added in varying thickness with opaque japan paint.

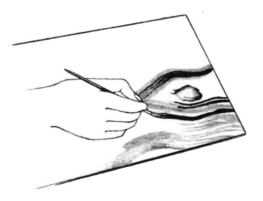

When the surface has dried for a week, the pores of the wood are put in by means of a brush lightly loaded with japan spattering fluid. A steel comb is held vertical to the surface and the brush is pushed backward and forward across it. This deposits a fine spray over the work. The spray is immediately brushed down with a badger blender or a whisk broom and the pores become visible. After this has dried overnight, a thin wash of oil paint and turpentine is applied to portions of the work for stylistic emphasis.

To heighten the luster of the surface after it has dried for a week, a second glaze so thin that hardly any color is perceptible is applied. With the brush well dried-out, the sharpest lights are effected by removing the glaze. This glazing loosens the initial paint surface just a little and the surface is quickly whisked with the badger blender to obtain the shimmer of fine wood.

Japan color may also be used effectively to render *faux bois*. As it is opaque, it should be used for extremely dramatic and stylistic versions. Japan color is used in all the methods as the ultimate finishing touch.

## PIEDMONTESE FAUX BOIS

From the Piedmontese comes a fantasy of *faux bois* which is direct and dramatic. Over a pale base hue rendered in the manner prescribed for all *faux bois*, a sharply contrasting oil glaze (made to the recipe in the section on cloudy grains) is stroked on with a pipe-over grainer in curving veins. One grainer stroke is placed adjacent to the preceding one to make a broader band, or three strokes are pulled together with a sable brush. For variety, India paper is crumpled into sharp points and pressed upon some of the bandings. The paint thus picked up is imprinted on the background areas between the grain. When the patterning has been completed, the surface is mat varnished. It is then antiqued with a pouncing of japan spattering fluid.

## ORIENTAL FAUX BOIS

Oriental *faux bois* called *mokume* was rendered in several ways: 1) the design was sometimes incised on the lacquer ground; 2) the graining was executed in yellow ochre and burnt sienna on a red-orange lacquered ground; 3) the graining was a brown-red powdered with gold on the usual black lacquer ground. The third method, which achieves a highly decorative effect, uses rubber cement as a resist on the black ground. A #3 sable brush is used to line the inner edge of the graining with size, and the remainder is heavily spattered with size. When these areas are tacky, a heavy deposit of gold flakes is tapped over the spatter with a flitter tube (see chapter on burnishing) and leaf is applied to the sized lines. After the drying interval, the rubber cement is rolled off. The highly stylized effect of *mokume* is stunning and would certainly add drama to contemporary furnishings.

## FAUX BOIS ON TOLE

A charming use of *faux bois* is to be found on French and English tole painted in a provincial manner with an exaggeration of color and a simplification of form. The effect is that of water color and it seems to have been achieved with gouache and casein over a japan-painted base. The *faux bois* is often combined with a freely rendered floral spray or an oval medallion.

In all the variations which have just been discussed, the delineation of *faux bois* is dramatic and decorative. Striking color combinations, stylized design, contrasting form, and spatial relationship provide the most effective, entertaining, and dynamic result.

## FAUX BOIS MARQUETRY

*Faux bois* in natural wood colors departs from exaggerated graining only when rendered as marquetry. Such fantasy calls for the design to be painted with exquisite precision—and the result is often more exciting than actual inlaid wood.

Marquetry is a branch of cabinetwork and consists of a decorative pattern applied on a wood surface. Both the field and the pattern material are veneers of equal thickness fitted together. The woods used for the ground and for the decorative sections are of differing color, grain, or specie. When the great examples of this work were done in the seventeenth and eighteenth centuries, the woods were dyed in brilliant colors. (Sycamore and maple were especially favored because they took the color so well.) The taste of the period demanded that the floral designs be as realistic as possible. Unfortunately, the dyes were not lasting, and the examples seen today have lost their original exuberant colors. Sometimes the woods were shaded (*ombré*) and outlined by burning, etching, or engraving with acid. The surface elements were cut from the wood in such a way that their veining would contribute to the inlay design itself or would give variety to the field around it.

In painting *faux bois* of this type, the geometric designs of parquetry are most decorative for small table desks, *poudreuses*, and miniature cabinets. *Trompe l'oeil* effects of interlocking and other three-dimensional members are particularly effective.

## WOODS TRADITIONALLY USED IN MARQUETRY

Most of the woods used in the eighteenth century were described with invented names which did not always designate a particular wood or which may have embraced a variety of woods with superficial resemblances. As F. J. B. Watson says:

> The trees from which these exotic woods were taken were quite unfamiliar to the Parisian craftsmen of the day and woods were grouped by colour and grain in a quite unscientific manner.

*Faux bois* painted in imitation of veneer was used in Italy during the late eighteenth century to camouflage poor wood. In France, where this was not necessary, it was more often used for panels and bandings.

## MARQUETRY—PREPARATION

The surface is finely prepared with four or five coats of the palest tone of the woods to be painted. If the woods differ widely from one another, it is well to mix a pale neutral tone, which can be washed with color, to the following formula:

6 volumes flat white paint
½ volume French yellow ochre japan color

Every second coat of base paint is tufbacked with 600 wet-or-dry paper and a soapy solution. The design is carefully laid out on tracing paper and transferred to the surface.

## MARQUETRY—PROCEDURE

After the placement of the various woods has been decided, each portion is tinted with a color wash made of oil paint and turpentine. After drying overnight, the surface is coated with diluted French varnish.

For genuine marquetry, the finest veneers are carefully selected. A common way of arranging them is book-matching: a pair of similar slices is opened up so that one member is a mirror image of the other. Each slice, of course, shows the slight variation of its growth; this must be kept in mind as work on the fantasy progresses.

The veining for marquetry is based on the patterns described at the beginning of this chapter. Here they will be rendered in miniature with only the 1-inch pipe-over grainer and the #3 and #6 sable brushes.

For each wood to be painted a series of washes of oil paint thinned with turpentine is required; at least three values (light, middle, and dark) are mixed. As they become darker, the mediums are thinned less and less. The thinnest of this group is applied with a pipe-over grainer to indicate the general flow of the grain. With a #6 sable brush the intermediary value is put on to indicate the placement of the veining. The deepest value is applied with a #3 sable brush as the grain becomes finer. Hairline grain and accents to the knots are added with denser japan paint. The shading and lining of

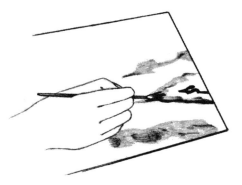

any elements of the pattern which were etched or burned in are rendered with raw or burnt umber japan color thinned with turpentine. To further define the fitting of the marquetry sections, hairlines of raw umber japan color are added.

It is recommended that the negative portions and the surround of the design be completed and protected before the design itself is painted.

## SATINWOOD FANTASY

Satinwood was used in the Neoclassic period, particularly in England. It is generally dappled or feathered. An area to be dappled is first painted over with a thin oil glaze (French yellow ochre oil paint and turpentine) applied in the direction of the pattern or grain. When partially dry, a small piece of natural cosmetic sponge is dropped on the area at random. The sponge marks are brushed back and forth with a small blender to soften their edges. This is allowed to dry and is protected with thinned French varnish.

Very fine veining is done with a feather which has been cut on one side to leave spaces between the ribs. It is dipped into water and then dipped into a somewhat thicker mixture of the oil glaze. The feather is then pulled through a comb to further separate the ribs. Next, the feather is run lightly in the direction of the grain across the surface in undulating waves. These are softened with a blender—particularly in the deeper areas of dappling, thus permitting the veins in the bright spots to stand out more.

If the ground is to be feathered, a deeper glaze—made so by the addition of a little raw sienna oil paint—is laid on. Parts of it are removed with a cosmetic sponge or brush, and the resultant effects have the plan of a feather, the tool breaking up any continuous line. The remaining glaze is now blended crosswise. Since satinwood is very pale, color must be applied sparingly; any overgraining on top of the dry feathered ground must be particularly fine.

After a satinwood panel has dried for a week, it is coated with thinned clear gloss varnish, every two coats of which are tufbacked with 600 wet-or-dry paper and a soapy solution. The final coat of varnish is rubbed down with a paste of rottenstone and lemon oil to produce the satin-like finish of fine wood.

Any *faux bois* rendered in marquetry may be further enhanced with ivory or ebony filletes or ormolu; the filletes are rendered in flat white paint or lampblack japan color, the ormolu in burnished gold.

*Faux bois* is a versatile expression of painted decoration. When rendered in brilliant color, it is as contemporary as the day. When applied to square forms, it erases the rigidity of their outline. It can be bold, dashing, and is always decorative. *Faux bois* reaches its zenith when it is rendered as marquetry in a dazzling tour de force of superb technique.

MALACHITE: *Top left, positive method; right, art nouveau.*
*Bottom left, negative method; right, veneer.*

# FAUX BOIS

*Materials*
Flat white paint
Japan colors
  French yellow ochre
  raw umber
  burnt umber
  lampblack
Oil paints
  earth colors
  Indian red
Acrylic fixative
White shellac
Alcohol
French varnish
Rottenstone
Alcohol solvent
Turpentine
Muslin
Mat varnish
Dry pigment powders
Beer or ale
Thinner
Flatting oil
Japan drier
Clear gloss varnish
Lemon oil

*Tools*
Spatter brush
Badger blender
Whisk brush

Several 1½" and 2" shellac
  brushes
Metal combs
Rubber combs
Stiff ½" and 1" round glue
  brushes
#3 and #6 sable brushes
Natural cosmetic sponges
Chamois
Child's rubber balloons
1" or 1½" pipe-over grainer
400 and 600 wet-or-dry paper
1" pounce brush
Orangewood sticks
Oxhair brushes
Feathers

*Miscellaneous*
Razors
Hammer
Knife
Carborundum
Cheesecloth
Tweezers
Manicure scissors
Brown paper
India ink
Cotton thread
Onion or garlic juice
Cotton swabs
India paper
Tracing paper

FANTASY FINISHES: *Top, native gold; bottom, tiger's eye.*

# MALACHITE

## GENUINE MALACHITE

In the *Historia Naturalis* written by Pliny the Elder in the first century A.D., a green jasper noted for its range of pattern is called *molochites*, the Latin word for precious stone. Pliny characterized the stone as possessing a kind of wavy pattern similar to poppies or bird feathers. The name malachite, a variant of Pliny's *molochites*, which described jasper, became the term used to designate this copper compound. Another explanation of the word malachite stems, in this case, from the Greek word *malache*, the term for mallow, because the green mineral resembles the green leaf of the mallow.

Malachite is one of the commonest and most stable of the secondary ores of copper. Because of its conspicuous green color, it is a most useful guide in prospecting for copper and is found in nearly all copper mining districts. Especially fine specimens have come from mines in Russia, Tanganyika, and the Congo.

Malachite is usually massive and generally occurs in rounded nodules. These may form in crusty aggregates or may occur as reniform (kidney-shaped) or botryoidal (grape cluster) surfaces with a radially fibrous internal structure. The pattern of malachite is infinitely variable, although it always follows the same principle—that of undulating lines of different widths and tones that form concentric rings around the characteristic circles and ovals of the mineral. In a cut and polished specimen, these bands are seen to intersect—or break off—or change direction. Since the nodules form at different levels and therefore reach different heights, they vary in a slab according to the point of formation at which they are cut. The successive layers frequently vary in color, from almost black dark-green through emerald and grass green to nearly white.

This magnificent stuff, the most precious of the semiprecious stones, was used by Romans and Egyptians alike for decoration on furnishings and for personal ornaments. In Russia, the stone was extravagently used in architecture, and for jewelry, inlay, and other decoration. Fabergé used it in many of his exquisite *objets de vertu*. The heady coloring and intricate detail of this beautiful stone give joy to the eye at close range. Except for small objects directly carved in the round, malachite has primarily been used because of its rarity as a thin veneer; for example, on the doors in the Chapultepec Palace in Mexico City or on the huge ornamental vases of the Winter Palace in Leningrad. For lesser objects, malachite is used either as veneer or as small wedge-like, irregular, fitted sections. The narrow spaces between sections are sometimes filled with finely crushed malachite particles.

# FAUX MALACHITE

Because of malachite's captivating color and its rarity, Venetian craftsmen were challenged to mimic the stone in paint. They did so with audacity, flaunting the painted image on chairs, tables, consoles, and furnishings, as well as on small objects. The unique color is entrancing in combination with other fantasy finishes.

Most imitated in decorative painting is globular malachite as it appears when the nodules are sliced through horizontally.

### THE NODULE AND ITS SURROUND

The rendering is a decorative and free one, not a painstaking copy of the stone, yet it does not ignore the logic of nature. The fantasy must evolve from the essential truth that the nodules dictate the forms that surround them. The nodules themselves differ in size and shape, indicating the various levels of development at the point of slicing. At times they may resemble double-yoked eggs. Each series of bands, waves, and swags emanates from a particular nodule—sometimes shown, sometimes not. No two series are alike, but each follows the same course of evolution: from small, rounded shapes to large, flattened curves. Ultimately one series comes up against others: at this point there may be a gentle diminution of one set of flattened curves into another set, or an abrupt confrontation of different forms. It is this endless variation that makes the pattern of malachite so fascinating.

### GEOMETRIC SECTIONS

When malachite is simulated with paint and brush, the technique is sometimes free and naive in a provincial manner. A more sophisticated concept is plotted to resemble the geometric sections of veneer composed of varied and irregular pieces. In the painted rendition, patterns within each section must vary. One section may show oval forms in different sizes and shapes surrounded by ribbon-like bandings. Another section may display only the surrounding bands, which resemble crystalline pleated swags or slow-curving waves. Other sections may contain the irregular parallel bandings revealed by the vertical slicing of the stone. Interspersed with these sections can be fillers representing small crystals of crushed malachite. The diversity of the rhythmic linear design of malachite affords a multitude of patternings for the painter. Nature's infinite variety should be consciously followed so that no pieces are exactly the same. Small objects in the round are envisioned as having been made from a single chunk of malachite, thus each plane revealed by the cutting must be indicated.

## THE NEGATIVE METHOD

### PREPARATION

Both the negative and the positive method are employed for simulating malachite in paint. In the negative method, the one generally practiced by nineteenth-century craftsmen, the design is revealed through a glaze. Preparation begins with the following:

YELLOW GREEN BASE    8 volumes emerald green japan color
2 volumes chrome yellow light light japan
    color
10% japan drier
turpentine (if needed for thinning)

Four or five coats of this base color are brushed on and, when dry, are tufbacked with 600 wet-or-dry paper and a soapy solution. The surface is then reserved with a coat of thinned white shellac or French varnish and is allowed to dry for an hour.

## *PROCEDURE*

The glaze coating is prepared:

> BLUE GLAZE    1 volume Prussian blue oil paint
> 4 to 6 volumes turpentine
> 3% japan drier

After the shellacked yellow green surface has been wiped over with cotton thinly saturated with flatting oil, the blue glaze is applied with an oxhair brush. The glaze is allowed to set for a few minutes. Fine metal graining combs that are held perpendicular to the surface are now run over the glaze to form the malachite patterns. Pink erasers cut into combs with teeth of uneven size irregularly spaced make versatile tools for this process. Some of the sections where combing has removed the glaze are further widened with an eraser stick. Some of the wide sections where glaze remains are fine-lined with a stylus. Fine lines can also be made with a thin wire brush, such as that used for cleaning hairbrushes. To form the silky fibers of malachite, a fan blender or a 1-inch whisk brush is used. The tool is pulled vertically through the existing patterns of bands, waves, or swags. In the studio a rubber date stamp turned to a combination of rounded letters and linear figures has been used in the same manner as a comb to make interesting waves and pleated swags around the nodules. To create a pleated swag, the stamp is pulled along in a 1-inch curve; then it is dipped down vertically ¼″, curved horizontally a fraction more than ¼″, and brought straight up again to the level of the first curve; this manipulation is re-

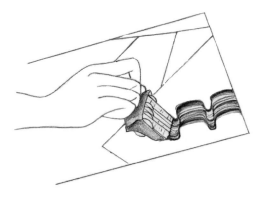

peated until a series of swags has been achieved. The eraser end of a pencil with a ⅛-inch hole cut in its center makes an effective tool for forming the central nodules. India paper crumpled into fine points and pressed on certain portions of the glaze will produce the small crystal areas. Fine lines surrounding the nodules are added with a quill. On some of the revealed ground, a fine spatter of Prussian blue oil paint simulates the beginning of crystallization. A close-pored cosmetic sponge pressed on the Prussian oil paint renders a more advanced stage of crystallization. A #3 or #6 sable brush wet with turpentine is used for any necessary clarification of the comb lines. Other furrows are filled in or emphasized, and additional dark lines are added, with a #3 sable brush dipped in Prussian blue oil paint. The negative method is most suitable for a free and inventive execution of the malachite pattern. Practice alone develops one's dexterity with the tools.

After completion, the work is set aside for a drying period of a week. In the nineteenth century malachite fantasies were finished with one coat of shellac, but surviving specimens have suffered from such casual protection. The best means of preservation is a protective coat of thinned white shellac followed by a number of thinned clear gloss varnish coatings. These are applied until the surface is level. Each coat is allowed to dry and then is tufbacked with 600 wet-or-dry paper and a soapy solution. If desired, the varnish may be tinted with thalo green oil paint. Genuine malachite, which is not hard enough to take a high glossy polish, has a soft lustrous finish. This is duplicated in the painted fantasy by rubbing the last varnish coat with a felt pad and a paste of rottenstone and lemon oil.

## THE POSITIVE METHOD

### PREPARATION
The surface is given at least five coats of flat white paint. These are tufbacked with 600 wet-or-dry paper and a soapy solution to satin smoothness, and the last one is protected with a coat of diluted French varnish. Over this base—which has been coated with flatting oil and then wiped almost dry—the following thin glaze is applied with a camel blender:

PALE GREEN GLAZE     1/2 volume thalo green oil paint (a paint
         made from phthalocyanine)
6 volumes turpentine
5 volumes undiluted clear gloss varnish
3% japan drier

When dry, the glaze is reserved with a coat of diluted French varnish.

### PROCEDURE
*Sections.* The painted surface is blocked out to resemble sections of malachite that have been fitted together. Each section is painted to imitate

different patterns of the stone, as if each were cut from a different level. For instance, a nodule with encircling bandings, a cluster of nodules, a swag surround with just the edge of a nodule showing, or a ribbon banding should all be placed so that they do not match nor run together. Whereas the sections of a fine piece of actual malachite are matched as closely as possible, a painted piece is more amusing when the sections are mismatched.

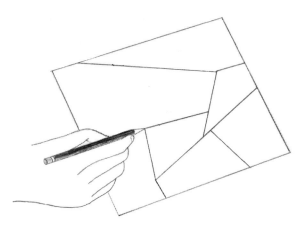

*Mediums.* The malachite pattern is rendered with a glaze made to this formula:

PATTERN GLAZE      ½ volume thalo green oil paint
3 volumes undiluted clear gloss varnish
4 volumes turpentine
3% japan drier

On completion of the pattern, dark lines to give accent and style to the malachite will be added with the following mixture:

ACCENT MEDIUM      1 volume thalo green oil paint
⅓ volume lampblack japan color
3 volumes turpentine
1/5 volume japan drier

*Tools.* The brushes needed for this rendition include the pipe-over grainer and #3 fan blenders. The bristles of one of the fan blenders should be shortened to ½"; in addition, ¼" of the bristles at each side of the fan should be cut off close to the ferrule. A metal comb is used to keep the bristles of the brushes separate. These tools are used to simulate the bandings, waves, and swags. Dexterity determines the choice of tool for each form. An eyedropper, India paper, a #12 red sable bright brush, and paper towels are also required.

*The pattern.* To create the malachite fantasy, a path of flatting oil is laid on the surface with a 1-inch oxhair brush; the color flowing from the tools used next will diffuse along this oil track. A brush is selected, loaded with Pattern Glaze, and knocked against the teeth of the metal comb in order to spread the bristles. The first stroke is rendered. Then successive curving strokes are laid on, overlapping the initial stroke. An eyedropper or the uncut fan blender, twirled and pivoted, produces the nodules. An eyedropper is also used to put in the dark center of a nodule. For the fine lines immediately surrounding a nodule, the #12 red sable bright brush is used. To create a crystalline effect, crumpled India paper is pressed on the edge of a banding at the point where it narrows in its flow around a nodule. A technique producing the silky fibers seen in the mala-chite formation involves pulling the whisk or fan brush vertically across the band to the crystalline area. Additional crystalline areas are produced by dropping the glaze medium into a float of water. After the water begins to evaporate, a paper towel crumpled into points is pressed against the section.

When the general pattern is achieved, a #3 sable brush moistened with turpentine is used to clarify the bandings and to clean up and complete

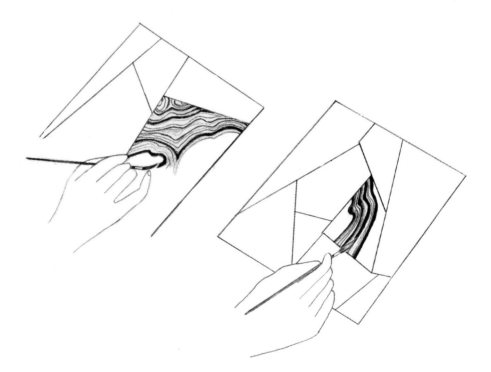

the pattern. The lines of the bandings, swags, and waves are varied both in width and in closeness to each other. Finally, dark accents are added with the Accent Medium, some of which are whisked. The work is then set aside to dry for a week, after which it is coated with a thin solution of French varnish.

*Additional glazes.* In the next stage of the procedure, the pattern is glazed with the following mixture:

<table>
<tr><td>VIRIDIAN</td><td>1 volume viridian green oil paint</td></tr>
<tr><td>GREEN GLAZE</td><td>2 volumes turpentine</td></tr>
<tr><td></td><td>2 volumes undiluted clear gloss varnish</td></tr>
<tr><td></td><td>3% japan drier</td></tr>
</table>

When this is dry, a second glaze made from blue-green—sometimes called malachite green—aniline powder (see aniline solutions, p. 200) is added so that the piece will attain the brilliancy of the real mineral.

*Final varnishes.* The entire surface is now varnished twice with thinned clear gloss and then is tufbacked with 600 wet-or-dry paper and a soapy solution. The remaining varnish coatings required to level the surface are tinted with terre-verte oil paint. After every two applications the surface is tufbacked with 600 wet-or-dry paper and a soapy solution. The terre-verte should be used only until a satisfactory color is reached. It is followed by coats of thinned clear gloss varnish. The final coating is polished with a paste of rottenstone and lemon oil, rubbed on with the heel of the hand or a felt pad.

# VARIATIONS

## CASEIN AND GOUACHE MALACHITE

There are a number of ways of rendering malachite in a positive technique. The following method starts with the same base of flat white paint. The base must not be shellacked or tinted. Three values of green are prepared with white casein and viridian green gouache: one value is pale green, one a middle green, and one two shades deeper than middle green. A fourth mixture, of dark green casein and viridian green gouache, provides the deepest value. The pattern is blocked out in the way previously described. The same brushes are used. In this instance, however, each brush tuft of the pipe-over grainer is loaded with a different color value. The fan blender brush is loaded with two values. When a wave or swag is rendered, a line of a value of green different from those used on the fan blender is added with a #3 sable brush and then is whisked into the wave. The lightest value is added with the sable brush and is whisked up into the darker portion of the wave. This produces the lustrous fibers of the mineral. Crystalline

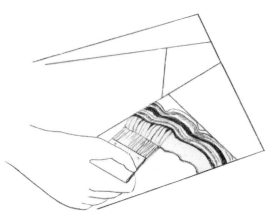

areas are added with India paper crumpled into fine points. A piece of the paper loaded with one value is pressed on the surface, and the same spot is immediately pressed by another piece loaded with a different value. The advantage of casein and gouache is that they dry in an hour.

The dry surface now receives an over-all coat of the following:

> GREEN GLAZE    1 volume thalo green oil paint
> FOR CASEIN     2 volumes turpentine
> 2 volumes undiluted clear gloss varnish
> 3% japan drier

This is applied with an oxhair brush. After the drying interval, the additional varnish coats are added and the procedure described for the other types of malachite is followed.

## MIXTION AND OIL PAINT MALACHITE
In the nineteenth century, French decorators painted malachite on a white ground, using a mixture of black and terre-verte oil paint. They first brushed the ground with a combination of flatting oil and japan drier called "mixtion." On this film, the forms of malachite were described with a brush loaded with a thinned solution of the oil paint mixture. The pattern was made up of a linking series of rounds and curling shapes, following the variations of nature on a curving principle, with intersections to divide and diversify. These forms resembled more nearly the simpler bandings of

agate. The thin paint blending with the mixtion diffused the forms, leaving color values ranging from light to dark. After the pattern had dried, intricate intersections and shadings were added by fanning a thin film of white paint through the darker tones. With this paint the nodule, called the "eye of the peacock," was inserted. In order to insure a lasting luster, the final coats of varnish are tinted with thalo green oil paint.

## *MALACHITE AND ART NOUVEAU*

One day a graceful version of malachite was brought to the studio, a gem rendered in black-green japan color on a green japan base by an early twentieth-century craftsman. These are the formulas:

| | |
|---|---|
| BASE | 2 volumes green japan color |
| | ½ volume flat white paint |
| COLOR FOR | 1½ volumes green japan color |
| MALACHITE PATTERN | ½ volume lampblack japan color |

The effect was achieved by the simple use of the deep color on the lighter ground. The craftsman had taken liberties with the curving form of malachite and turned it into an *art nouveau* treasure. The study of malachite forms will make clear that the *art nouveau* curve is readily translated into malachite fantasy.

# MALACHITE

*Materials*

Emerald green japan color
Chrome yellow light
   light japan color
Dark green casein
Turpentine
Japan drier
White shellac
Alcohol (for thinning shellac)
Prussian blue oil paint
Flatting oil
Clear gloss varnish
Thalo green oil paint
Rottenstone
Lemon oil
Flat white paint
French varnish
Lampblack japan color
Green japan color
Viridian green oil paint
Blue-green aniline powder
   (malachite)
White casein
Viridian green gouache
Thinner
Terre-verte oil paint

*Tools*

1″ oxhair brush
Metal graining combs
Pink pearl erasers
Eraser stick
Stylus
Thin wire brush
Two #3 fan blenders
1″ whisk brush
Rubber date stamp
Fine quill
Varnish brush
Shellac brush
Camel-hair blender

Close-pored cosmetic sponge
#3 and #6 sable brushes
Pipe-over grainer
Eyedropper
#12 red sable bright brush
Pencil with eraser
600 wet-or-dry paper

*Miscellaneous*

India paper
Paper towels
Absorbent cotton
Felt pad

# SIX FANTASIES

This series was fostered by a growing fascination with the flamboyant color and the intricacy of line and form found in the mineral world. It seemed unsporting to reproduce these natural wonders with painstaking brush-work. The challenge was to create similitude by using the miscible and immiscible elements of paint as well as a variety of solvents. The formulas that follow came out of experiment and play and were devised to enhance twentieth-century decoration. They demonstrate that familiarity with the techniques explained in this book can lead to improvisation and produce new and original finishes. As were the *faux* finishes in centuries past, they are rendered as fantasies of nature.

The first three fantasies employ miscible fluids; the last three call for certain immiscible fluids.

## AZURITE

### DESCRIPTION

Azurite is a copper carbonate generally found above copper mines; it often turns to malachite. The rosette form rather than the crystal form has been used as the basic idea for this fantasy. Like malachite, azurite sometimes is found in small nodules resembling a bunch of grapes. When this assemblage is cut through horizontally, the deep ultramarine blue section, dotted with constellations of tiny concentric circles of the same blue ranging from dark to light, is exposed. The dots and circles seem to have exploded deep below the glossy surface of the mineral.

## PREPARATION

The base coverage consists of four to five coats (applied with an oxhair brush) of this mixture:

> 8 volumes ultramarine blue japan color
> 1/10 volume japan drier
> 1 volume turpentine (for thinning to the
>     consistency of light cream)

When dry, these coats are tufbacked with 400 wet-or-dry paper and a soapy solution. The surface is then protected with thinned white shellac, which is allowed to dry for one hour.

## PROCEDURE

Three mixtures are now prepared. A light and a medium value of ultramarine blue japan color are mixed with flat white paint, then are thinned to the consistency of spattering fluid with:

> 4 volumes turpentine
> 1 volume flatting oil

In addition, a portion of the base paint is thinned with flatting oil and turpentine to the consistency of skim milk. Wax paper is used as a palette for each of these mixtures. First, the thinned base paint is rapidly applied to the shellacked surface. While this coating is still wet, the lightest blue solution is spattered—by means of a wooden block held 1′ from the surface, and a 2-inch spattering brush—over 95 per cent of the surface; the diameter of the spattered dots should range from ⅛″ to ¼″. This spatter is immediately followed with a spatter of medium blue, directed diagonally, which simulates the color drifts of azurite. The thinned base color is used again, this time spotted on with a brush to eliminate any previous excessively fine spattering. The whole is now spattered with large drops of turpentine, into some of which the contrasting blues are immediately dropped with a fully loaded #3 sable brush. During the drying, the same brush is used to surround existing circles with fine circles of another hue. At this point the

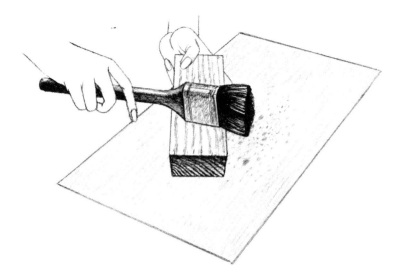

work is examined closely and any dots smaller than $\frac{1}{16}''$ in diameter are blocked out with the base hue. The work is allowed to dry for a week before the varnishing begins.

In order to level the surface, the varnishing for this fantasy sometimes consists of more than twenty coats, every second one of which is tufbacked with 600 wet-or-dry paper and a soapy solution. The final coat of thinned clear gloss varnish is applied so smoothly that it can be left unpolished.

## AZURITE

*Materials*
  Ultramarine blue japan color
  Japan drier
  Turpentine
  White shellac
  Flat white paint
  Flatting oil
  Wax paper
  Clear gloss varnish
  Alcohol solvent

*Tools*
  400 wet-or-dry paper
  600 wet-or-dry paper
  Shellac brush
  Varnish brush
  Wooden block
  2″ spatter brush
  #3 sable brush
  1″ or 2″ oxhair brush

## NATIVE GOLD

### DESCRIPTION

Granite is the most common deep-seated igneous rock in the earth's crust. Gold in crystallized quartz is the outcropping on granite which has been partially weathered away. The fantasy here described simulates this opulent manifestation of nature's work. The matrix from which the gold emerges is gray, tinted with a touch of iron to a rosy tone, and with a bluish green reminiscent of a copper oxide.

### PREPARATION

With an oxhair brush, the surface is prepared with three coats of a darker than middle gray:

> 2 volumes flat white paint
> 1 volume lampblack japan color

These coats are tufbacked with 400 wet-or-dry paper and a soapy solution. The whole is coated with thinned white shellac, then is left to dry for one hour.

### PROCEDURE

The procedure here is somewhat similar to marbleizing. A thin solution is made of the middle gray paint by adding flatting oil and turpentine in equal amounts. The surface is coated with this mixture. Into it are floated the three following solutions thinned with equal amounts of turpentine and flatting oil:

> 1.  1 volume chrome green oil paint
>     $\frac{1}{4}$ volume cadmium yellow light oil paint
>     6 volumes flat white paint
>
> 2.  1 volume cadmium red medium oil paint
>     $\frac{1}{2}$ volume flat white paint
>
> 3.  1 volume flat white paint
>     3 volumes flatting oil

The first two fluids are drifted into the wet surface with turkey feathers. The resulting irregular masses of color should cover no more than 5 per cent of the surface. While these are wet, the thinned white paint is

FANTASY FINISHES: *Top, azurite; bottom, rhodochrosite.*

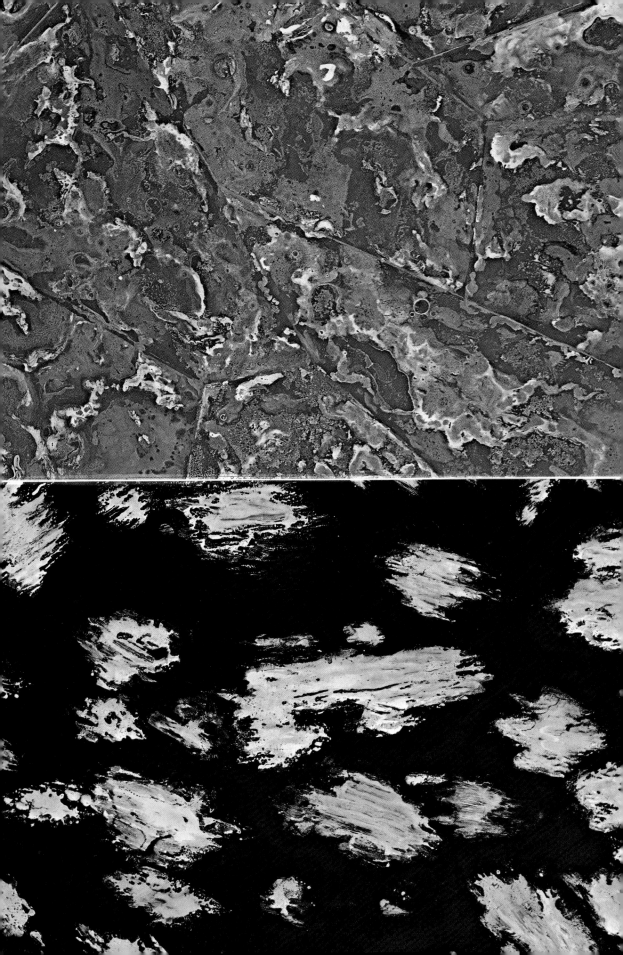

spattered with a 1-inch spatter brush rapped against a block of wood. A feather dipped into a 1:1 mixture of flatting oil and turpentine is whisked over the surface to blend the pattern of white, green, and rose. With absorbent cotton dipped in turpentine and wrung out, some of the white spatters are lifted in order to reveal the darker base hue. When this surface has dried for a week, a coat of thinned white shellac is applied. Then, with a #6 sable brush dipped in quick size tinted with yellow ochre oil paint, the irregular areas are coated on the surface where the gold outcroppings are to occur. When these areas have reached a tacky stage somewhat wetter than that for actually laying leaf, they are heaped with skewings and crumpled and shredded sheets of Dutch metal. These gold outcroppings are tamped down; nevertheless they should be slightly raised above the level of

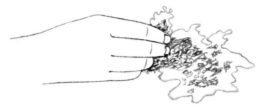

the support—but in the case of a table, not enough to prevent its normal use. Next day the leaf is brushed off, and if sections of the golden areas are too thin, size is re-applied and more skewings are laid down. After the drying period, any scattered fragments outside the intended areas are cleared away. An eraser stick is used around the outcroppings to create jagged irregular edges. With a #6 brush, some portions of the outcroppings are tinted with burnt sienna oil paint thinned with turpentine, others with raw umber oil paint thinned with turpentine, thus producing the effect of weathered gold. However, some of the Dutch metal is left untouched to glint among the weathered segments.

After a week's drying, the *entire* surface is coated four times with thinned clear gloss varnish. Only the background areas unadorned by the gold are tufbacked with 600 wet-or-dry paper and a soapy solution. After the four coats have been applied, the varnishing continues—*excluding* the portions of gold—until a fine smooth surface has been attained.

FANTASY FINISHES: *Top, variscite; bottom, snowflake obsidian.*

## NATIVE GOLD

*Materials*
- Flat white paint
- Lampblack japan color
- White shellac
- Alcohol solvent
- Flatting oil
- Turpentine
- Chrome green oil paint
- Cadmium yellow light oil paint
- Cadmium red medium oil paint
- Quick size
- Yellow ochre oil paint
- Burnt sienna oil paint
- Raw umber oil paint
- Dutch metal
- Clear gloss varnish

*Tools*
- Shellac brush
- Varnish brush
- Gilder's tamper
- 400 and 600 wet-or-dry paper
- Turkey feathers
- 1″ spatter brush
- Wood block
- #6 sable brush
- Eraser stick
- 1″ or 2″ oxhair brush

*Miscellaneous*
- Absorbent cotton

## TIGER'S EYE

### DESCRIPTION

Tiger's Eye is a beautiful stone used for jewelry and other types of ornament. Its name must emanate from its similarities to the markings of a tiger. The structure of the quartz is fibrous with long silky filaments which contribute to the chatoyancy—a changeable luster with an undulating band of light. This glamorous stone in addition has iridescent eyes combined with the translucent to dark brown bands which glow against its golden tone.

### PREPARATION

With an oxhair brush, the surface is prepared with japan bole (see chapter on gilding); when dry, it is coated with diluted orange shellac. Then Dutch metal leaf is applied over all with quick size.

## *PROCEDURE*

On the surface a series of sections is marked out with a pencil to indicate that the stone has been used like a veneer. The supposed thin slabs should be geometric but irregular. It should be determined which of them will contain the characteristic Tiger's Eye. Each step in the procedure is carried out in all of these sections before the next step is undertaken.

*Sections with eyes.* This fantasy is more dramatic when the scale is enlarged, therefore the innermost ovals, which represent the eyes, should be about 2″ long and 1½″ wide. They are outlined with a fine erratic line rendered with a #3 sable brush dipped in India ink. The two oval bands immediately surrounding each eye are similarly outlined with India ink: the first is about ½″ distant from the eye; the second, more than 1″ distant from the first. The total distance from the eye is a little more than the width of the eye.

The eye itself is laid in with silver leaf, and next day is oxidized with liver sulfate (pea-size nugget in 2 ounces water applied with cotton). The silver goes through the usual color changes, finally reaching a bluish iridescence. At this point any surface moisture is gently blotted with fresh cotton before the leaf burns. The eye is allowed to dry overnight, then it alone is coated with thinned clear gloss varnish. The first oval band is oxidized with sodium sulfide solution (pea-size nugget in 2 ounces water), which is kept within the India ink outline. The third surrounding band of gold is masked off with thinned orange shellac, as is the rest of the section; the remaining part of the surface not spotted with eyes is also protected with shellac. This leaves only the second band surrounding the eye unprotected. A solution of sodium sulfide is spattered on the unprotected area.

The clear gold band comes next. It should be about one-half the width of the first oval band. It is bordered by a shaded band made with the following medium:

> 2 volumes burnt umber japan color
> ⅛ volume chrome yellow light japan color
> 4 volumes flatting oil
> turpentine (as needed to make a transparent
>   wash)

The band is shaded from the outer edge inward with a #3 sable brush and this mixture.

From this point on, the brown mixture is used to fill out the section with concentric curves that vary in width from narrow to wide. They are transparent—the gold leaf being allowed to glimmer through. These bandings should be darker near the reserved gold band. If the bands are too opaque, additional flatting oil makes them transparent. A fine dark overline may be added to the wider light curve with a #3 sable brush dipped in a full-strength mixture of the japan colors. This variety creates the interplay of light called chatoyancy.

Other eyes are rendered by changing the spattered oxidized portion to the band nearer the oxidized eyes, and surrounding it with an oxidized band and then with the narrow gold reserve band. The transparent gold bands are lighter as they reach the periphery.

*Sections with brown and gold stripes.* These sections have no eyes, instead contain only a succession of bandings lying parallel to each other. Each section is at an angle to, or directly counter to, the adjacent sections. The direction intended is laid in with flatting oil with a 1-inch oxhair brush. Over this the pipe-over grainer loaded with the dark brown paint makes parallel undulating bands across the section. Sometimes the pipe-over

grainer renders contiguous bands; sometimes it leaves various widths of untouched gold between the bands. Some of the denser bands are lightened with flatting oil. With additional brown paint, fine dark lines are added here and there. The mixtures have been so thinned with flatting oil that it is necessary to allow two weeks' drying time. Then twenty coats of thinned clear gloss varnish are applied. Every second coat is tufbacked with 600 wet-or-dry paper and a soapy solution—however, the last coat of varnish should *not* be tufbacked.

## TIGER'S EYE

*Materials*
Alcohol solvent
Japan bole
Orange shellac
Dutch metal leaf
Quick size
India ink
Silver leaf
Liver sulfate
Clear gloss varnish
Sodium sulfide
Burnt umber japan color
Chrome yellow light japan color
Flatting oil
Turpentine

*Tools*
#3 and #6 sable brushes
Shellac brush
Varnish brush
Spatter brush
Pipe-over grainer
400 and 600 wet-or-dry paper
1″ or 2″ oxhair brush

*Miscellaneous*
Pencil
Absorbent cotton

The fantasies described to this point have largely been created with the use of miscible fluids. Those that follow show the eccentricities that occur when immiscible fluids are combined.

## VARISCITE

### DESCRIPTION
Variscite is formed near the surface of the earth by the alteration of aluminum-bearing rocks that are rich in phosphates. Large polished pieces have a pictorial resemblance to miniature mountains and limpid blue lakes. Other specimens are cool green to blue-green, and are run through with white veinlets like the froth of ocean waves. It is variscite of the latter type that has been chosen for the fantasy.

## PREPARATION

The base is prepared with japan paint made to this formula:

> 1½ volumes blue-green medium japan color
> 1 volume chrome yellow light light japan
>     color
> 5 volumes flat white paint

Four to five coats are applied with a 1-inch or 2-inch oxhair brush, and tufbacked with 400 wet-or-dry paper and a non-detergent soapy solution. When they are finally dry, a protective coat of thinned white shellac is applied. The surface is lightly sanded with 100 garnet paper to give it tooth.

## PROCEDURE

Since a variscite surface resembling a veneer is to be created, various rectangular and triangular shapes fitted together are marked off with a pencil. Next, a mixture of 1 volume flat white paint and 1 volume turpentine is made. One of the sections outlined with pencil is flooded with water, then drifts of the white mixture are floated in with a #6 sable brush. The paint crawls in the water, forming tendrils and frothy flecks. When the shapes

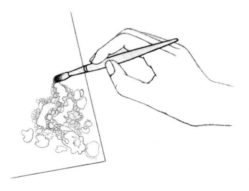

of white have become established, some of the base paint—further thinned with flatting oil and turpentine—is floated in to break up any solid spots of white. For contrast, some of the base color should remain exposed. The water evaporates, leaving the paint in its variegated green and white veinlets.

Now the non-adjacent sections are filled in. When they have dried, the intervening sections are rendered. The paint is allowed to dry for a week before coats of thinned clear gloss varnish are applied. These continue until the surface is leveled; tufbacking with 600 wet-or-dry paper and a soapy solution follows every second coat of varnish. The final coat is rubbed down with a paste of rottenstone and lemon oil.

## VARISCITE

*Materials*
Blue-green medium japan color
Chrome yellow light
   light japan color
Flat white paint
White shellac
Alcohol solvent
Turpentine
Flatting oil
Clear gloss varnish
Rottenstone
Lemon oil

*Tools*
#6 sable brush
Shellac brush
Varnish brush
1″ or 2″ oxhair brush
400 wet-or-dry paper
600 wet-or-dry paper
100 garnet paper

*Miscellaneous*
Pencil

## SNOWFLAKE OBSIDIAN

### DESCRIPTION
Bowls of obsidian were made in Mesopotamia as early as 3200 B.C. Obsidians are volcanic glasses usually found among lavas rich in silica. These glassy materials are not minerals, but rock melts of variable chemical composition which cooled before much crystallization could develop.

Volcanic glass contains white rounded bodies ranging from microscopic size to several feet in diameter. The ones called spherulites are often composed of radiating fiber-like crystals believed to have evolved from scattered inclusions of embryo crystals after the glass became rigid. In a section of obsidian, they appear like soft fallen snowflakes, and in such manner they are rendered against a dark background in the painted fantasy.

### PREPARATION
The surface medium is prepared to this formula:

5 volumes flat black paint
½ volume burnt umber japan color
⅓ volume japan drier
¼ volume spar varnish

Four coats are applied with an oxhair brush and the last coat is tufbacked with 600 wet-or-dry paper and a soapy solution.

### PROCEDURE

First, ¼ teaspoon nigrozine black alcohol-soluble aniline powder is dissolved in ½ pint alcohol. One-third of this mixture is reserved. To the rest is added an equal portion of 5-pound cut undiluted orange shellac; this is rubbed over the surface with a cotton fabric bob. After drying for an hour, the surface is lightly smoothed with ooo steel wool and tack-clothed. Then it is given one coat of diluted clear gloss varnish, which should dry for 24 hours.

Flat white paint is thinned with a half-and-half mixture of flatting oil and turpentine. With a 1-inch shellac brush and the reserved aniline-alcohol solution, the areas for the snowflakes of a single cluster are painted in on the black surface. Immediately afterward, the thin white paint is floated into the wet areas with a #6 sable brush. Because the flat white and the aniline-alcohol solution do not combine, the white separates and crawls— a fragmentation that simulates the fiber-like design of the snowflake. When the flakes have set for a few moments, a straight whisk brush is dipped into

alcohol and brushed through them, fraying their edges and revealing some of the base coat. The striation is done in the same direction for each snowflake. When the snowflakes in the first cluster appear sufficiently delicate and crystal-like, they are allowed to dry. The operation is repeated until the surface is scattered with clusters.

After drying for a week, the surface is coated with thinned clear gloss varnish tinted with cobalt blue oil paint to increase the illusion of volcanic glass. The varnish coats are continued until the surface is level. Every second coat is tufbacked with 600 wet-or-dry paper and a soapy solution. The final varnish is applied so smoothly that it need not be tufbacked.

# SNOWFLAKE OBSIDIAN

*Materials*

Flat black paint
Burnt umber japan color
Japan drier
Spar varnish
Clear gloss varnish
Nigrozine black alcohol-soluble
   aniline powder
Alcohol solvent
Orange shellac (5-lb. cut)
Flat white paint
Flatting oil
Turpentine
Cobalt blue oil paint

*Tools*

1″ or 2″ oxhair brush
600 wet-or-dry paper
000 steel wool
1″ shellac brush
Varnish brush
#6 sable brush
Whisk brush

*Miscellaneous*

Tack cloth
Cotton fabric bob

# RHODOCHROSITE

## DESCRIPTION

Rhodochrosite, its name stemming from *rhodos,* the Greek word for the rose, is a pink to rose-colored mineral consisting mainly of carbonate of manganese. It somewhat resembles malachite, for its formation is botryoidal (resembling grape clusters) and, when cut vertically, it reveals a ribboned pattern. Sometimes its beautiful forms are interspersed with a green matrix and crystalline fissures. This fantasy is rendered as if it were a thin veneer of stone, with sections cut both with and across the grain.

## PREPARATION

With an oxhair brush, the surface is given four to five coats of flat white paint and every other one is tufbacked with 400 wet-or-dry paper and a soapy solution. It is then protected with a thin coat of diluted French varnish. After the drying interval, the geometric sections of veneer are marked off with a pencil.

## *PROCEDURE*

Three mixtures are prepared. The first is:

> ROSE   1 volume rose madder oil paint
> $\frac{1}{8}$ volume Indian red oil paint
> $\frac{1}{32}$ volume viridian green oil paint

This mixture is combined with turpentine and a few drops of japan drier to a thin solution.

The second mixture is:

BLUE-GREEN MATRIX   1 volume blue-green japan
$\frac{1}{4}$ volume chrome yellow light light japan
    color
6 volumes flat white paint

The third mixture:

> WHITE   1 volume flat white paint
> 1 volume flatting oil
> 1 volume turpentine

This white medium should have the consistency of skim milk.

*Ribbon bands.* The bandings resemble ribbons having from four to six stripes. To render a banding, a wavering path of flatting oil is laid on with a 1-inch oxhair brush. A pipe-over grainer is dipped in the rose paint and is manipulated over the path in a pleated swag movement. The swag is produced by drawing the brush along in a curve for about an inch. Next, the pleat is made by moving the brush quickly downward, then upward—in both cases radial to the curve—for about $\frac{1}{4}''$ to $\frac{1}{2}''$. This swag-and-pleat effect is rendered the length of the ribbon. If the banding is to exceed the original four stripes created by the pipe-over grainer, the succeeding stripe overlaps the preceding one, the grainer being held so that two of its clumps of bristles move along the course of the paint that has just been applied. The rose color is diffused by the flatting oil underneath each stripe.

Striped bandings are added in parallel fashion until the entire section is filled; they are separated from each other by $\frac{1}{4}''$ to $\frac{1}{2}''$ of white space.

With a #6 sable brush, some of the bands are re-touched with the rose paint. While the bands are wet, a crumpled paper towel is pressed on the bottom edge of each one to create a crystalline effect. The ribbon bands are further accented with fine radial lines of rose and white put in with a #3 sable brush.

When the section has dried overnight, a #6 sable brush is used to lay in rivulets of the blue-green matrix; these appear in irregular and jagged widths between the ribbon bands and swags. A crumpled towel pressed on the matrix varies the texture if additional crystallization is desired. Water is floated into the edges of both the bands and their stripes when they are dry. Into this a little of the thinned white paint is floated. As the water begins to evaporate, these portions are pressed with a crumpled towel.

*Sections with nodules.* When the nodule section is rendered, it is essential that the working surface be completely level.

With an eyedropper loaded with flatting oil, the section is touched with a number of separate droplets. When they have become stationary, a

drop of rose paint is added to each one with a #3 sable brush. The paint is allowed to spread. After a few moments a tiny drop of turpentine is added to the center of each of the nodules. When the drop no longer spreads and is semi-dry, fine concentric circles of rose color are painted around the periphery with a #3 sable brush. If the color in the center of the nodule is dissipated by the turpentine, rose color is added.

The section should be filled with large and small nodules. Here and there between them the blue-green matrix is painted in irregularly, then is

pressed with a crumpled towel. When the nodules have dried, their crystal-line effect may need intensifying: this is done by placing droplets of water in their centers, followed by a touch of rose or white paint. The nodules may also be ringed with rose or white paint, which is whisked in toward the center; or rose paint may be placed in the center and whisked outward. Any nodule that seems too small is enlarged with a drop of water, then with one of thin paint. When this has settled, the crumpled paper towel is used as a control.

Two weeks of drying time must elapse before coats of thinned clear gloss varnish are added. Every second one is tufbacked with 600 wet-or-dry paper and a soapy solution. The final coat is rubbed down with a paste of rottenstone and lemon oil.

# RHODOCHROSITE

*Materials*
  Flat white paint
  French varnish
  Alcohol solvent
  Rose madder oil paint
  Indian red oil paint
  Viridian green oil paint
  Turpentine
  Japan drier
  Blue-green japan color
  Chrome yellow light
    light japan color
  Flatting oil
  Rottenstone
  Lemon oil

*Tools*
  Shellac brush
  Varnish brush
  400 wet-or-dry paper
  600 wet-or-dry paper
  1″ or 2″ oxhair brush
  Pipe-over grainer
  #3 sable brush
  #6 sable brush
  Eyedroppers

*Miscellaneous*
  Pencil
  Paper towels

# SUBJECT OUTLINE

## CRAFTSMEN & STUDENTS
## WHOSE WORK IS SHOWN IN THE COLOR PLATES

Page 17, *Faux* Bamboo: Mirror frame, Mrs. Richard Krauss; footstool, Mrs. George LaBranche, Jr.; "male" striped-bamboo desk, Isabel O'Neil; chair, Mrs. Burnham Carter; five-drawer chest, Mrs. Beverly Pascal; three-drawer chest, Mrs. Lester C. Brion, Jr.

Page 18: Top left, Italian-casein chair, Charles Bohme; top right, French-casein chair, Mrs. Clifford Nellissen. Bottom, console with distressed base, *faux-marbre* top, Mrs. Charles H. Mott.

Page 35: *Faux* natural-tortoise box, Mrs. Willis Mills.

Page 36: Armchair, basic antiquing and striping, Mrs. Elizabeth Byrne.

Page 69, Basic Antiquing: Top left, pounced, wax and japan antiquing medium, Mrs. Nelson Eliscu; right, japan spattering fluid, Mrs. Clifford Nellissen. Bottom left, flyspecks, wax and powder, Mrs. Nelson Eliscu; right, striation, wax and powder, Mrs. Clifford Nellissen.

Page 70, Distressing: Top left, distressing in three colors, Mrs. James McKinnon; right, peeled finish, Isabel O'Neil. Bottom left, peeled finish, Mrs. James McKinnon; right, peeled finish, Isabel O'Neil.

Page 87, Distressing:   Settee, Mrs. James McKinnon.

Page 88, Glazing:   Top left, striated, Mrs. Nelson Eliscu; right, blended with cheesecloth, Mrs. James Abrams. Bottom left, patted with sponge and spattered, Isabel O'Neil; right, sponged, Mrs. Nelson Eliscu.

Page 105, Lacquer:   Seven-drawer chest, Mrs. Ramsay Wilson; library steps, Mrs. John Corroon; wall brackets, Mrs. Stanley Mortimer, Jr.; hexagonal box, Mrs. Thure Peterson; miniature chest, Mrs. Donald Bierman; bentwood table mirror, Mrs. George Hamilton Combs; Oriental table, Mrs. Stanley Mortimer, Jr.; Parsons table with red and black marquetry, Ina Marx; box with eggshell-inlay flowers, Mrs. Kenneth Skelton; round taboret table, Mrs. Winston Frost; Chinese canister, Ina Marx.

Page 106, Lacquer:   Top left, variant, Mrs. Ramsay Wilson; right, coromandel, Mrs. James Abrams. Bottom left, dragon's blood, Larri B. Tillman; right, antiqued Chinese linen, Isabel O'Neil.

Page 123, Eggshell-inlay Lacquer:   Obelisk, Mrs. E. B. Bowring; gilt-drawered chest, Mrs. Ethel S. Rodgers; eggshell-and-gilt box, Mrs. George Hamilton Combs; box with gilt insects, George S. Ewald, Jr.; box with eggshell-mosaic circles, Mrs. Jacques Smit; box with black-ink zig-zag, Mrs. Stanley Mortimer, Jr.; four-drawer chest, Mrs. Ramsay Wilson.

Page 124, Lacquer:   Top left, *vernis Martin*, Mrs. James Abrams; right, rice kernel, Mrs. Ramsay Wilson. Bottom left, antiqued Chinese, Mrs. James Abrams; right, with eggshell inlay, Mrs. Kenneth Skelton.

Page 157, Casein:   Top left, sponge board; right, pounce-brush stipple; bottom left, rolled chamois; right, rubber roller; all, Mrs. Ramsay Wilson.

Page 158, Casein:   Top left, corrugated checkerboard; right, wash-lye spatter; both, Mrs. Ramsay Wilson. Bottom left, with cartouche, Mrs. Nelson Eliscu; right, striation, Mrs. Ramsay Wilson.

Page 175, Mat Gilding:   Top left, mat gold and sand, Mrs. George Hamilton Combs; right, black ground etched through gold, Mrs. Carlos Routh. Bottom left, Renaissance finish, Mrs. Nelson Eliscu; right, relief design, Mrs. Ramsay Wilson.

Page 176: Mat-gilded coffee table with Oriental ink brushwork, Mrs. Bernard Greenfield.

Page 225, Antique Patinas for Leaf: Top left, Chinese bronze (Dutch metal and distemper) ; right, aluminum leaf with japan spatter; bottom left, gold leaf with bole exposed; all, Mrs. John Corroon. Bottom right, Italian, acid-on-silver, Mrs. George Hamilton Combs.

Page 226, Burnishing: Top left, burnished-gold *graffiti;* right, tooled burnished gold; bottom left, mat leaf and raised burnished design; right, *pastiglia;* all, Mrs. Clifford Nellissen.

Page 243, *Faux* Bamboo, left to right: Lacquer, Mrs. Winston Frost; conceit, Mrs. Kenneth Skelton; "female," Mrs. Brook Nelson; piece of antique *faux bois;* with leaf spray, Mrs. Kenneth Skelton; "male," Mrs. Brook Nelson; variation, Isabel O'Neil.

Page 244, Porphyry: Top left, with inlay; right, granite; both, Mrs. Henry Cook. Bottom left, purple, Mrs. Brook Nelson; right, French, Mrs. Henry Cook.

Page 261: Chest of drawers, distressed, with *faux-marbre* top, George S. Ewald, Jr.

Page 262, *Faux Marbre:* Top left, serpentine, Mrs. James C. Cope; right, trompe-l'oeil, Mrs. Kenneth Skelton. Bottom left, fossiliferous; right, floating; both, Mrs. James C. Cope.

Page 279, *Faux Marbre:* Top left, black-and-gold, negative; right, *breche;* both, Mrs. James C. Cope. Bottom left, feather, Isabel O'Neil; right, trompe-l'oeil, Mrs. Brook Nelson.

Page 280, Tortoise Shell: Top left, Italian, Mrs. Nelson Eliscu; right, green Boulle fantasy, Mrs. Kenneth Skelton. Bottom left, red Boulle fantasy, Mrs. Nelson Eliscu; right, English, Ina Marx.

Page 297, Tortoise Shell: Top left, natural, Mrs. Willis Mills; right, conceit, with oil, Mrs. Brook Nelson. Bottom left, lace; right, conceit, with aniline; both, Mrs. Nelson Eliscu.

Page 298, Lapis Lazuli: Top left, French; right, Italian with gold skewings; both, Mrs. Kenneth Skelton. Bottom left, provincial, Isabel O'Neil; right, jewel, Mrs. Kenneth Skelton.

Page 315, *Faux Bois*:   Top left, Oriental with gold, Mrs. Nelson Eliscu; right, provincial, Mrs. Stanley Mortimer, Jr. Bottom left, Oriental, Mrs. Nelson Eliscu; right, crotch *faux bois*, Mrs. Kenneth Skelton.

Page 316, *Faux Bois*:   Top left, stylized, Mrs. Brook Nelson; right, North Italian, Mrs. George Hamilton Combs. Bottom left, marquetry, Mrs. James Abrams; right, pecky *faux bois*, Mrs. Willis Mills.

Page 333, Malachite:   Top left, positive method; right, art nouveau; both, Mrs. Winston Frost. Bottom left, negative method, Ina Marx; right, veneer, Mrs. Winston Frost.

Page 334, Fantasy Finishes:   Top, native gold, bottom, tiger's eye; both, Isabel O'Neil.

Page 351, Fantasy Finishes:   Top, azurite, bottom, rhodochrosite; both, Isabel O'Neil.

Page 352, Fantasy Finishes:   Top, variscite, bottom, snowflake obsidian; both, Isabel O'Neil.

# SUGGESTED READING

ALBERS, JOSEF. *Interaction of Color*. New Haven & London: Yale University Press, 1963.

MAYER, RALPH. *The Artist's Handbook of Materials and Techniques*. New York: Viking Press, 1959.

KAY, REED. *The Painter's Companion*. Cambridge, Mass.: Webb Books Inc., 1961.

DOERNER, MAX. *The Materials of the Artist*. New York: Harcourt, Brace & World, Inc., 1934; rev. ed., 1962.

LAURIE, A. P. *The Painter's Methods and Materials*. London: Seeley Service and Company, Ltd., 1960.

HERBERTS, KURT. *Oriental Lacquer: Art and Technique*. New York: H. N. Abrahms, 1963.

JENYNS, R. ROANES, AND WATSON, WILLIAM. *Chinese Art*. New York: University Books, Inc., 1963.

JOURDAIN, MARGARET. *English Decoration and Furniture of the Later XVIIIth Century (1760–1820), An Account of Its Development and Characteristic Forms*. London: B. T. Batsford, Ltd., 1922.

KOIZUMI, G. *Lacquer Work*. London: Sir Isaac Pitman & Sons, Ltd., 1925.

STALKER, JOHN, AND PARKER, GEORGE. *A Treatise of Japanning and Varnishing*. 1688. Reprint. Chicago: Quadrangle Books, 1960.

CENNINI, CENNINO. *The Craftsman's Handbook*. New York: Dover Publications, Inc., 1933.

THOMPSON, DANIEL V. *The Materials and Techniques of Medieval Painting*. New York: Dover Publications, Inc., 1956.

THOMPSON, DANIEL V. *The Practice of Tempera Painting*. New York: Dover Publications, Inc., 1936.

WHITLOCK, NATHANIEL. *The Decorative Painter's and Glazier's Guide*. London: Isaac Taylor Hinton, 1827.

VAN DER BURG, A. R., AND VAN DER BURG, P. *School of Painting for the Imitation of Woods and Marbles*. London: Technical Press, Ltd., 1936.

METZ, RUDOLPH. *Precious Stones and Other Crystals*. New York: Viking Press, 1965.

ODOM, WILLIAM M. *A History of Italian Furniture*, Vol. 2. New York: Doubleday, Page & Co., 1919.

MACQUOID, PERCY R. I. *A History of English Furniture*. London: Laurence & Bullen, Ltd., 1938.

*About the Author . . .*

Mrs. O'Neil is known nationally as an authority on painted finishes. In New York City, she conducts the Isabel O'Neil Studio-Workshop which is both school and laboratory. Her background—of art education at Skidmore College and Yale University, ten years of professional work for New York interior designers, research in France and Italy, and constant study of old methods plus long experimentation in the development of new finishes— led to the establishment of the curriculum at the Studio-Workshop. The accumulated knowledge of Mrs. O'Neil and of her students has at last been documented in this, the only comprehensive, contemporary work on the art of the painted finish.